WRITER'S JOURNAL

explorations

domains
in language and composition

WRITER'S JOURNAL
explorations

Dalton H. McBee

HARCOURT BRACE JOVANOVICH, INC.
New York   Chicago   San Francisco   Atlanta   Dallas

DALTON H. McBEE has taught in secondary schools in New Hampshire and Florida. For the past sixteen years he has been an instructor in English at Phillips Academy, Andover, Massachusetts, where he currently serves as Admissions Officer and Director of Financial Aid.

ACKNOWLEDGMENTS: For permission to reprint copyrighted material, grateful acknowledgment is made to the following publishers, authors, and agents:

APPLETON-CENTURY-CROFTS: From *Understanding Fiction,* 2nd edition, by Brooks and Warren.

ATLANTIC-LITTLE, BROWN AND COMPANY: "The Toaster" from *Laughing Time* by William Jay Smith, copyright 1955 by William Jay Smith.

THE ATLANTIC MONTHLY COMPANY, BOSTON, MASSACHUSETTS: From "Urbanity and Sophistication" by Richard Brown Baker from *The Atlantic Monthly,* copyright © 1965 The Atlantic Monthly Company, Boston, Massachusetts.

THE ATLANTIC MONTHLY COMPANY, BOSTON, MASSACHUSETTS and ROLAND FLINT: "August from My Desk" by Roland Flint from *The Atlantic Monthly,* February, 1965, copyright © 1965 by The Atlantic Monthly Company, Boston, Massachusetts.

BEACON PRESS and ROBERT LANTZ-CANDIDA DONADIO LITERARY AGENCY: From "Autobiographical Notes" from *Notes of a Native Son* by James Baldwin, copyright © 1955 by James Baldwin.

G. BELL & SONS LTD.: From "Thoughts on Various Subjects" from *The Prose Works of Jonathan Swift, D.D.,* edited by Temple Scott, Volume I.

BRANDT & BRANDT: From "The New England Prep School" by Stephen Birmingham from *Holiday Magazine,* February 1964.

BRANDT & BRANDT and A. M. HEATH & COMPANY LTD. representing MISS SONIA BROWNELL and SECKER & WARBURG, LTD.: From *Down and Out in Paris and London* by George Orwell, copyright 1933 by George Orwell; copyright renewed 1960 by Sonia Pitt-Rivers. Published by Harcourt Brace Jovanovich, Inc.

TRUMAN CAPOTE: From "Greek Paragraphs" by Truman Capote. Originally published in *Travel & Camera,* May 1969.

THE CLUB OF ODD VOLUMES: From *What Is Time?* by Karl Vogel, M.D.

COLLINS-KNOWLTON-WING, INC. and DOROTHY EDITH COLLINS: From "On R.L.S." from *Generally Speaking* by G. K. Chesterton, copyright © 1929, 1957 by Oliver Chesterton. Published by Books for Libraries, Inc.

COMMUNICATIONS/RESEARCH/MACHINES/INC.: From "A Conversation with Ray Bradbury & Chuck Jones, the Fantasy-Makers" by Mary Harrington Hall from *Psychology Today,* April 1968, copyright © Communications/Research/Machines/Inc.

CORNELL UNIVERSITY PRESS: From *A Study of Literature* by David Daiches, copyright 1948 by Cornell University.

J. M. DENT & SONS LTD. PUBLISHERS and THE TRUSTEES OF THE JOSEPH CONRAD ESTATE: From the Preface to *The Nigger of the Narcissus* by Joseph Conrad.

DODD, MEAD & COMPANY, INC.: From *How to Write* by Stephen Leacock, copyright 1943 by Dodd, Mead & Company, Inc. "On Novels and the Art of Writing Them" from *Autobiography of Anthony Trollope.*

DOUBLEDAY & COMPANY, INC.: "Dolor," copyright 1943 by Modern Poetry Association, Inc., from *The Collected Poems of Theodore Roethke.* From *Penrod* by Booth Tarkington, copyright 1914 by Doubleday & Company, Inc. From "Writing About Science" by David O. Woodbury from *Writers On Writing,* edited by Herschel Brickell, copyright 1949 by Doubleday & Company, Inc., 1949 by Saturday Review Associates, Inc.

DOUBLEDAY & COMPANY, INC. and THE LITERARY EXECUTOR OF W. SOMERSET MAUGHAM AND WILLIAM HEINEMANN LTD.: From "The Summing Up" from *The Maugham Reader* by W. Somerset Maugham, copyright 1938 by W. Somerset Maugham. Published in England under the title of *Writer and Reader.*

DOUBLEDAY & COMPANY, INC. and A. P. WATT & SON representing MRS. GEORGE BAMBRIDGE and MACMILLAN COMPANY OF CANADA LTD.: From "The Jewel Game" from *Kim* by Rudyard Kipling.
DOUBLEDAY & COMPANY, INC. and A. P. WATT & SON representing MRS. D. CHESTON BENNETT: From *Things That Have Interested Me* by Arnold Bennett, copyright 1921 by George H. Doran Company. From Part I, Section III from *The Author's Craft* by Arnold Bennett, copyright 1914 by George H. Doran Company. From "Mental Calisthenics" from *Mental Efficiency* by Arnold Bennett, copyright 1911 by George H. Doran Company.
E. P. DUTTON & COMPANY, INC.: From "They Grind Exceeding Small" from *Thrifty Stock and Other Stories* by Ben Ames Williams, copyright 1923 by E. P. Dutton & Co., Inc.; renewal 1951 by Ben Ames Williams.
ANGEL FLORES: "The Albatross" by Charles Baudelaire, translated by Kate Flores from *Anthology of French Poetry from Nerval to Valery in English Translation,* edited by Angel Flores.
R. W. GERARD: From "The Biological Basis of Imagination" by Dr. R. W. Gerard from *The Scientific Monthly,* June 1946.
HARCOURT BRACE JOVANOVICH, INC.: From "The Love Song of J. Alfred Prufrock" from *Collected Poems 1909–1935* by T. S. Eliot. From "Some Thoughts on the Common Toad" from *Shooting an Elephant and Other Essays* by George Orwell. From *A Walker in the City* by Alfred Kazin.
HARCOURT BRACE JOVANOVICH, INC., QUENTIN BELL, ANGELICA GARNETT and THE HOGARTH PRESS LTD.: From *The Death of the Moth* by Virginia Woolf, copyright 1942 by Harcourt Brace Jovanovich, Inc.
HARPER & ROW, PUBLISHERS, INCORPORATED: Abridged from pp. 104–112 in *A Fragment of Autobiography* by John Gunther, copyright © 1961, 1962 by John Gunther. From "My Face" by Robert Benchley in *The Benchley Roundup: A Selection by Nathaniel Benchley,* copyright 1938 by Robert C. Benchley. From Chapter XXVI of "In South Africa" from *Mark Twain's Notebook,* edited by Albert Bigelow Paine. Published by Harper & Row, 1935. Abridgment of *How "Bigger" Was Born* by Richard Wright, copyright 1940 by Richard Wright. Abridged from pp. 28, 29, 31, 33, 35, 36 and p. 42 in *The Art of Readable Writing* by Rudolf Flesch, copyright 1949 by Rudolf Flesch. From "On Various Kinds of Thinking" from *The Mind in the Making* by James Harvey Robinson. Published by Harper & Row, 1921.
SIR RUPERT HART-DAVIS: From "Bird of Bright Plumage—Will Herries Dines at Westaways" from *Judith Paris* by Hugh Walpole.
HARVARD UNIVERSITY PRESS: From *My Class in Composition* by Julien Bezard.
THE BELKNAP PRESS OF HARVARD UNIVERSITY PRESS: From *Letters and Journals of James Fenimore Cooper,* Vol. I, edited by James Franklin Beard.
D. C. HEATH AND COMPANY: From "What Is Thought" from *How We Think* by John Dewey, copyright 1933 by D. C. Heath and Company, Lexington, Massachusetts. From "The Daily Theme Eye" from *Essays and Essay-Writing Based on Atlantic Monthly Models,* edited by William M. Tanner, copyright © 1941 by William M. Tanner; copyright © 1945 by D. C. Heath and Company, Lexington, Massachusetts.
THE HOGARTH PRESS: From *Talks with Tolstoi* by A. B. Goldenweizer.
HOLT, RINEHART AND WINSTON, INC.: "The Woodpile," "Birches," "Desert Places" from *The Poetry of Robert Frost,* edited by Edward Connery Lathem, copyright 1916, 1930, 1939, © 1969 by Holt, Rinehart and Winston, Inc. Copyright 1936, 1944, 1958 by Robert Frost. Copyright © 1964, 1967 by Lesley Frost Ballantine. "Steam Shovel" from *Upper Pasture* by Charles Malam, copyright 1930, © 1958 by Charles Malam. From *A Creative Approach to Writing* by Roger H. Garrison, copyright 1951 by Holt, Rinehart and Winston, Inc. From *Constructive Theme Writing* by Mary Ellen Chase, copyright 1929 by Holt, Rinehart and Winston, Inc., copyright © 1957 by Mary Ellen Chase. From *Lives in Progress,* Second Edition by Robert W. White. From "Introduction" from *The Logic and Rhetoric of Exposition* by H. C. Martin. From "On *A Portrait of the Artist as a Young Man*" from *The English Novel: Form and Function* by Dorothy Van Ghent. From "Habit" from *Psychology* by William James.
HOUGHTON MIFFLIN COMPANY: From Chapter IV from *Journal of Henry David Thoreau,* Vol. IV. From "Ethan Brand's Lime-Kiln" from *The Heart of Hawthorne's Journals,* edited by Newton Arvin. "Ars Poetica" from *Collected Poems of Archibald MacLeish 1917–1952.*
INDIANA UNIVERSITY PRESS, CANADIAN BROADCASTING CORPORATION and NORTHROP FRYE: From *The Educated Imagination* by Northrop Frye, copyright © 1964 by Indiana University Press. Copyright © 1963 by Canadian Broadcasting Corporation. Published in Canada by CBC Publications.
ALFRED A. KNOPF, INC.: From Preface to "Pierre et Jean," copyright 1925; renewed 1953 by Alfred A. Knopf, Inc., from *The Collected Novels and Stories of Guy de Maupassant,* translated by Ernest Boyd. From "The Feel" from *Farewell to Sport* by Paul Gallico, copyright 1938 and renewed 1966 by Paul Gallico. From "The Necklace," copyright 1924 and renewed 1952 by Alfred A. Knopf, Inc., from *The Collected Novels and Stories of Guy de Maupassant,* translated by Ernest Boyd.

For Lee and Alice,
Coles and Joel

Contents

Unit 4
Reflection

Unit 5
Develop your Powers of Perception

UNIT 1

Start a Journal

> *Keep a Journal. Pay so much honor*
> *to the visits of truth to your mind*
> *as to record them.*—RALPH WALDO EMERSON

1|1

ANYBODY CAN LEARN TO WRITE

. . . Writing is essentially *thinking,* or at least involves thinking as its first requisite. All people can think, or at least they think they think. But few people can say what they think, that is, say it with sufficient power of language to convey it to the full. Even when they have conveyed it, it may turn out to be not worth conveying. But there are some people whose thoughts are so interesting that other people are glad to hear them, or to read them. Yet even these people must learn the use of language adequate to convey their thoughts; people may sputter and gurgle in a highly interesting way but without the full equipment of acquired language their sputters won't carry far. This, then, is what is meant by writing—to have thoughts which are of interest to other people and to put them into language which reveals the thoughts. These thoughts may come in part from native originality, in part from deliberate search and reflection. In all that concerns writing, spontaneous originality, what we call native gift, is mingled with the result of conscious effort. The threads are interwoven in the cloth, till they blend and often seem indistinguishable.

So much for native ability to seize an opportunity that comes by chance. But what are we to say of the writer who sits down and struggles, even agonizes, to get something funny to write? Here we have Mr. A. A. Milne, whose native ability is at the saturation point, telling us in his autobiography of such struggles and agonies when he had to turn out his copy, week by week, for *Punch*. This seems very different from accident or inspiration. In reality, it is just the same thing. What Mr. Milne, and lesser people, are doing in this brute effort at being funny, is to [recall] . . . scenes and people. . . . Something half-perceived and subconsciously recorded is there as obvious as a partridge sitting on a bough. We have only to fire with both barrels. It may not be "sportsmanlike," in comparison with inspiration, but it gets the bird. . . .

We have decided then that writing has got to be done deliberately. We can't wait for it to come. On these terms, I claim that anybody can learn to write, just as anybody can learn to swim. Nor can anybody swim without learning how. A person can thus learn to swim up to the limits imposed by his aptitude and physique. The final result may not be worth looking at, but he can swim. So with writing. Nobody can learn to write without having learned how, either consciously or unconsciously. But it fortunately happens that what we call our education supplies to all of us the first basis for writing, the ability to read and to spell. Indeed our ordinary education, even in any elementary school, gives us a certain training in putting words together. Under the name of "composition" we go through a harrowing set of little exercises in correcting errors in the use of English; we put poetry back into prose, and go so far as to reach up to writing a composition on "An Autumn Walk" or "The Fidelity of the Dog." This is not "writing" in the sense adopted in this book, but it is as essential a preliminary to it as learning to drive a nail into a board is to carpentry. People of exceptional native ability and no schooling sometimes write, and sometimes have reached great eminence without such training. But that is because the bent of their minds was so strong in that direction that unconsciously they weighed and measured words and phrases, fascinated with the power of expression, as an artistic genius, a young Giotto, with the pictured line.

Indeed, an ordinary environment of today gives us an even further start, and nowadays our sight and hearing, through moving pictures, introduce us to a vast world of history, of actual events, and imaginary stories. These and the little circumstances of our own life give us plenty of material for thought. If we put our thoughts into words and write them down, that is *writing*. There's no more to it. It's just as simple as that.

In other words, anybody can write who has something to say and knows how to say it. Contrariwise, nobody can write who has nothing to say, or nothing that he can put into words.

But the main point is that writing . . . has got to be done for and by oneself. If you want to write, start and write down your thoughts. If you haven't any thoughts, don't write them down. But if you have, *write* them down; thoughts about anything, no matter what, in your own way, with no idea of selling them or being an author. Just put down your thoughts. If later on it turns out that your thoughts are interesting and if you get enough practice to be able to set down what they really are in language that conveys them properly—the selling business comes itself. There are many things in life, as we have said, that come to us as it were "at back rounds." Look for happiness and you find dust. Look for "authorship" and you won't find it; look for self-expression in words, for its own sake, and an editor's check will rustle down from heaven to your table. Of course you really hoped for it; but you won't get it unless and until self-expression for its own sake breaks through.

What do you write about? You write about anything. Your great difficulty will be, as soon as you apprehend this method, that you can *think* things but can't say them. Most people live and die in that state; their conversation is stuffed with smothered thought that can't get over.

Take an example: Two people are walking out with the crowd from the roar and racket of a football game, just over. One says, "I don't know that I quite believe in all that rooting stuff, eh?" And the other answers, reflectively, "Oh, I don't know; I'm not so sure." That's as far as they can get. What the first man means is that organized hysteria is a poor substitute for spontaneous enthusiasm; and what the other means is that after all even genuine enthusiasm *unless* organized, unless given the aid of regularity and system—even spontaneous enthusiasm degenerates into confusion; our life, itself artificial, compels a certain "organization." They can't say this, but either of these two spectators would read with pleasure a well-written magazine article under such a title as "Should Rooting Be Rooted Out?" The articles we think really good are those that express the things that we think but can't say.

Now when people begin to write down their thoughts, some of them will find that their thoughts take the form of judgments or opinions on things that are. Others will find that their thoughts instinctively run into fancies, that is, ideas of things that might happen, and these become stories. Stories are just new editions of what might happen to somebody based on what did happen to somebody else. Hence, for many people the desire to write assumes the form of a sort of wish, or instinct to write "stories." . . . They turn with impatience from all talk of preparation, of practice, of words. All that seems artificial. The natural idea, to them, is to try to write a story and then try to sell it to a magazine; and thus by practice learn how to write and get paid for it at the same time.

It is more reasonable to suppose that most beginners underestimate the difficulty of storytelling. What they write at first is not apt to be really worth a selling price. It is a pity to stake their literary future on their first efforts. Few people begin at their best, or even at their average level. The exceptions, such as Rudyard Kipling, who began at the top with what seems effortless excellence—well, they're exceptional.

Stories, I repeat, that are really worthwhile are hard to write. Most people who aspire to be story writers think that stories depend upon incidents, upon a plot. This is not so. They depend on telling. As to incident or plot, there are fundamentally only three of them, that So-and-So was born, that he fell in love and got married, that he died—with the variation that he fell in love and didn't get married, and that he nearly died but didn't. Stories about how a man nearly died and didn't are called Adventure Stories, and stories about how a person got married, or didn't, are called Love Stories. But the main thing in any story is to be able to think the character into reality, and then find the words to convey what you think. Once you can create a character, as the phrase runs (catch a character would be better), anything and everything about him is a story.

Now you may feel very vividly that there's a character to be caught but you've got to catch him first. There is a waiter, let us say, in a restaurant you frequent, whom you feel to be a regular character. But saying that won't make him one. You've got to catch and convey something about him that makes him one, and then you don't need to tell your reader that the waiter is a character. He'll say so first. What makes so many stories stupid and unreadable is that the writer, instead of making characters, announces them. He says, "The waiter was one of the quaintest characters whom our hero had ever looked upon." Was he? But we don't see him. Or else the writer thinks to succeed by piling up an accumulation of details so that the sum total must at least come to something. But this, except to fill space against a price, is all wrong. The best descriptions are the shortest; their point is in their effective suggestion; the reader does the rest. The best lesson in this respect is to learn to admire and linger over the work of others; if it is true that Shakespeare (so he said) often found himself admiring "this man's art and that man's scope," there is no doubt that the process helped to make him Shakespeare.

We are still talking then of how to begin. I would like to offer as a practical suggestion the keeping of a sort of "commonplace book" in which one writes all kinds of random attempts at expression. If you have just read a book, write a few words down about it. If a moving picture has deeply moved you, write down the fact and try to explain why. Cultivate admiration of other people's words and phrases that seem to express much, and write them down. Soon you will write your own. In a certain sense all literature begins with imitation. Divergence comes later.

It is often thought that writing a diary is, par excellence, the most natural and effective way to begin writing. I don't think so at all. A diary is apt to throw the person on the wrong track. It tends to be such an artificial business. What are you to put in it—all your most intimate thoughts? But most people haven't got any, or none that they care to put on paper. The young heroine in novels spreads out her diary and tells it that it is to be her dearest friend. "I will put into it, my dear diary," she says, "all that I think, all that I feel, all that I don't know." It sounds a large order. In reality it only means that this is the author's way of writing the book, by pretending that the heroine wrote it.

On the other hand, if a diary is written as a simple record of what happens, done in the writer's own ordinary language, it is apt to be of no great value as literary practice. Example: diary of J. Smith, on vacation:

July 8: went bass fishing: got six. July 9: didn't go bass fishing: lake too rough: played poker: lost

a dollar twenty. July 10: bass fishing: didn't get
any——

Nor would it make it any better if J. Smith used
his diary for the kind of fits of affectation described
[elsewhere] in connection with correspondence:

July 8: We went out to fish for bass, the lake a
beautiful amethyst gray, very calm as if stilled into
expectancy. Our piscatorial efforts were rewarded
by the capture of six bass, the largest of which we
could easily see without the need of scales to repre-
sent a weight of five pounds, at least, while all possessed a beauty of shimmering color, a length of
fin and a breadth of jaw characteristic of the large-
mouthed black bass (*ranunculus silva*) at its largest.

On the whole, therefore, I think we may say
good-by to diary-making and personal correspondence as methods of beginning to write.

But let us come back for the moment and take
the other alternative of the dilemma spoken of
above. Suppose a would-be writer can't begin. I
really believe there are many excellent writers who
have never written because they never could begin.
This is especially the case of people of great sensi-
tiveness, or of people of advanced education. Pro-
fessors suffer most of all from this inhibition. Many
of them carry their unwritten books to the grave.
They overestimate the magnitude of the task; they
overestimate the greatness of the final result. A
child in a "prep" school will write "The History
of Greece" and fetch it home finished after school.
"He wrote a fine 'History of Greece' the other day,"
says his proud father. Thirty years later the child,
grown to be a professor, dreams of writing the history of Greece—the whole of it from the first Ionic
invasion of the Aegean to the downfall of Alex-
andria. But he dreams. He never starts. He can't.
It's too big.

Anybody who has lived around a college knows
the pathos of these unwritten books. Moreover,
quite apart from the nonstart due to the appalling
magnitude of the subject, there is a nonstart from

the mere trivial difficulty of "how to begin" in the smaller sense, how to frame the opening sentences. In other words how do you get started?

The best practical advice that can be given on this subject is, don't start. That is, don't start anywhere in particular. Begin at the end, begin in the middle, but begin. If you like, you can fool yourself by pretending that the start you make isn't really the beginning and that you are going to write it all over again. Pretend that what you write is just a note, a fragment, a nothing. Only get started.

STEPHEN LEACOCK
from How to Write

A sentence must be compelled to say a single thing; a paragraph, a single thing; an essay, a single thing. Each part is to be a preliminary whole and the total a finished whole.

GEORGE H. PALMER
from Self-Cultivation in English

Assignment 1

1. Read the excerpt from *How to Write* by Stephen Leacock.
2. In your journal do *one* of the following:
   a. If you were to test a reader on this first chapter, what would be your three best questions? Write them in your journal together with your answers.
   b. In your own words rewrite the Leacock essay. Avoid redundancy; cover the topic in a page or two.
   c. Reconsider Leacock's essay in light of the statement by George H. Palmer that precedes this assignment. Show how Leacock does or does not violate the requirements of "a finished whole." Be specific.

Assignment 2

In your journal, write on any topic or choose a little circumstance from your own life. Give it thought. Put your thoughts into words—prose or poetry—and write them down.

This is the suggested form to use at the beginning of each new journal entry:

> Unit 1, Chapter 1, Assignment 2, Date
> My entry #2
> Objective:

Here is an example of a student response to this assignment, written by Dan Braunlin. See if you can do as well.

A boy was wandering around Fuess House this afternoon, but not finding the friend for whom he was looking, he wandered into my room to talk for a while, I guess.

But he had barely muttered a "Hello" when he spotted a campaign poster of the late Senator Kennedy on my wall. "Why in heaven do you put pictures of dead men on your wall?" he demanded. "Oh, I guess I just like to," I casually replied, not really giving much thought to either the question or my answer. "Boy, that's stupid," he retorted.

I didn't think much about it then, but later I found myself wondering if perhaps this boy was trying to be funny or if to him Robert Kennedy was just a dead man now—nothing more.

I must confess that I got the impression that the ideas and achievements of the late Senator meant nothing to the boy and I was, quite frankly, shocked. I don't know why I feel so strongly about this, but I do. I was twelve when President Kennedy was assassinated, and although I realized that we had lost a great man, it meant nothing more to me. All his ideas, his dreams for the future, his great accomplishments, his failure—they meant nothing to me. But I suppose I was too young.

Again when Dr. King became the victim of fatal rifle bullets in April, I thought that we had lost another great man and I realized that equality for all in this country would suffer from this loss—but nothing more. Perhaps I was too caught up in school.

But when Robert Kennedy died of bullet wounds

in his skull, I again realized that we had lost another great man, full of ideas, proud of his accomplishments—yet dead in his prime.

Yet more than that I wept, at least inwardly, for this country of ours which seems so sick—full of war, violence, and hatred. When Bobby Kennedy was shot, I finally realized that something has to be done in this country and that I and my classmates are the ones that have to do it.

Perhaps my visitor hasn't realized this yet.

DAN BRAUNLIN

Assignment 3

In your journal do *one* of the following:

a. If you have a story to write, write it. Don't aim at style or finish; just try to get the rough notes down with enough repetition of your core idea to have your reader feel the impact of your theme. With each incident provide variation of outcome as well as variation of event, but make each incident point to what you are really trying to say. Assignments 6, 12, and 15 in this unit will provide additional working time. Here, simply do what you can in the allotted time.

b. Write out a conversation of "smothered thoughts." Then "unsmother" them. Leacock's paragraph about the talk of the two people leaving with the crowd after the football game suggests the sort of thing that is wanted.

c. Write your thoughts on any topic about which you feel strongly.

1|2

MENTAL CALISTHENICS

I have dealt with the state of mind in which one should begin a serious effort toward mental efficiency, and also with the probable causes of failure in previous efforts. We come now to what I may call the calisthenics of the business, exercises which may be roughly compared to the technical exercises necessary in learning to play a musical instrument. It is curious that a person studying a musical instrument will have no false shame whatever in doing mere exercises for the fingers and wrists while a person who is trying to get his mind into order will almost certainly experience a false shame in going through performances which are undoubtedly good for him. Herein lies one of the great obstacles to mental efficiency. Tell a man that he should join a memory class, and he will hum and haw, and say . . . that memory isn't everything; and, in short, he won't join the memory class, partly from indolence, I grant, but more from false shame. (Is not this true?) He will even hesitate about learning things by heart. Yet there are few mental exercises better than learning great poetry or prose by heart. Twenty lines a week for six months: What a "cure" for debility! The chief, but not the only, merit of learning by heart as an exercise is that it compels the mind to concentrate. And the most important preliminary to self-development is the faculty of concentrating at will. Another excellent exercise is to read a page of no-matter-what, and then immediately to write down—in one's own words or in the author's—one's full recollection of it. A quarter of an hour a day! No more! And it works like magic.

This brings me to the department of writing. I am a writer by profession; but I do not think I have any prejudices in favor of the exercise of writing. Indeed, I say to myself every morning that if there is one exercise in the world which I hate, it is the exercise of writing. But I must assert that in my opinion the exercise of writing is an indispensable part of any genuine effort toward mental efficiency. I don't care much what you write, so long as you compose sentences and achieve continuity. There are forty ways of writing in an unprofessional manner, and they are all good. You may keep "a full diary," as Mr. Arthur Christopher Benson says he does. This is one of the least good ways. Diaries, save in experienced hands like those of Mr. Benson, are apt to get themselves done with the very minimum of mental effort. They also tend to an exaggeration of egotism, and if they are left lying about they tend to strife. Further, one never knows when one may not be compelled to produce them in a court of law. A journal is better. Do not ask me to define the difference between a journal and a diary. I will not and I cannot. It is a difference that one feels instinctively. A diary treats exclusively of one's self and one's doings; a journal roams wider, and notes whatever one has observed of interest. A diary relates that one had lobster mayonnaise for dinner and rose the next morning with a headache, doubtless attributable to mental strain. A journal relates that Mrs. _____, whom one took into dinner, had brown eyes, and an agreeable trick of throwing back her head after asking a question, and gives her account of her husband's strange adventures in Colorado, etc. A diary is

All I, I, I, I, itself I

(to quote a line of the transcendental poetry of Mary Baker G. Eddy). A journal is the large spectacle of life. A journal may be special or general. I know a man who keeps a journal of all cases of current superstition which he actually encounters.

He began it without the slightest suspicion that he was beginning a document of astounding interest and real scientific value; but such was the fact. In default of a diary or a journal, one may write essays (provided one has the moral courage); or one may simply make notes on the book one reads. Or one may construct anthologies of passages which have made an individual and particular appeal to one's tastes. Anthology construction is one of the pleasantest hobbies that a person who is not mad about golf and bridge—that is to say, a thinking person—can possibly have; and I recommend it to those who, discreetly mistrusting their power to keep up a fast pace from start to finish, are anxious to begin their intellectual course gently and mildly. In any event, writing—the act of writing—is vital to almost any scheme. . . .

After writing comes thinking. (The sequence may be considered odd, but I adhere to it.) In this connection I cannot do better than quote an admirable letter which I have received from a correspondent who wishes to be known only as "An Oxford Lecturer." The italics (except the last) are mine, not his. He says: "Till a man has got his physical brain completely under his control—*suppressing its too-great receptivity, its tendencies to reproduce idly the thoughts of others, and to be swayed by every passing gust of emotion*—I hold that he cannot do a tenth part of the work that he would then be able to perform with little or no effort. Moreover, work apart, he has not entered upon his kingdom, and unlimited possibilities of future development are barred to him. Mental efficiency can be gained by constant practice in meditation—i.e., by concentrating the mind, say, for but ten minutes daily, but with absolute regularity, on some of the highest thoughts of which it is capable. Failures will be frequent, but they must be regarded with simple indifference and dogged perseverance in the path chosen. If that path be followed *without intermission* even for a few weeks the results will speak for themselves." I thoroughly agree with what this correspondent says, and am obliged to him for having so ably stated the case. But I regard such a practice of meditation as he indicates as being rather an "advanced" exercise for a beginner. After the beginner has got under way, and gained a little confidence in his strength of purpose, and acquired the skill to define his thoughts sufficiently to write them down—then it would be time enough, in my view, to undertake what "An Oxford Lecturer" suggests. . . .

So much for the more or less technical processes of stirring the mind from its sloth and making it exactly obedient to the aspirations of the soul. And here I close. Numerous correspondents have asked me to outline a course of reading for them. In other words, they have asked me to particularize for them the aspirations of their souls. My subject, however, was not self-development. My subject was mental efficiency as a means to self-development. Of course, one can only acquire mental efficiency in the actual effort of self-development. But I was concerned, not with the choice of route; rather with the manner of following the route. You say to me that I am busying myself with the best method of walking, and refusing to discuss where to go. Precisely. One man cannot tell another man where the other man wants to go.

If he can't himself decide on a goal he may as well curl up and expire, for the root of the matter is not in him. I will content myself with pointing out that the entire universe is open for inspection. Too many people fancy that self-development means literature. They associate the higher life with an intimate knowledge of the life of Charlotte Brontë, or the order of the plays of Shakespeare. The higher life may just as well be butterflies, or funeral customs, or county boundaries, or street names, or mosses, or stars, or slugs, as Charlotte Brontë or Shakespeare. Choose what interests you. Lots of finely organized, mentally efficient persons can't read Shakespeare at any price, and if you asked them who was the author of *The Tenant of Wildfell Hall* they might proudly answer Emily Brontë, if they didn't say they never heard of it. An accurate knowledge of *any* subject, coupled with a carefully nurtured sense of the relativity of that subject to other subjects, implies an enormous self-development. With this hint I conclude.

ARNOLD BENNETT
from *Mental Efficiency*

Assignment 4

1. Read the preceding observations presented by Arnold Bennett.
2. In your journal do *one* of the following:
   a. Distinguish as best you can between a journal and a diary.
   b. Explain why "the exercise of writing is an indispensable part of any genuine effort toward mental efficiency."
   c. As an exercise in "mental efficiency," and as an example of "the faculty of concentrating at will," learn by heart twenty lines of poetry (pick a poem that you like). Then copy them out from *memory* into your journal.

Assignment 5

Nine Rules for Writers

1. Have something to say.
2. Let your ideas take form in your mind before you begin to write. If you can't hold the ideas in your mind, how can the reader?
3. Don't write when tired; tired writing makes tired reading.
4. Choose a time and place free from interruption.
5. Write down the words just as they come without much attention to detail.

6. Rewrite the article carefully with your readers in mind.
7. Check through to get rid of big words and fancy phrases.
8. Check through again to see that the sequence of ideas is right.
9. Check through once more to see if you can add something personal, human, or concrete.

ANONYMOUS

1. Read "Nine Rules for Writers" above.
2. In your journal do *one* of the following:
   a. Write an article that might be used for your school newspaper. Pay special attention to Rules 1 and 5.
   b. "One man cannot tell another man where the other man wants to go." Agree, disagree, discuss.
   c. Start an anthology of "Short Story Starts." Copy out the first paragraph of a story you particularly admire. Then explain in some detail why you think this particular start is effective.

Assignment 6

In your journal do *one* of the following:
   a. If you started a story in Chapter 1, Assignment 3, then start here to fill in the gaps.
   b. Write about coincidence as it occurs in life and fiction.
   c. Write down your thoughts about anything, but remember that "writing has got to be done deliberately. We can't wait for it to come." Pick a topic (don't spend more than two minutes making your choice); then reveal your thoughts in language that will interest your reader.

1|3

WHAT TO DO
WITH THE SENSES

I began to wonder at about this time just what
one saw when one looked at anything, really looked
at anything.

GERTRUDE STEIN

Perception requires more than eyes. One perceives with all
his senses and sensitivities. Lear and Oedipus both perceived
best when blind.

Optic responses are purely mechanical; what we perceive
is the product of our total experience. Our perceptions carry
not only optic reports but our psychological interpretations
of them.

Here is part of an essay by Paul Gallico that shows us something about perception. As you read see how a writer uses
(1) *selection* to make his material fit his purpose and desired
result. Note how (2) *point of view* both physical and psychological organizes and controls the fullness of the original experience. Note, too, Gallico's (3) *tone of voice,* (4) *vocabulary,*
and (5) *frame of reference.* All these—as well as his previous
experience—affect what he reports. Consider his use of (6)
metaphor to reveal relationships. Finally consider his use of
(7) *the senses.*

A child, wandering through a department store
with its mother, is admonished over and over again
not to touch things. Mother is convinced that the
child only does it to annoy or because it is a child,
and usually hasn't the vaguest inkling of the fact
that Junior is "touching" because he is a little blot-
ter soaking up information and knowledge, and
"feel" is an important adjunct to seeing. Adults
are exactly the same, in a measure, as you may ascer-

tain when some new gadget or article is produced for inspection. The average person says: "Here, let me see that," and holds out his hand. He doesn't mean "see," because he is already seeing it. What he means is that he wants to get it into his hands and feel it so as to become better acquainted.

As suggested in the foregoing chapter, I do not insist that a curiosity and capacity for feeling sports is necessary to be a successful writer, but it is fairly obvious that a man who has been tapped on the chin with five fingers wrapped up in a leather boxing glove and propelled by the arm of an expert knows more about that particular sensation than one who has not, always provided he has the gift of expressing himself. . . .

I was always a child who touched things and I have always had a tremendous curiosity with regard to sensation. If I knew what playing a game felt like, particularly against or in the company of experts, I was better equipped to write about the playing of it and the problems of the men and women who took part in it. And so, at one time or another, I have tried them all. . . .

It all began back in 1922 when I was a cub sportswriter and consumed with more curiosity than was good for my health. I had seen my first professional prize fights and wondered at the curious behavior of men under the stress of blows, the sudden checking and the beginning of a little fall forward after a hard punch, the glazing of the eyes and the loss of locomotor control, the strange actions of men on the canvas after a knockdown as they struggled to regain their senses and arise on legs that seemed to have turned into rubber. I had never been in any bad fist fights as a youngster, though I had taken a little physical punishment in football, but it was not enough to complete the picture. Could one think under those conditions?

I had been assigned to my first training-camp coverage, Dempsey's at Saratoga Springs, where he was preparing for his famous fight with Luis Firpo. For days I watched him sag a spar boy with what seemed to be no more than a light cuff on the neck, or pat his face with what looked like no more than a caressing stroke of his arm, and the fellow would come all apart at the seams and collapse in a useless heap, grinning vacuously or twitching strangely. My burning curiosity got the better of prudence and a certain reluctance to expose myself to physical pain. I asked Dempsey to permit me to box a round with him. I had never boxed before, but I was in good physical shape, having just completed a four-year stretch as a galley slave in the Columbia eight-oared shell.

When it was over and I escaped through the ropes, shaking, bleeding a little from the mouth, with rosin dust on my pants and a vicious throbbing in my head, I knew all that there was to know about being hit in the prize ring. It seems that I had gone to an expert for tuition. I knew the sensation of being stalked and pursued by a relentless, truculent professional destroyer whose trade and business it was to injure men. I saw shock as a bony, leather-bound fist lands on cheek or mouth. I learned more (partly from photographs of the lesson, viewed afterwards, one of which shows me ducked under a vicious left hook, an act of which I never had the slightest recollection) about instinctive ducking and blocking than I could have in ten years of looking at prize fights, and I learned, too, that as the soldier never hears the bullet that kills him, so does the fighter rarely, if ever, see the punch that tumbles blackness over him like a mantle, with a tearing rip as though the roof on his skull were exploding, and robs him of his senses.

There was just that—a ripping in my head and then sudden blackness, and the next thing I knew, I was sitting on the canvas covering of the ring floor with my legs collapsed under me, grinning idiotically. How often since have I seen that same silly, goofy look on the faces of dropped fighters— and understood it. I held on to the floor with both hands, because the ring and the audience outside were making a complete clockwise revolution, came to a stop, and then went back again counterclockwise. When I struggled to my feet, Jack Kearns, Dempsey's manager, was counting over me, but I neither saw nor heard him and was only conscious that I was in a ridiculous position and that the thing to do was to get up and try to fight back. The floor swayed and rocked beneath me like a fishing dory in an offshore swell, and it was a welcome respite when Dempsey rushed into a clinch, held me up, and whispered into my ear: "Wrestle around a bit, son, until your head clears." And then it was that I learned what those little love taps to the back of the neck and the short digs to the ribs can mean to the groggy pugilist more than half knocked out. It is a murderous game, and the fighter who can escape after having been felled by a lethal blow has my admiration. And there, too, I learned that there can be no sweeter sound than the bell that calls a halt to hostilities.

From that afternoon on, also, dated my antipathy for the spectator at prize fights who yells: "Come on, you bum, get up and fight! Oh, you big quitter! Yah yellow, yah yellow!" Yellow, eh? It is all a man can do to get up after being stunned by a blow, much less fight back. But they do it. And how a man is able to muster any further interest in a combat after being floored with a blow to the pit of the stomach will always remain to me a miracle of what the human animal is capable of under stress.

PAUL GALLICO
from *Farewell to Sport*

Experience comes through the senses. Don't neglect them. Here is further advice on how to speak to your reader:

There are three main matters of prime importance in writing (and in writing science). These are Your Audience, Your Purpose, and Your Structure. That is their proper order.

Audience comes first. Since the only reason you write is to say something to somebody, it is certainly a good idea to know whom you are talking to and how he will react. Most people who write to sell don't think beyond the editor who is their immediate target. He is important, to be sure. But if you want to be outstanding, *or to last,* aim your mind over his head toward the hypothetical person with your writing before him. What can that person understand? What is to make him want to read your stuff? What are you trying to do to *him?* Do you want to amuse him? Inform him? Frighten him? Persuade him? Anger him? Or is it a combination of several of these? It is important to know.

It is important because when he reads your piece you won't be there to add a syllable, and he can flip the page any moment and forget you. Your object is to prevent that. To do so you must appeal to him on *his* terms. Before you write, you must imagine yourself in your reader's shoes, visualizing how he will react to your subject and to the way you present it.

A great deal of modern writing is done without thought of the reader. It is self-conscious or sterile, sometimes both at once. Frequently it is obtuse, occasionally downright opaque. This represents a disdain for the reader that is rarely permissible; never, in science writing. Often ignorance of the subject makes you commit these errors unintentionally. To avoid them, try this exercise before setting anything to paper. Ask yourself: How would I handle this matter if my reader were here before me and could talk back?

DAVID O. WOODBURY
from "Writing About Science"

Honest John Bunyan was the first that I know of who mixed narration and dialogue—a method of writing very engaging to the reader who in the most interesting parts, finds himself, as it were, brought into the company and present at the discourse.

BENJAMIN FRANKLIN

Assignment 7

1. Read the preceding observations.
2. In your journal do *one* of the following:
    a. Report what you can about Gallico's use of any *one* of the seven points numbered and italicized at the opening of this chapter.
    b. Rewrite a portion of the Gallico essay, paraphrasing if you wish. In rewriting make a shift in *point of view* and in *vocabulary*. For example, report the same experience but as it might have been told by Jack Dempsey, Luis Firpo, Gallico's younger brother, etc.
    c. Write an entry that mixes narration and dialogue. Consider each of the seven italicized terms at the opening of this chapter before you begin to write.

Assignment 8

There is always something better to be said than anything that has ever been said, but in the meantime somebody has got to agree to say something, and he can't take forever.

WILLIAM SAROYAN

In your journal do *one* of the following:
    a. Write an imaginary conversation with an imaginary reader about a subject you know "from the inside"—a sport, a hobby, or an interest.
    b. Review a short story and make an entry in which you comment on the author's use of sensory detail.

c. List the vocabulary words you have mastered this week. Then list as many synonyms for each word as you can find.

Assignment 9

Just get into the habit of putting words down, and try not to miss a day. I don't mean to say that anyone should stick at something that isn't going right. I often have to put a piece aside and come back to it later after I've switched to something else for a bit. But it's important just to write, consistently, persistently. Reading is probably just as important. Read everything you can put your hands on and have time for.

EMILY HAHN
from "Journal Keeping"

In your journal do *one* of the following:
   a. Recount a personal experience from which you learned something. Tell about the part that sensory impression played in the experience.
   b. Present a situation or event that shows the difference between observing and being personally involved.
   c. Write on a topic of your own choice.

1|4

HOW AN OBJECT
BECOMES A SYMBOL

What never seems to come quite clear is the simple fact that art is art. It is not life.

The life of the imagination will always remain separated from the life of reality. It feeds upon the life of reality, but it is not that life—cannot be. Mr. John Marin painting Brooklyn Bridge, Henry Fielding writing *Tom Jones,* are not trying in the novel and the painting to give us reality. They are striving for a realization in art of something out of their imaginative experiences, fed to be sure upon the life immediately about. A quite different matter from making an actual picture of what they see before them.

And here arises a confusion. For some reasoning —I myself have never exactly understood very clearly—the imagination must constantly feed upon reality or starve. Separate yourself too much from life and you may at moments be a lyrical poet, but you are not an artist. Something within dries up, starves for the want of food. Upon the fact in nature the imagination must constantly feed in order that the imaginative life remain significant.

SHERWOOD ANDERSON
from *Sherwood Anderson's Notebook*

Robert Frost understood the need of keeping one's feet on the ground and also the seemingly contradictory need of separating oneself from life. He tells about these needs in a poem that starts in a series of clear, accurate, down-to-earth observations, but with line 40 he transforms the physical into symbol and moves from the concrete to the abstract—from earth to heaven (or near there), from fact to dream. At the end he brings his fancy and himself safely down to earth.

This poem, "Birches," bears reading and rereading. It is a poem that dramatizes an experience—an experience in escape and rooted fact. And as the reader is set down gently upon the earth in the last line, he realizes the good of reaching out and coming back.

This poem is effective as statement, experience, and idea, partly because the central symbol works. One does not feel it is contrived, or reached for, but rather that it is natural and intimately understood. So, too, in the selection by Orwell later in this chapter, symbol represents as well as presents. Note Orwell's use of the dining-room door. Both he and Frost are masters at presenting detail, but by making a central object take on symbolic significance they are able to strengthen and enlarge their observations.

The ability to use the objects of daily life with an easy certainty, and at the same time to give them symbolic importance, is a way of relating art to life.

Birches

When I see birches bend to left and right
Across the lines of straighter darker trees,
I like to think some boy's been swinging them.
But swinging doesn't bend them down to stay
As ice storms do. Often you must have seen them
Loaded with ice a sunny winter morning   6
After a rain. They click upon themselves
As the breeze rises, and turn many-colored
As the stir cracks and crazes their enamel.
Soon the sun's warmth makes them shed crystal
    shells   10
Shattering and avalanching on the snow crust—
Such heaps of broken glass to sweep away
You'd think the inner dome of heaven had fallen.
They are dragged to the withered bracken by the
    load,
And they seem not to break; though once they are
    bowed   15

So low for long, they never right themselves;
You may see their trunks arching in the woods
Years afterwards, trailing their leaves on the
   ground
Like girls on hands and knees that throw their hair
Before them over their heads to dry in the sun.   20
But I was going to say when Truth broke in
With all her matter-of-fact about the ice storm,
I should prefer to have some boy bend them
As he went out and in to fetch the cows—
Some boy too far from town to learn baseball,   25
Whose only play was what he found himself,
Summer or winter, and could play alone.
One by one he subdued his father's trees
By riding them down over and over again
Until he took the stiffness out of them,   30
And not one but hung limp, not one was left
For him to conquer. He learned all there was
To learn about not launching out too soon
And so not carrying the tree away
Clear to the ground. He always kept his poise   35
To the top branches, climbing carefully
With the same pains you use to fill a cup
Up to the brim, and even above the brim.
Then he flung outward, feet first, with a swish,
Kicking his way down through the air to the
   ground.   40
So was I once myself a swinger of birches.
And so I dream of going back to be.
It's when I'm weary of considerations,
And life is too much like a pathless wood
Where your face burns and tickles with the
   cobwebs   45
Broken across it, and one eye is weeping
From a twig's having lashed across it open.
I'd like to get away from earth awhile
And then come back to it and begin over.
May no fate willfully misunderstand me   50
And half grant what I wish and snatch me away
Not to return. Earth's the right place for love:
I don't know where it's likely to go better.

I'd like to go by climbing a birch tree,   54
And climb black branches up a snow-white trunk
Toward heaven, till the tree could bear no more,
But dipped its top and set me down again.
That would be good both going and coming back.
One could do worse than be a swinger of birches.

ROBERT FROST

My bad day was when I washed up for the dining
room. I had not to wash the plates, which were
done in the kitchen, but only the other crockery,
silver, knives and glasses; yet, even so, it meant
thirteen hours' work, and I used between thirty
and forty dishcloths during the day. The anti-
quated methods used in France double the work of
washing up. Plate-racks are unheard-of, and there
are no soap flakes, only the treacly soft soap, which
refuses to lather in the hard, Paris water. I worked
in a dirty, crowded little den, a pantry and scullery
combined, which gave straight on the dining room.
Besides washing up, I had to fetch the waiters' food
and serve them at table; most of them were intol-
erably insolent, and I had to use my fists more than
once to get common civility. The person who nor-
mally washed up was a woman, and they made her
life a misery.

It was amusing to look around the filthy little
scullery and think that only a double door was
between us and the dining room. There sat the
customers in all their splendor—spotless tablecloths,
bowls of flowers, mirrors and gilt cornices and
painted cherubim; and here, just a few feet away,
we in our disgusting filth. For it really was disgusting filth. There was no time to sweep the floor till
evening, and we slithered about in a compound of
soapy water, lettuce-leaves, torn paper, and trampled food. A dozen waiters with their coats off,
showing their sweaty armpits, sat at a table mixing
salads and sticking their thumbs into the cream
pots. The room had a dirty, mixed smell of food
and sweat. Everywhere in the cupboards, behind

the piles of crockery, were squalid stores of food that the waiters had stolen. There were only two sinks, and no washing basin, and it was nothing unusual for a waiter to wash his face in the water in which clean crockery was rinsing. But the customers saw nothing of this. There were a coconut mat and a mirror outside the dining-room door, and the waiters used to preen themselves up and go in looking the picture of cleanliness.

It is an instructive sight to see a waiter going into a hotel dining room. As he passes the door a sudden change comes over him. The set of his shoulders alters; all the dirt and hurry and irritation have dropped off in an instant. He glides over the carpet, with a solemn priestlike air. I remember our assistant maître d'hôtel, a fiery Italian, pausing at the dining-room door to address an apprentice who had broken a bottle of wine. Shaking his fist above his head, he yelled (luckily the door was more or less soundproof). . . .

Words failing him, he turned to the door; and as he opened it he delivered a final insult in the same manner as Squire Western in *Tom Jones*.

Then he entered the dining room and sailed across it dish in hand, graceful as a swan. Ten seconds later he was bowing reverently to a customer. And you could not help thinking, as you saw him bow and smile, with that benign smile of the trained waiter, that the customer was put to shame by having such an aristocrat to serve him.

This washing up was a thoroughly odious job— not hard, but boring and silly beyond words. It is dreadful to think that some people spend their whole decades at such occupations. The woman whom I replaced was quite sixty years old, and she stood at the sink thirteen hours a day, six days a week, the year round; she was, in addition, horribly bullied by the waiters. . . .

GEORGE ORWELL
from *Down and Out in Paris and London*

Assignment 10

1. Read the chapter up to this point.
2. In your journal do *one* of the following:
   a. Make your own statement of the basic ideas about writing presented in this chapter. You may wish to use supporting examples from your own reading or other experience.
   b. Explain as best you can the difference between art and life.
   c. If experience comes to you through the senses, how does it come to a reader? Examine a short story you know and *list* the words used to transmit sense impression.

Assignment 11

"*My method is to make a memorandum every night of what I have seen during the day. By this means I have my materials always secured. Sometimes I am three, four, five days without journalizing. When I have time and spirits, I bring up this my Journal as well as I can in the hasty manner in which I write it.*" . . . Like all diary-keepers, indeed, he [Boswell] dreamed of a Journal which should be "full" and always up to date. But more than most he fell short. Dissipation, laziness, hypochondria are excuses he alternately makes. But he had taken to heart Johnson's warning of the dangers of "dilatory notation" and every night, or next morning, he jotted down in "shorthand" a summary of the day's events and the day's conversation. And this was done not as a permanent record, but simply to serve as a reminder when in a few days or weeks he found time to "bring up" his Journal. Now and again the ideal of a full Journal keeping pace with the events was realized for a few days, after the birth of a son, a New Year, an arrival in London, or at some other "fresh start"; and on these occasions he resolves never again to fall back. But he invariably reverts to the stopgap "short-hand" Notes.

It is no exaggeration to say that Boswell regarded his Journal as the principal duty and aim of his existence; life unrecorded was not life. He goes so far as to make this singular pronouncement: "I should live no more than I can record, as one should not have more corn growing than one can get in. There is a waste of good if it be not preserved. . . ."

Nevertheless in every act of life he is registering the scene, and analyzing the sensation, with a view to putting it on record. As for disagreeable experiences, there is nothing, he says, that he cannot go through, *if only I am to give an account of it.*

from *The Making of the Life of Johnson*

1. Read the introductory statement by Boswell.
2. In your journal do *one* of the following:
   a. Write an entry in which you use a simple object from daily life as a symbol.
   b. Reread the statement by Boswell. Make a memorandum of what you have seen today. Do this not as "journalizing" but as a way of making your "materials always secured." You may use these notes as a reminder for a later journal entry.
   c. Write on any topic you wish.

Assignment 12

"Fool!" said my muse to me, "look in thy heart, and write."

SIR PHILIP SIDNEY
from *Astrophel and Stella*

In your journal do *one* of the following:
   a. If you have been working on a short story, now start a final draft.

b. ". . . the imagination must constantly feed upon reality or starve." Consider and comment.

c. Take the notes of what you have seen, as recorded in Assignment 11, and expand them into a full entry.

1|5

WRITING FROM EXPERIENCE

It is equally excellent and inconclusive to say that one must write from experience; to our suppositious aspirant such a declaration might savor of mockery. What kind of experience is intended, and where does it begin and end? Experience is never limited, and it is never complete; it is an immense sensibility, a kind of huge spider web of the finest silken threads suspended in the chamber of consciousness, and catching every air-borne particle in its tissue. It is the very atmosphere of the mind; and when the mind is imaginative—much more when it happens to be that of a man of genius—it takes to itself the faintest hints of life, it converts the very pulses of the air into revelations. The young lady living in a village has only to be a damsel upon whom nothing is lost to make it quite unfair (as it seems to me) to declare to her that she shall have nothing to say about the military. Greater miracles have been seen than that, imagination assisting, she should speak the truth about some of these gentlemen. I remember an English novelist, a woman of genius, telling me that she was much commended for the impression she had managed to give in one of her tales of the nature and way of life of the French Protestant youth. She had been asked where she learned so much about this recondite being; she had been congratulated on her peculiar opportunities. These opportunities consisted in her having once, in Paris, as she ascended a staircase, passed an open door where, in the household of a *pasteur,* some of the young Protestants were seated at table round a finished meal.

The glimpse made a picture; it lasted only a moment, but that moment was experience. She had got her direct personal impression, and she turned out her type. She knew what youth was, and what Protestantism; she also had the advantage of having seen what it was to be French, so that she converted these ideas into a concrete image and produced a reality. Above all, however, she was blessed with the faculty which when you give it an inch takes an ell, and which for the artist is a much greater source of strength than any accident of residence or of place in the social scale. The power to guess the unseen from the seen, to trace the implications of things, to judge the whole piece by the pattern, the condition of feeling life in general so completely that you are well on your way to knowing any particular corner of it—this cluster of gifts may almost be said to constitute experience, and they occur in country and in town, and in the most differing stages of education. If experience consists of impressions, it may be said that impressions are experience, just as (have we not seen it?) they are the very air we breathe. Therefore, if I should certainly say to a novice, "Write from experience and experience only," I should feel that this was rather a tantalizing monition if I were not careful immediately to add, "Try to be one of the people on whom nothing is lost!"

HENRY JAMES
from "The Art of Fiction"

But how do you become one of those people "on whom nothing is lost"? By using your luck, your talent—if you are born that way, and if you are not, then by working at it. Respond! See, Savor, Say—that technique succeeds.

Emily Dickinson is a model of such a person. Although her experience was limited—no college, no travel, nineteenth-century Amherst, Massachusetts—she nevertheless converted ugliness and beauty into statements that show how little was lost upon her. Here are two of her poems:

A Narrow Fellow in the Grass

A narrow fellow in the grass
Occasionally rides;
You may have met him—did you not?
His notice sudden is.

The grass divides as with a comb,
A spotted shaft is seen;
And then it closes at your feet
And opens further on.

He likes a boggy acre,
A floor too cool for corn,
Yet when a boy, and barefoot,
I more than once, at noon,

Have passed, I thought, a whiplash
Unbraiding in the sun—
When, stopping to secure it,
It wrinkled, and was gone.

Several of nature's people
I know, and they know me;
I feel for them a transport
Of cordiality;

But never met this fellow,
Attended or alone,
Without a tighter breathing,
And zero at the bone.

Indian Summer

These are the days when birds come back,
A very few, a bird or two,
To take a backward look.

These are the days when skies put on
The old, old sophistries of June,—
A blue and gold mistake.

Oh, fraud that cannot cheat the bee,
Almost thy plausibility
Induces my belief,

Till ranks of seeds their witness bear,
And softly through the altered air
Hurries a timid leaf!

Oh, sacrament of summer days,
Oh, last communion in the haze,
Permit a child to join,

Thy sacred emblems to partake,
Thy consecrated bread to break,
Taste thine immortal wine!

EMILY DICKINSON

Now here is a very different person—Thomas Wolfe—who represents another time and experience. But his words explain what is meant by "working at it" and what is meant by being one of those people "on whom nothing is lost."

In my own experience, my wedding guests were the great ledgers in which I wrote, and the tale which I told to them would have seemed, I am afraid, completely incoherent, as meaningless as Chinese characters, had any reader seen them. I could by no means hope to give a comprehensive idea of the whole extent of this labor because three years of work and perhaps a million and a half words went into these books. It included everything from gigantic and staggering lists of the towns, cities, counties, states, and countries I had been in, to minutely thorough, desperately evocative descriptions of the undercarriage, the springs, wheels, flanges, axle rods, color, weight, and quality of the day coach of an American railway train. There were lists of the rooms and houses in which I had lived or in which I had slept for at least a night, together with the most accurate and evocative descriptions of those rooms that I could write—their

size, their shape, the color and design of the wall-
paper, the way a towel hung down, the way a chair
creaked, a streak of water rust upon the ceiling.
There were countless charts, catalogues, descriptions that I can only classify here under the general
heading of Amount and Number. What were the
total combined populations of all the countries in
Europe and America? In how many of those countries had I had some personal and vital experience?
In the course of my twenty-nine or thirty years of
living, how many people had I seen? How many
had I passed by on the streets? How many had I
seen on trains and subways, in theaters, at baseball
or football games? With how many had I actually
had some vital and illuminating experience,
whether of joy, pain, anger, pity, love, or simple
casual companionship, however brief?

In addition, one might come upon other sections
under some such cryptic headings as "Where now?"
Under such a heading as this, there would be brief
notations of those thousands of things which all of
us have seen for just a flash, a moment in our lives,
which seem to be of no consequence whatever at
the moment that we see them, and which live in our
minds and hearts forever, which are somehow preg-
nant with all the joy and sorrow of the human
destiny, and which we know, somehow, are therefore more important than many things of more
apparent consequence. "Where now?" Some quiet
steps that came and passed along a leafy nighttime
street in summer in a little town down South long
years ago; a woman's voice, her sudden burst of
low and tender laughter; then the voices and the
footsteps going, silence, the leafy rustle of the trees.
. . . Where now—in these great ledger books,
month after month, I wrote such things as this, not
only the concrete, material record of man's ordered
memory, but all the things he scarcely dares to
think he has remembered; all the flicks and darts
and haunting lights that flash across the mind of

man that will return unbidden at an unexpected moment: a voice once heard; a face that vanished; the way the sunlight came and went; the rustling of a leaf upon a bough; a stone, a leaf, a door. . . .

For the first time I was forced to consider squarely this problem: where does the material of an artist come from? What are the proper uses of that material, and how far must his freedom in the use of that material be controlled by his responsibility as a member of society? This is a difficult problem, and I have by no means come to the bottom of it yet. Perhaps I never shall, but as a result of all the distress which I suffered at that time and which others may have suffered on account of me, I have done much thinking and arrived at certain conclusions.

My book was what is often referred to as an autobiographical novel. I protested against this term in a preface to the book upon the grounds that any serious work of creation is of necessity autobiographical and that few more autobiographical works than *Gulliver's Travels* have ever been written. I added that Dr. Johnson had remarked that a man might turn over half the volumes in his library to make a single book, and that in a similar way, a novelist might turn over half the characters in his native town to make a single figure for his novel. In spite of this the people in my native town were not persuaded or appeased, and the charge of autobiography was brought against me in many other places.

As I have said, my conviction is that all serious creative work must be at bottom autobiographical, and that a man must use the material and experience of his own life if he is to create anything that has substantial value. But I also believe now that the young writer is often led through inexperience to a use of the materials of life which are, perhaps, somewhat too naked and direct for the purpose of a work of art. The thing a young writer is likely to do is to confuse the limits between actuality and reality. He tends unconsciously to describe an event in such a way because it actually happened that way, and from an artistic point of view, I can now see that this is wrong. It is not, for example, important that one remembers a beautiful woman of easy virtue as having come from the state of Kentucky in the year 1907. She could perfectly well have come from Idaho or Texas or Nova Scotia. The important thing really is only to express as well as possible the character and quality of the beautiful woman of easy virtue. But the young writer, chained to fact and to his own inexperience, as yet unliberated by maturity, is likely to argue, "she must be described as coming from Kentucky because that is where she actually did come from."

In spite of this, it is impossible for a man who has the stuff of creation in him to make a literal transcription of his own experience. Everything in a work of art is changed and transfigured by the personality of the artist. And as far as my own first book is concerned, I can truthfully say that I do not believe that there is a single page of it that is true to fact. And from this circumstance, also, I learned another curious thing about writing. For although my book was not true to fact, it was true to the general experience of the town I came from and I hope, of course, to the general experience of all men living. The best way I can describe the situation is this: it was as if I were a sculptor who had found a certain kind of clay with which to model. Now a farmer who knew well the neighborhood from which this clay had come might pass by and find the sculptor at his work and say to him, "I know the farm from which you got that clay." But it would be unfair of him to say, "I know the figure, too." Now I think what happened in my native town is that having seen the clay, they became immediately convinced that they recognized the figure, too, and the results of this misconception were so painful and ludicrous that the telling of it is almost past belief.

THOMAS WOLFE
from *The Story of a Novel*

And the most important preliminary to self-development is the faculty of concentrating at will.

ARNOLD BENNETT
from *Mental Efficiency*

Assignment 13

1. Read the chapter up to this point.
2. In your journal do *one* of the following:
   a. Discuss one of the key ideas in this chapter.
   b. In your own words explain what Henry James said in the excerpt presented here from "The Art of Fiction."
   c. What questions would you ask were you to test a reader on this chapter? Write out the questions and your answers to them.

Assignment 14

In your journal do *one* of the following:
   a. Write about the poem "Indian Summer" or about your own experience with a season.
   b. Demonstrate your own ability to guess the unseen from the seen.
   c. Explain what you mean by "writing from experience."

Assignment 15

The truth of fiction involves such matters as the following: (1) the consistency and comprehensibility of character; (2) the motivation and credibility of action; and (3) the acceptability of the total meaning. As for the method of fiction, it should also be evident, even at this point, that these three matters —character, action, and theme—are intimately bound up together.

CLEANTH BROOKS and ROBERT PENN WARREN
from *Understanding Fiction*

In your journal do *one* of the following:
a. If you have been working on a short story, bring it to completion, or at least to the point where it can be read and commented on in class.
b. Write a "Where now?" entry of your own.
c. Outline a story that is not true to fact, but true to experience. You may invent your story or use one you have read. If you choose the latter, be sure to give author, title, and source.

1 Review

For some useful suggestions on writing autobiography, see the following comments by Mary Ellen Chase and by James Baldwin. Baldwin gives an example of what can be done within a short space. Note in particular his use of ideas.

There are three inescapable problems before the student who is to write an autobiography: (1) that of incident and detail; (2) that of evaluation and choice; (3) that of plan and organization.

A conversation, not imaginary, and only recently held with a college freshman, may serve to illustrate this first problem:

"I wish I could write a different theme, Miss C——. This one is bound to be stupid. There isn't a thing in my life worth telling."

"That's too bad. Why such a dull life?"

"Oh, I've lived in the country and in Nebraska —of all places!"

"What's the matter with Nebraska? Miss Cather seems to have found something interesting."

"Well—yes. But *I* can't. She's different."

"When were you born?"

"Oh, eighteen years ago—in the winter."

"On just an ordinary day?"

"No, not exactly. They say there was a blizzard."

"That's not a bad start for anyone. Remember the blizzard in *My Antonia?*"

"Yes, but—well, anyway, I guess it was a bad blizzard. The doctor couldn't get through the snow."

"Better still. What about your childhood?"

"Oh, just going to a country school on the prairie."

"Well, the prairie. What about that? Weren't there flowers or storms or cold days? How did you get to school—walk or ride? Were there animals about? What were the teachers like? Were your neighbors foreign or American born? What did you raise on your farm? Did you ever have a scourge of locusts or a hailstorm or a cyclone?"

In half an hour by means of somewhat impatient labor, for it is irritating to find a person so blind to the drama of environment, I discovered that this girl, who had had nothing in her life worth telling, had been born in a blizzard, had learned to ride when she was four years old, for seven years had ridden three miles morning and afternoon in all weathers to and from school, had made a collection of prairie wildflowers, which had won first prize at the State Fair, had herself earned five hundred dollars toward her college expenses by growing a plot of wheat, and had lived through a cyclone which tore the roof from the schoolhouse and killed three children! And yet her theme was bound to be stupid! I recommended more of Willa Cather and Anna Howard Shaw's *The Story of a Pioneer* and with a long sigh sent her to the library.

Many lives which seem bare of drama are yet rich in detail. Had the freshman under consideration missed both blizzard and cyclone, she would still have had the morning and evening rides over the prairie with its sunlight and rain, its stretches of snow, its spring awakenings. Indeed, she might well have written her theme about her interest in Nebraskan wildflowers since they clearly had greatly influenced her life. The gathering of flowers may or may not be a dramatic incident—that will depend upon the viewpoint of the gatherer—but at least it may afford an abundance of bright detail.

The Nebraskan freshman was not unusual in her point of view. She could not feel that her life on the prairie, interesting to her in spite of her insistence upon its worthlessness as theme material, could possibly interest others. Now that attitude is a great mistake which must be corrected at the outset. No one but yourself can evaluate the happenings and the emotions of your life; and it is safe to say that, given genuine interest on your part, your theme, no matter what its other and lesser defects, cannot be dull.

MARY ELLEN CHASE
from *Constructive Theme Writing*

I was born in Harlem thirty-one years ago. I began plotting novels at about the time I learned to read. The story of my childhood is the usual bleak fantasy, and we can dismiss it with the restrained observation that I certainly would not consider living it again. In those days my mother was given to the exasperating and mysterious habit of having babies. As they were born, I took them over with one hand and held a book with the other. The children probably suffered, though they have since been kind enough to deny it, and in this way I read *Uncle Tom's Cabin* and *A Tale of Two Cities* over and over and over again; in this way, in fact, I read just about everything I could get my hands on— except the Bible, probably because it was the only book I was encouraged to read. I must also confess that I wrote—a great deal—and my first professional triumph, in any case, the first effort of mine to be seen in print, occurred at the age of twelve or thereabouts, when a short story I had written about the Spanish revolution won some sort of prize in an extremely short-lived church newspaper. I remember the story was censored by the lady editor, though I don't remember why, and I was outraged.

Also wrote plays, and songs, for one of which I received a letter of congratulations from Mayor La Guardia, and poetry, about which the less said, the better. My mother was delighted by all these goings-on, but my father wasn't; he wanted me to be a preacher. When I was fourteen I became a preacher, and when I was seventeen I stopped. Very shortly thereafter I left home. For God knows how long I struggled with the world of commerce and industry—I guess they would say they struggled with *me*—and when I was about twenty-one I had enough done of a novel to get a Saxton Fellowship. When I was twenty-two the fellowship was over, the novel turned out to be unsalable, and I started waiting on tables in a Village restaurant and writing book reviews—mostly, as it turned out, about the Negro problem, concerning which the color of my skin made me automatically an expert. Did another book, in company with photographer Theodore Pelatowski, about the store-front churches in Harlem. This book met exactly the same fate as my first—fellowship, but no sale. (It was a Rosenwald Fellowship.) By the time I was twenty-four I had decided to stop reviewing books about the Negro problem—which, by this time, was only slightly less horrible in print than it was in life—and I packed my bags and went to France, where I finished, God knows how, *Go Tell It on the Mountain*.

Any writer, I suppose, feels that the world into which he was born is nothing less than a conspiracy against the cultivation of his talent—which attitude certainly has a great deal to support it. On the other hand, it is only because the world looks on his talent with such a frightening indifference that the artist is compelled to make his talent important. So that any writer, looking back over even so short a span of time as I am here forced to assess, finds that the things which hurt him and the things which helped him cannot be divorced from each other; he could be helped in a certain way only because he was hurt in a certain way; and his help is simply to be enabled to move from one conundrum to the next—one is tempted to say that he moves from one disaster to the next. When one begins looking for influences one finds them by the score. I haven't thought much about my own, not enough anyway; I hazard that the King James Bible, the rhetoric of the store-front church, something ironic and violent and perpetually understated in Negro speech—and something of Dickens's love for bravura—have something to do with me today; but I wouldn't stake my life on it. Likewise, innumerable people have helped me in many ways; but finally, I suppose, the most difficult (and most rewarding) thing in my life has been the fact that I was born a Negro and was forced, therefore, to effect some kind of truce with this reality. (Truce, by the way, is the best one can hope for.)

One of the difficulties about being a Negro writer (and this is not special pleading, since I don't mean to suggest that he has it worse than anybody else) is that the Negro problem is written about so widely. The bookshelves groan under the weight of information, and everyone therefore considers himself informed. And this information, further-more, operates usually (generally, popularly) to reinforce traditional attitudes. Of traditional atti-tudes there are only two—For or Against—and I, personally, find it difficult to say which attitude has caused me the most pain. I am speaking as a writer; from a social point of view I am perfectly aware that the change from ill-will to good-will, however motivated, however imperfect, however expressed, is better than no change at all.

But it is part of the business of the writer—as I see it—to examine attitudes, to go beneath the sur-face, to tap the source. From this point of view the Negro problem is nearly inaccessible. It is not only written about so widely; it is written about so badly. It is quite possible to say that the price a Negro pays for becoming articulate is to find him-self, at length, with nothing to be articulate about. ("You taught me language," says Caliban to Pros-pero, "and my profit on't is I know how to curse.") Consider: the tremendous social activity that this problem generates imposes on whites and Negroes alike the necessity of looking forward, of working to bring about a better day. This is fine, it keeps the waters troubled; it is all, indeed, that has made possible the Negro's progress. Nevertheless, social affairs are not generally speaking the writer's prime concern, whether they ought to be or not; it is absolutely necessary that he establish between himself and these affairs a distance which will allow, at least, for clarity, so that before he can look forward in any meaningful sense, he must first be allowed to take a long look back. In the context of the Negro problem neither whites nor blacks, for excellent reasons of their own, have the faintest desire to look back; but I think that the past is all that makes the present coherent, and further, that the past will remain horrible for exactly as long as we refuse to assess it honestly.

I know, in any case, that the most crucial time in my own development came when I was forced to recognize that I was a kind of bastard of the West; when I followed the line of my past I did not find myself in Europe but in Africa. And this meant that in some subtle way, in a really profound way, I brought to Shakespeare, Bach, Rembrandt, to the stones of Paris, to the cathedral at Chartres, and to the Empire State Building, a special attitude. These were not really my creations, they did not contain my history; I might search in them in vain forever, for any reflection of myself. I was an interloper; this was not my heritage. At the same time I had no other heritage which I could possibly hope to use—I had certainly been unfitted for the jungle or the tribe. I would have to appropriate these white centuries, I would have to make them mine —I would have to accept my special attitude, my special place in this scheme—otherwise I would have no place in *any* scheme. What was the most difficult was the fact that I was forced to admit something I had always hidden from myself, which the American Negro has had to hide from himself as the price of his public progress; that I hated and feared white people. This did not mean that I loved black people; on the contrary, I despised them, possibly because they failed to produce Rembrandt. In effect, I hated and feared the world. And this meant, not only that I thus gave the world an altogether murderous power over me, but also that in such a self-destroying limbo I could never hope to write.

One writes out of one thing only—one's own experience. Everything depends on how relentlessly one forces from this experience the last drop, sweet or bitter, it can possibly give. This is the only real concern of the artist, to re-create out of the disorder of life that order which is art. The difficulty then, for me, of being a Negro writer was the fact that I was, in effect, prohibited from examining my own experience too closely by the tremendous demands and the very real dangers of my social situation.

I don't think the dilemma outlined above is uncommon. I do think, since writers work in the disastrously explicit medium of language, that it goes a little way toward explaining why, out of the enormous resources of Negro speech and life, and despite the example of Negro music, prose written by Negroes has been generally speaking so pallid and so harsh. I have not written about being a Negro at such length because I expect that to be my only subject, but only because it was the gate I had to unlock before I could hope to write about anything else. I don't think that the Negro problem in America can be even discussed coherently without bearing in mind its context; its context being the history, traditions, customs, the moral assumptions and preoccupations of the country; in short, the general social fabric. Appearances to the contrary, no one in America escapes its effects and everyone in America bears some responsibility for it. I believe this the more firmly because it is the overwhelming tendency to speak of this problem as though it were a thing apart. But in the work of Faulkner, in the general attitude and certain specific passages in Robert Penn Warren, and, most significantly, in the advent of Ralph Ellison, one sees the beginnings—at least—of a more genuinely penetrating search. Mr. Ellison, by the way, is the first Negro novelist I have ever read to utilize in language, and brilliantly, some of the ambiguity and irony of Negro life.

About my interests: I don't know if I have any, unless the morbid desire to own a sixteen-millimeter camera and make experimental movies can be so classified. Otherwise, I love to eat and drink—it's my melancholy conviction that I've scarcely ever had enough to eat (this is because it's *impossible* to eat enough if you're worried about the next meal)—and I love to argue with people who do not disagree with me too profoundly, and I love to laugh. I do *not* like bohemia, or bohemians, I do not like people whose principal aim is pleasure, and I do not like people who are *earnest* about anything. I don't like people who like me because I'm a Negro; neither do I like people who find in the same accident grounds for contempt. I love America more than any other country in the world, and, exactly for this reason, I insist on the right to criticize her perpetually. I think all theories are suspect, that the finest principles may have to be modified, or may even be pulverized by the demands of life, and that one must find, therefore, one's own moral center and move through the world hoping that this center will guide one aright. I consider that I have many responsibilities, but none greater than this: to last, as Hemingway says, and get my work done.

I want to be an honest man and a good writer.

JAMES BALDWIN
from *Notes of a Native Son*

Review Assignment

Check with your instructor for time allowance on this assignment.

In your journal do *one* of the following:
  a. Write a biography of yourself. This is a writing assignment required by many college application forms and

by many freshman English courses. In treating it as a journal assignment, try to do your best piece of writing to date. Have in mind that the experience will be of practical value to you.

b. List the chief events in your life. Then choose one that had special significance for you. Describe the event and tell why it was significant.

c. List the chief events in your life. Then choose one event that you feel lends itself to fiction. Write a factual narrative of the event. Then write a fictional account of the same happening.

UNIT 2

Observation

A person whose eyesight or hearing is faulty may not be aware of his difficulty until he tests his faculties. Just as some people go for years without discovering that one of their senses is impaired, most people probably go through life with underdeveloped powers of observation.—FRED MORGAN

2|1

BUT HOW IS IT DONE?

In this unit you'll be expected to start each writing assignment with notations and sentences that catch your own best ideas and observations of the day; comment on what you see in nature and in the world around you. As Leacock suggested (Unit 1, page 8), keep "a sort of 'commonplace book' in which one writes all kinds of random attempts at expression. If you have just read a book, write a few words down about it. If a moving picture has deeply moved you, write down the fact and try to explain why. Cultivate admiration of other people's words and phrases that seem to express much, and write them down." There will not be time to develop these jottings at length, but set them down much in the way James Boswell keep his notes (Unit 1, page 31). Devote about half a page to this work before starting your regular assignment. Use this prewriting as a kind of warmup for the more directed writing required by each lesson.

In Unit 2 the focus is on Observation, an important skill in itself and one upon which all subsequent work is built. Although your final goal is to unify a variety of skills, the need at the moment is to develop skill in making your writing concrete and in involving the senses of your reader.

As you begin this unit, you are in the foothills of a long climb. Don't be discouraged. There is every assurance that you will get where you want to go provided you work in an orderly way. For nothing you'll get nothing, but every effort will move you forward. Of course, there are learning plateaus; there will be periods without apparent upward progress, but if you write regularly, you will improve, a fact demonstrated by every writer who has moved from novice to professional.

In *The Summing Up*, W. Somerset Maugham tells us:

> It is evident that no professional writer can afford
> only to write when he feels like it. If he waits 'til

he is in the mood, 'til he has the inspiration as he says, he waits indefinitely and ends by producing little or nothing. The professional writer creates the mood. He has his inspiration too, but he controls and subdues it to his bidding by setting himself regular hours of work. But in time writing becomes a habit, and like the old actor in retirement who gets restless when the hour arrives at which he has been accustomed to go down to the theater and make up for the evening performance, the writer itches to get to his pens and paper at the hours at which he has been used to write. . . . Every production of an artist should be the expression of an adventure of his soul. This is a counsel of perfection and in an imperfect world a certain indulgence should be bestowed on the professional writer; but this surely is the aim he should keep before him.

One of the best ways to realize a goal is to start acting on the wish. If you want to experience some of the sense of achievement that goes with a professional job, then you must do what the professionals do—write regularly. We all know that we aren't at our best every day, and there is a great disposition to wait until we are at our best before we start a writing job—letters, essay, or what you will. The "optimum moment" approach is comfortable but not realistic. A runner must run on the days he doesn't feel like it—even a jogger has to practice three or four times a week. If you write regularly, incorporate your optimum moments into your work; you'll find yourself experiencing more optimum moments. So place your pen on paper and start pushing. The more you've thought about your topic before you write, the better. As you go about your daily tasks think about your next piece of writing.

Yes, I know what you are about to say, and there is some truth in it. If you write a lot, you may perforce be substituting quantity for quality. So you may, but don't be afraid of it. You can always edit out the bad, and if you are all bad on some days, face that fact too. It happens to all of us. But you've got to go beyond getting stuck if you want to succeed, and you can't let the fear of failure short-circuit your potential performance.

If you want to find out what a person is like, go on a trip with him. If you want to know what your own writing is made of, see how it holds up over the long stretch of regular composition. That will bring out your real faults so that you and others can see them. There is no criticism like group criticism—write and be judged.

But if you would write, you must first observe, for observation is the footing upon which all you say must be built. Observation is seeing—seeing with the eye, the mind, and the heart. All men have some skill in this way, though some more than others. Necessity may prompt this faculty, curiosity may whet it, but nothing develops this skill like practice. If you would be a good observer, you must train yourself. In part, this can be done by keeping notes on the things you see— much as Boswell kept his journal. You will find it helpful too, in both observing and in writing, to keep in mind the distinction between literal, selective or subjective, and imaginative description. You will by turns want to try your hand at each. For your convenience here are the terms in review: (1) *Literal description* is visual, factual, accurate, photographic reportage of what one has seen, felt, or thought. (2) *Selective or subjective description* makes no attempt to see or report all, but rather it filters experience through some particular bias or angle of vision. (3) *Imaginative description* presents what is seen in speculation, or in anticipation. The normal controls of fact and event are transformed by wish and by the magic of the inward eye, and, in consequence, such observation may be as accurate or fanciful as the mind of the viewer dictates. These distinctions, while useful, do not pretend that writing is in fact compartmentalized. They simply make more distinct the approaches that you should practice. Most writing, of course, involves a synthesis of observation, imagination, and reflection, which brings together a medley of techniques. But for now, and because we are consciously trying to improve, the focus is on observation.

Nathaniel Hawthorne's journal is a model of the kind of observation you should be making in your entries for this unit. The first example given here presents literal description, the second selection illustrates selective or subjective description, and the third example uses in its last paragraph imaginative description. Here are his entries:

(1)

Mr. Leach and I took a walk by moonlight, last evening, on the road that leads over the mountain. Remote from houses, far up on the hillside, we found a limekiln, burning near the roadside; and, approaching it, a watcher started from the ground, where he had been lying at his length. There are several of these limekilns in this vicinity; they are built circular, with stones, like a round tower, eighteen or twenty feet high; having a hillock heaped around in a considerable portion of their circumference, so that the marble may be brought and thrown in by cartloads at the top. At the bottom there is a doorway, large enough to admit a man in a stooping posture. Thus an edifice of great solidity is composed, which will endure for centuries, unless needless pains are taken to tear it down. There is one on the hillside, close to the village, wherein weeds grow at the bottom, and grass and shrubs too are rooted in the interstices of the stones, and its low doorway has a dungeon-like aspect, and we look down from the top as into a roofless tower. It apparently has not been used for many years, and the lime and weather-stained fragments of marble are scattered about.

But in the one we saw last night a hardwood fire was burning merrily beneath the superincumbent marble—the kiln being heaped full; and shortly after we came, the man (a dark, black-bearded figure, in shirt sleeves) opened the iron door, through the chinks of which the fire was gleaming, and thrust in huge logs of wood, and stirred the immense coals with a long pole; and showed us the glowing limestone—the lower layer of it. The glow of the fire was powerful, at the distance of several yards from the open door. He talked very sociably with us, being doubtless glad to have two visitors to vary his solitary nightwatch. . . .

(2)

Returning by the almshouse, I stopped a good while to look at the pigs—a great herd—who seemed to be just finishing their suppers. They certainly are types of unmitigated sensuality—some standing in the trough, in the midst of their own and others' victuals—some thrusting their noses deep into the food—some rubbing their backs against a post—some huddled together between sleeping and waking, breathing hard—all wallowing about; a great boar swaggering round, and a big sow waddling along with her huge paunch. Notwithstanding the unspeakable defilement with which these strange sensualists spice all their food, they seem to have a quick and delicate sense of smell. What ridiculous-looking animals! Swift himself could not have imagined anything nastier than what they practice by the mere impulse of natural genius.

(3)

In a wood, a heap or pile of logs and sticks, that had been cut for firewood, and piled up square, in order to be carted away to the house when convenience served—or, rather, to be sledded in sleighing time. But the moss had accumulated on them, and leaves falling over them from year to year and decaying, a kind of soil had quite covered them, although the softened outline of the woodpile was perceptible in the green mound. It was perhaps fifty years—perhaps more—since the woodman had cut and piled those logs and sticks, intending them for his winter fires. But he probably needs no fire now. There was something strangely interesting in this simple circumstance. Imagine the long-dead woodman, and his long-dead wife and family, and one old man who was a little child when the wood was cut, coming back from their graves, and trying to make a fire with this mossy fuel.

from *The Heart of Hawthorne's Journals*
edited by Newton Arvin

You will note Hawthorne's observations in this last selection are factual and objective, but that he treats his topic in a way that is both speculative and imaginative.

The following poem, "The Wood-pile" by Robert Frost, treats the subject in the same spirit, but here the imaginative aspect is more fully drawn. It is interesting to note, however, that both writers rely heavily on factual observations as the basis of thought and imaginative description.

The Wood-pile

Out walking in the frozen swamp one gray day,
I paused and said, "I will turn back from here.
No, I will go on farther—and we shall see."
The hard snow held me, save where now and then
One foot went through. The view was all in lines
Straight up and down of tall slim trees
Too much alike to mark or name a place by
So as to say for certain I was here
Or somewhere else: I was just far from home.
A small bird flew before me. He was careful
To put a tree between us when he lighted,
And say no word to tell me who he was
Who was so foolish as to think what *he* thought.
He thought that I was after him for a feather—
The white one in his tail; like one who takes
Everything said as personal to himself.
One flight out sideways would have undeceived him.
And then there was a pile of wood for which
I forgot him and let his little fear
Carry him off the way I might have gone,
Without so much as wishing him good-night.
He went behind it to make his last stand.
It was a cord of maple, cut and split
And piled—and measured, four by four by eight.
And not another like it could I see.
No runner tracks in this year's snow looped near it.
And it was older sure than this year's cutting,
Or even last year's or the year's before.
The wood was gray and the bark warping off it

And the pile somewhat sunken. Clematis
Had wound strings round and round it like a bundle.
What held it, though, on one side was a tree
Still growing, and on one a stake and prop,
These latter about to fall. I thought that only
Someone who lived in turning to fresh tasks
Could so forget his handiwork on which
He spent himself, the labor of his ax,
And leave it there far from a useful fireplace
To warm the frozen swamp as best it could
With the slow smokeless burning of decay.

ROBERT FROST

But by now you may fairly ask, "How is it done?" Here is an explanation.

Rudyard Kipling presents the answer in his novel *Kim*—where Lurgan Sahib and his pupil teach the Jewel Game to Kim.

> The child dried his tears at once, and dashed to the back of the shop, whence he returned with a copper tray.
>
> "Give me!" he said to Lurgan Sahib. "Let them come from thy hand, for he may say that I knew them before."
>
> "Gently—gently," the man replied, and from a drawer under the table dealt a half handful of clattering trifles into the tray.
>
> "Now," said the child, waving an old copy of a paper. "Look on them as long as thou wilt, stranger. Count and, if need be, handle. One look is enough for *me*." He turned his back proudly.
>
> "But what is the game?" Kim asked.
>
> "When thou hast counted and handled and art sure that thou canst remember them all, I cover them with this paper, and thou must tell over the tally to Lurgan Sahib. I will write mine."
>
> "Oah!" The instinct of competition waked in his breast. He bent over the tray. There were but fifteen stones on it. "That is easy," he said after a minute. The child slipped the paper over the wink-

ing jewels and scribbled in a limp-backed native account-book.

"There are under that paper five blue stones— one big, one smaller, and three small," said Kim, all in haste. "There are four green stones, and one with a hole in it; there is one yellow stone that I can see through, and one like a pipe stem. There are two red stones, and—and—I made the count fifteen, but two I have forgotten. No! Give me time. One was of ivory, little and brownish; and— and—give me time. . . ."

"One—two—" Lurgan Sahib counted him out up to ten. Kim shook his head.

"Hear my count!" the child burst in, trilling with laughter. "First, are two flawed sapphires—one of two ruttees and one of four as I should judge. The four-ruttee sapphire is chipped at the edge. There is one Turkestan turquoise, plain with green veins, and there are two inscribed—one with a Name of God in gilt, and the other being cracked across, for it came out of an old ring, I cannot read. We have now the five blue stones. Four flawed emeralds there are, but one is drilled in two places, and one is a little carven——"

"Their weight?" said Lurgan Sahib impassively.

"Three—five—five and four ruttees as I judge it. There is one piece of old greenish amber, and a cheap cut topaz from Europe. There is one ruby of Burma, of two ruttees, without a flaw, and there is a ballas ruby, flawed, of two ruttees. There is a carved ivory from China representing a rat sucking an egg; and there is last—ah ha!—a ball of crystal as big as a bean set in a gold leaf."

He clapped his hands at the close.

"He is thy master," said Lurgan Sahib, smiling.

"Huh! He knew the names of the stones," said Kim, flushing. "Try again! With common things such as he and I both know."

They heaped the tray again with odds and ends gathered from the shop, and even the kitchen, and every time the boy won, till Kim marveled.

"Bind my eyes—let me feel once with my fingers, and even *then* I will leave thee open-eyed behind," he challenged.

Kim stamped with vexation when the lad made his boast good.

"If it were men—or horses," he said, "I could do better. This playing with tweezers and knives and scissors is too little."

"Learn first—teach later," said Lurgan Sahib. "Is he thy master?"

"Truly. But how is it done?"

"By doing it many times over till it is done perfectly—for it is worth doing."

RUDYARD KIPLING
from *Kim*

The good observer is able to see not only events but also relationships. He notes their spirit and ethos. He sees how things are done and also why.

And so we come back to Kim's question and the Sahib's answer:

"Truly. But how is it done?"

"By doing it many times over till it is done perfectly—for it is worth doing."

A mere description of unconverted, unpossessed reality cannot be a work of creation. The work of art does not need to be adequate to the outside material—"true to life"; it must be true to itself within that singleness of mood from which it arises.

AUGUSTO CENTENO
from *The Intent of the Artist*

Assignment 1

1. Read the chapter up to this point.
2. In your journal do *one* of the following:
   a. Play the Jewel Game and record your experience. You have only to look into a shop window and look away to check on your accuracy of vision.

b. Write about one object or event you observed today. Present it literally, subjectively, and imaginatively.

c. Describe an object from the outside; then describe the same object from the inside. First write a physical description, then one based on empathy—one that catches the mood, inner feeling, or significance of the object.

Remember you can't possibly report everything. Limit yourself to that which can reasonably be seen from where you are viewing. First, decide where you stand in a physical sense. Then decide on your metaphorical position. Are you giving the object a sentimental, a romantic, or a hard look? Again, you can't do everything; a singleness of mood should control your vision. For example, the prose passage that follows shows how a professional manages this assignment.

But above the gray land and the spasms of bleak dust which drift endlessly over it, you perceive, after a moment, the eyes of Doctor T. J. Eckleburg. The eyes of Doctor T. J. Eckleburg are blue and gigantic—their retinas are one yard high. They look out of no face, but, instead, from a pair of enormous yellow spectacles which pass over a nonexistent nose. Evidently some wild wag of an oculist set them there to fatten his practice in the borough of Queens, and then sank down himself into eternal blindness, or forgot them and moved away. But his eyes, dimmed a little by many paintless days under sun and rain, brood on over the solemn dumping ground.

F. SCOTT FITZGERALD
from *The Great Gatsby*

Assignment 2

"You * must scrutinize whatever you want to express, so long, and so attentively, as to enable you to find some aspect of it which no one has yet seen

* Gustave Flaubert is addressing Guy de Maupassant.

and expressed. There is an unexplored side to everything, because we are wont never to use our eyes but with the memory of what others before us have thought of the things we see. The smallest thing has something unknown in it; we must find it. To describe a blazing fire, a tree on a plain, we must stand face to face with that fire or that tree, till to us they are wholly unlike any other fire or tree. Thus we may become original. . . .

"When you pass a grocer sitting in his doorway," he would say, "a concièrge smoking his pipe, or a cab-stand, show me that grocer and that concièrge, their attitude and their whole physical aspect, including, as indicated by the skill of the portrait, their whole moral nature, in such a way that I shall never mistake them for any other grocer or concièrge; and by a single word give me to understand wherein one cab-horse differs from fifty others before or behind it. . . ."

GUY DE MAUPASSANT
from the Preface to *Pierre et Jean*

1. In your journal practice observation. Help yourself by paying attention to "the power of a word put in the right place."
2. Choose *one* of the quotations given below; discuss and illustrate it by an entry of your own, or copy out an example taken from a professional short story.
   a. ". . . we are wont never to use our eyes but with the memory of what others before us have thought of the things we see."
   b. "The good observer is able to see not only events but also relationships. He notes their spirit and ethos. He sees how things are done and also why."
   c. "You must scrutinize whatever you want to express, so long, and so attentively, as to enable you to find some aspect of it which no one has yet seen and expressed . . . including, as indicated by the skill of the portrait, [its] whole moral nature, in such a way that I shall never mistake [it] for any other. . . ."

Assignment 3

A perception, for a moment, of one's eventual and moral self as if it were another person—the observant faculty being separated, and looking intently at the qualities of the character. There is a surprise when this happens—this getting out of one's self—and then the observer sees how queer a fellow he is.

from *The Heart of
Hawthorne's Journals*
edited by Newton Arvin

The poem "Dolor," which appears below, is by Theodore Roethke. In the poem Roethke makes observations that carry the surprise that comes from getting outside a situation and seeing the familiar in new perspective.

Dolor

I have known the inexorable sadness of pencils,
Neat in their boxes, dolor of pad and paper-weight,
All the misery of manila folders and mucilage,
Desolation in immaculate public places,
Lonely reception room, lavatory, switchboard,
The unalterable pathos of basin and pitcher,
Ritual of multigraph, paper-clip, comma,
Endless duplication of lives and objects.
And I have seen dust from the walls of institutions,
Finer than flour, alive, more dangerous than silica,
Sift, almost invisible, through long afternoons of
    tedium,
Dropping a fine film on nails and delicate eye-
    brows,
Glazing the pale hair, the duplicate gray standard
    faces.

THEODORE ROETHKE

The object of this assignment is to help you find material for your own short story. One of the ways to find such material is to see the familiar from a new perspective.

1. Read the material by Hawthorne and Roethke.
2. In your journal do *one* of the following:
    a. Write about a familiar object, person, or situation from a point of view that permits you to see the familiar in a new way.
    b. Show the reader a remarkable character, one whom you have observed closely. Insofar as time permits, let your sketch show his whole moral nature.
    c. Present a character as he might see himself and as he might be seen by others.

2|2

THINGS WORTH SEEING

In the first lesson in this unit you were asked to write objective descriptions; you were also asked to give your sense
of the inner feeling or significance of an object, and then you
were invited to observe events and relationships in varying
perspectives.

In this lesson you will be getting practice in finding topics
worth seeing and describing—that is, in "seeing copy." The
trick here, of course, is to find something that genuinely interests you, and then to find something to say about it that
genuinely interests your reader. Of course, there is no formula
for finding topics to write about, but there is a way of looking
at events that often turns them into topics you want to write
about. Here is a statement that explains how one person
developed his capacity to see copy. As you read his report
consider ways of adapting his technique to your own writing
needs.

> When I was an undergraduate at Harvard our
> instructors in English composition endeavored to
> cultivate in us a something they termed "the daily
> theme eye." This peculiar variety of optic, I fear, al-
> ways remained a mystery to a majority of the toilers
> after clearness, force, and elegance. Clearness, force,
> and even a certain degree of elegance may be ac-
> quired; but the daily theme eye, like the eye for
> the sights of a rifle, may be discovered, developed,
> trained—but not acquired. It comes by the grace of
> Heaven, not of the Harvard or any other English
> department, and its possession is often one of the
> marks of the man whose destiny compels him to
> write. The Harvard English department has but
> given it a name; it has no local habitation. . . .
> The fairy who stood over my cradle, though he

forgot the gold spoon and much else besides, at least bestowed the gift of this wonderful optic. It brought me my college degree; for when other courses failed—which means when I failed in other courses—there was always English; it has brought me a living since; but more than all else it has brought me enjoyment, it has clothed the daily walk with interest, the teeming, noisy town with color and beauty, "the society of my contemporaries," to use Emerson's big phrase for my little purpose, with stimulating excitement. It has turned the panorama of existence into a play, or rather a thousand plays, and brought after sorrow or pain the great comfort of composition.

Daily themes in my day had to be short, not over a page of handwriting. They had to be deposited in a box at the professor's door not later than ten-five in the morning. A classmate of mine, when an epigram was called for, once wrote, "An epigram is a lazy man's daily theme written at ten-three A.M." And because of this brevity, and the necessity of writing one every day whether the mood was on you or not, it was not always easy—to be quite modest—to make these themes literature, which, we were told by our instructors, is the transmission through the written word, from writer to reader, of a mood, an emotion, a picture, an idea. I hate to think how few, in fact, of all the thousands that were poured into that yawning box were literature, how seldom the poor instructors could dip their pens into their pots of red ink and write the magic "A" on the back. Their sarcastic comments were surely excusable. . . . Well, the effort of those of us who were sincere and comprehending in our pursuit of the elusive power to write was to make our themes literature as often as possible; and to do this the first essential was the choice of a subject. Not everything one sees or does or thinks can take shape on a page of paper and reproduce itself for the reader. Selection was the first requirement.

It became needful, then, to watch for and treas-

ure incidents that were sharply dramatic or poignant, moods that were clear and definite, pictures
that created a single clean impression. The tower
of Memorial seen across the quiet marshes against
the cool, pink sky of evening; the sweep of a shell
under the bridge and the rush of the spectators to
the other rail to watch the needlelike bow emerge,
and the bent, brown backs of the crew; the chorus
girls, still rubbing the paint from their cheeks with
a tiny handkerchief wrapped over the forefinger,
coming out of a stage entrance into the snow; the
first sharp impression of a book just read or a play
just seen—these were the things we cherished, for
these we could put on a page of paper with a beginning, a middle, and an end, and with some show of
vividness. What we came to do, then, was to keep
a notebook of our impressions, and when in June
our themes were returned to us we had a precious
record for the year. By training the daily theme eye,
we watched for and found in the surroundings of
our life, as it passed, a heightened picturesqueness,
a constant wonder, an added significance. That
hardened cynic, the professional writer, will smile
and say, "You saw copy." Yes, we saw copy; but to
see copy is to see the significant, to clarify what the
ear and heart and eye receive, to add light and
shadow to the monochrome of life.

My college roommate, a blessed boy full of good
humor and serious purpose, was as incapable of
acquiring the daily theme eye as a cat of obeying
the eighth commandment. His idea of a daily
theme was a task, not a pleasure. If there was no
chance to write a political editorial, he supplied
an anecdote of his summer vacation. Once he described a cliff he had seen in Newfoundland, and,
determined to be pictorial, he added "tumbling
waterfalls" and "sighing pines." Unfortunately, the
instructor who read it had also been in Newfoundland, and he pointed out that his investigations of
the cliff in question had failed to disclose either
"tumbling waterfalls" or "sighing pines." My room-

mate treated the matter as a joke; he could not see that he had been guilty of any fault. And yet he is a much more moral man than I, with a far more troublesome conscience. Truth to his principles he would die for. But truth to the picture his mind retained and his hand tried to portray in the medium of literature, to him so trivial and unimportant, he could not grasp. What did it matter? So it would never occur to him to record in his themes the fleeting impressions of his daily life, to sit up half the night trying to pack into the clumsy frame of words the recollection of a strangely innocent face seen suddenly in the flash of an opened door down a dark, evil alley where the gusts of winter swirled. He went to bed and never knew a headache or jumpy nerve. Yet I could not help thinking that there was something in life he was missing besides the ultimate mark in our composition course. And I cannot help thinking that there is something in life he misses still. . . .

from "The Daily Theme Eye"
in *Essays and Essay-Writing*
edited by William M. Tanner

Assignment 4

Observation endows our day and our street with the romantic charm of history, and stimulates charity—not the charity which signs checks, but the more precious charity which puts itself to the trouble of understanding. The one condition is that the observer must never lose sight of the fact that what he is trying to see is life, is the woman next door, is the man in the train—and not a concourse of abstractions. To appreciate all this is the first inspiring preliminary to sound observation.

ARNOLD BENNETT
from *The Author's Craft*

1. Read the chapter up to this point.
2. In your journal do *one* of the following:
   a. Summarize in your own words what the author of "The Daily Theme Eye" is saying. Do you agree or disagree? What are the essential differences between this writer and his roommate? Characterize each man in a few words.
   b. Choose a specific mood, emotion, picture, or idea and write about it with vividness. Aim at sharing with your reader your own thoughts and feelings about the topic. Write at least one full page. Provide a beginning, a middle, and an end.
   c. Present an incident that is sharply dramatic or poignant. Here is a poem that shows how a poet managed this problem.

Auto Wreck

Its quick soft silver bell beating, beating
And down the dark one ruby flare
Pulsing out red light like an artery,
The ambulance at top speed floating down
Past beacons and illuminated clocks
Wings in a heavy curve, dips down,
And brakes speed, entering the crowd.
The doors leap open, emptying light;
Stretchers are laid out, the mangled lifted
And stowed into the little hospital.
Then the bell, breaking the hush, tolls once,
And the ambulance with its terrible cargo
Rocking, slightly rocking, moves away,
As the doors, an afterthought, are closed.

We are deranged, walking among the cops
Who sweep glass and are large and composed.
One is still making notes under the light.
One with a bucket douches ponds of blood
Into the street and gutter.
One hangs lanterns on the wrecks that cling,
Empty husks of locusts, to iron poles.

Our throats were tight as tourniquets,
Our feet were bound with splints, but now
Like convalescents intimate and gauche,
We speak through sickly smiles and warn
With the stubborn saw of common sense,
The grim joke and the banal resolution.
The traffic moves around with care,
But we remain, touching a wound
That opens to our richest horror.

Already old, the question Who shall die?
Becomes unspoken Who is innocent?
For death in war is done by hands;
Suicide has cause and stillbirth, logic.
But this invites the occult mind,
Cancels our physics with a sneer,
And spatters all we knew of dénouement
Across the expedient and wicked stones.

KARL SHAPIRO

Assignment 5

The writer does not copy his originals; he takes
what he wants from them, a few traits that have
caught his attention, a turn of mind that has fired
his imagination, and therefrom constructs his character.

This [*Le Rouge et le Noir*] is a very great novel,
but it is generally acknowledged that the end is unsatisfactory. The reason is not hard to find. Stendhal
got the idea for it from an incident that at the time
made a great stir: a young seminarist killed his
mistress, was tried and guillotined. But Stendhal
put into Julien Sorel, his hero, not only a great
deal of himself, but much more of what he would
have liked to be and was miserably conscious that
he was not; he created one of the most interesting
personages of fiction and for fully three quarters of
his book made him behave with coherence and

probability; but then he found himself forced to return to the facts that had been his inspiration. He could only do this by causing his hero to act incongruously with his character and his intelligence. The shock is so great that you no longer believe, and when you do not believe in a novel you are no longer held. The moral is that you must have the courage to throw your facts overboard if they fail to comply with the logic of your character. I do not know how Stendhal could have ended his novel; but I think it would have been hard to find a more unsatisfactory end than the one he chose.

I have been blamed because I have drawn my characters from living persons, and from criticisms that I have read one might suppose that nobody had ever done this before. That is nonsense. It is the universal custom. From the beginning of literature authors have had originals for their creations. . . .

I should say that the practice of drawing characters from actual models is not only universal but necessary. I do not see why any writer should be ashamed to acknowledge it. As Turgenev said, it is only if you have a definite person in your mind that you can give vitality and idiosyncrasy to your own creations. . . .

We know very little even of the persons we know most intimately; we do not know them enough to transfer them to the pages of a book and make human beings of them. People are too elusive, too shadowy, to be copied; and they are also too incoherent and contradictory. . . . He [the author] is not concerned whether it is a truthful likeness; he is concerned only to create a plausible harmony convenient for his own purposes. So different may be the finished product from the original that it must be a common experience of authors to be accused of having drawn a lifelike portrait of a certain person when they had in mind someone quite different. Further, it is just chance whether the author chooses his models from persons with whom he is intimately connected or not. It is often enough for him to have caught a glimpse of someone in a teashop or chatted with him for a quarter of an hour in a ship's smoking room. All he needs is that tiny, fertile substratum which he can then build up by means of his experience of life, his knowledge of human nature and his native intuition.

W. SOMERSET MAUGHAM
from *The Summing Up*

1. Read the observations by Maugham.
2. In your journal do *one* of the following:
   a. Present a character. Aim at making the reader believe in your creation.
   b. Demonstrate your ability to find in your own surroundings one or more of these qualities: picturesqueness, wonder, significance.
   c. Copy out (giving complete source) the best piece of description you have read this week. Explain briefly why it works, why it appeals to you. Be specific.

Assignment 6

Of course any writer in any field whatever, every time he sets down a sentence, is translating his observation of life as he has known it. But when it comes to drawing a character from life and setting his personality upon the printed page, nearly every writer whom I have ever met will tell you that no actual human being is convincing in this highly artificial environment. Living men and women are too limited, too far from being typical, too greatly lacking in a universal appeal, to serve in a properly planned piece of fiction. A successful character in a novel is a conglomerate, a combination of dozens of traits, drawn from experience with hundreds of individuals, many of them half known and half forgotten; and all these traits have been transformed by passing through the writer's mind. From a writer's standpoint it takes a vast number of disconnected memories and impressions to create a satisfactory illusion of reality.

JOHN P. MARQUAND
from the Preface to
H. M. Pulham, Esquire

From your observations you will need to create "a satisfactory illusion of reality" when you write a short story. Here is an assignment designed to help you.

1. Read the excerpt by Marquand.
2. In your journal do *one* of the following:
   a. Present a person as he is in real life. Then combine some of his traits with those of other people to make a fictional character.
   b. Present a scene as it exists in fact. Then describe the same scene as it might be used in the opening of a story.
   c. Copy out a passage of dialogue from a story you like. Then write the conversation as it might have occurred in real life.

2|3

THE ANGLE OF VISION

How do you talk about a subject after you have observed it closely? You talk about it as it looks, feels, smells, tastes, or in some way impinges on you. But very often you are "all mixed up" and don't know where to begin or what to present first. So many aspects of the topic present themselves that crosscurrents of thought and feeling seem to cancel one another out, and you are left paralyzed in front of your topic and your page. This lesson is intended to help you manage that problem and to "get you started" by directing your angle of vision. It is an exercise in sorting things out until you find what you are looking for—that aspect of your subject that will work best in directing and structuring your writing. Of course, you can always just start and hope things work out; often they do. But here you will be asked to give deliberate thought to the best way of approaching your topic. Some very good and very practical advice is found in *The Art of Readable Writing* by Rudolf Flesch. Here is an excerpt.

> Let me do a little translating for you. In the original German, the word *Gestalt* means nothing particularly exciting; it simply means *shape*. And that's what this whole business is about: when you do this kind of just-sitting-and-thinking, you are trying to grasp the *shape* of your ideas. The *configurations,* the *recentering,* the *restructuring*—all these words mean that your mind is operating just like your eye—or your camera—when it is looking at an object. To see the object clearly, you have to find the right focus, the right perspective, the right angle of vision. Only when all these things are taken care of do you really see what the object is like.
>
> The same way, in your writing you must first go over your material in your mind, trying to find

the focus, the perspective, the angle of vision that will make you see clearly the shape of whatever it is you are writing about. There has to be one point that is sharply in focus, and a clear grouping of everything else around it. Once you see this clearly, your reader will see it too. And that, the shape of your ideas, is usually all he is going to carry away from his reading. . . .

The most widely used device for getting ideas in shape is to buttonhole some unsuspecting victim— the kind of person who is apt to read later what you have written—and to rehearse your ideas aloud. This has two advantages: first, it forces you to funnel your ideas into a limited number of words; and second, the other person will tell you what your ideas look like from where he sits. Allan Nevins, the historian, puts it this way: "Catch a friend who is interested in the subject and talk out what you have learned, at length. In this way you discover facts of interpretation that you might have missed, points of argument that had been unrealized, and the form most suitable for the story you have to tell." . . .

. . . A good way of using someone else for focus and perspective is to put such a person right into your piece of writing. You present your facts and ideas as seen by an observer with a detached point of view. This will make things clearer to yourself and will help your reader in catching on. . . .

This sounds simple, but there is a pitfall in it. It's hard to look away from the eye-catching, out-standing—and therefore not typical—members of the group. . . .

So much for groups and types. How about describing a series of events? The principle is the same: focus on one point that is so significant that you can hang your story onto it. Invariably there is such a point—the turning point, the key event that explains everything before and after. The only problem is to find it; and it is important, with events just as with people, not to overlook the simple because of the more glamorous or spectacular. Turning points have a way of happening long before the big fireworks start. . . .

Proper focusing becomes difficult when you have neither a group of people nor a series of events. Then what? There is a way, but it's rather hard to put in simple words. Let me try.

What you are after, as you are turning your material over in your mind, is something like the one-sentence headline, the typical group member, the turning point in the chain of events—some one thing that will point up the significance of the subject as a whole. Even if your material looks at first like a shapeless mass of totally different items, there must be one point at which they all converge—otherwise you wouldn't, or shouldn't, treat them all together in one piece of writing. The trouble is that this common denominator is usually so simple and obvious that it's practically invisible. It's the thing you take so much for granted that you never bother to give it a second thought. And that's exactly the trick: find the underlying feature that you have taken for granted and try to give it a second thought.

To come back, for instance, to Jack Alexander's *Saturday Evening Post* article on St. Louis. Alexander's problem was this: he had returned from St. Louis with a heap of notes but didn't know how to pull them together into an understandable whole. After having spent a day in thinking, he hit upon the solution. The obvious way to describe a city is to stress the things in which it is outstanding; but somehow, in the case of St. Louis, these things were hard to find. Alexander gave that a second thought and decided to write his piece around the theme that St. Louis made a virtue of not being outstanding in anything. He wrote:

> The spell which the city exerts is paradoxical. . . . St. Louis pursues the commercial strategy of limited objectives. It has no vast industries. . . . [Its] citizenry is simultane-

ously hospitable and suspicious of the East, gay and stubborn, serious about living and yet fun-loving. . . . A booster crude enough to preach the common American gospel of giantism achieves no more than a dry rattle in his throat. . . . St. Louis has never fallen for skyscrapers. . . . St. Louis might have grown up to be another Chicago or Detroit—a fate which now seems to St. Louis to be worse than death. . . .

In this fashion, Alexander wrote a memorable article by turning the underlying theme upside down.

RUDOLF FLESCH
from *The Art of Readable Writing*

Assignment 7

1. Read the chapter up to this point.
2. In your journal do *one* of the following:
   a. Study the "angle of vision" used by three different writers dealing with the same subject. Report your findings.
   b. Name a subject about which you might write an extended paper on some occasion. Explore the "angle of vision" that might work best; that is, "find the underlying feature that you have taken for granted and try to give it a second thought." Name that underlying feature and explain what you discovered as the result of giving it a second thought.
   c. Write a full page journal entry about a group of people whom you have observed.

Assignment 8

The one subject you might think it possible to write about without considering observation, or shaping ideas, or finding an angle of vision is you. Just expressing yourself would seem natural enough not to call for a set of special instructions. But before you start "communicating," read what Walker Gibson says on that subject in the first chapter of his text, *Seeing and Writing*. His statement that appears here poses a fundamental question.

What do you want to accomplish as a writer, as a student of writing in a composition course? You might try to list some of your aims. For example, you might say that you want to convey your thoughts to others through a skillful use of words. You want to communicate clearly so that other people will really grasp your meaning. You want to express yourself, accurately, vividly. These are reasonable aims, you might say, for a course in composition.

But as a matter of fact they are not reasonable at all—they are impossible. Consider your own thoughts, for instance, and your desire to convey them to others. What *are* your thoughts? Think about your own thinking for a moment—think about your own thinking right *now*. What is in your mind? You are sitting in a chair, probably, just slightly aware of its touch on you, just slightly aware that it is or isn't upholstered. You are aware of being alone (or not alone), of the time, the temperature, the state of your stomach. How many thoughts are competing in your head, now that you think of them? A date, a game, the shape of this sentence, sleepiness, anxiety, boredom. Life! The more you think about your thinking, the more it's a mess. And if you ask yourself, now, what has happened to the state of your mind since you started thinking about it like this, your answer would have to be that it has certainly changed by the very process of trying to express it. Were you really aware of your hunger a minute ago, or is it just that you are now, being reminded of it? The more we try to describe our thoughts at a given moment, the more we do them an injustice by that very effort.

The state of our minds, as it really is at this moment, is inexpressible, and we can't "convey" that state to anybody, not even to ourselves.

Well, then, what *is* expressible? It would be possible to say, in answer to that question, that strictly speaking nothing is, that no idea can be "conveyed" precisely from the mind of one person to the mind of another. Yet we need only look around us to admire the proofs of some kind of communicating going on in the world. The business of the day gets done, on the whole marvelously well. Airplanes take off, often on time, and they land safely in dense fog without ever seeing the ground. Someone has been talking to someone else, and, if he has not expressed the state of his thoughts, he has at least gotten something done. A man in the dark, watching the pips on a radar screen, tells the pilot that he should lower his wheels, that he is nearing the runway, that he is all right—and this miracle of communication is enough to silence any skepticism.

But the practical question that confronts us in the situation of the composition class is still unanswered. What shall we write about? If we can't convey "ourselves" and the state of our minds, and if we aren't landing planes in a fog, what alternatives do we have in our search for useful problems of communication? What area of experience can we examine as a fruitful and controllable field for expression?

There are probably many answers to this question: the one adopted by this book is an obvious one. It proposes that we begin by *looking* at something simple, or at any rate something that seems simple, and that we try to render an experience of this thing in words.

In the following statement, Arthur C. Benson makes some comments that you should find helpful as you begin *looking* at simple things.

. . . when we first begin to write, we find how difficult it is to keep the thread of our thoughts; we keep turning out of the main road to explore attractive bypaths; we cannot arrange our ideas. All writers who produce original work pass through a stage in which they are conscious of a throng of kindred notions, all more or less bearing on the central thought, but the movements of which they cannot wholly control. Their thoughts are like a turbulent crowd, and one's business is to drill them into an ordered regiment. A writer has to pass through a certain apprenticeship; and the cure for this natural vagueness is to choose small precise subjects, to say all that we have in our minds about them, and to stop when we have finished; not to aim at fine writing, but at definiteness and clearness.

ARTHUR C. BENSON
from *From a College Window*

1. Read the observations by Gibson and Benson.
2. In your journal do *one* of the following:
   a. Observe a "small precise subject." Then say all that you have to say about it, and stop. Aim at definiteness and clearness.
   b. Look at something simple and try "to render an experience of this thing in words."
   c. Describe a single object that you can now observe.

Assignment 9

Life is a jungle of events whose meanings are at once too casual and to that extent insignificant and too full of possible implications (without offering us any guidance as to which implication or set of implications we should choose). The skilled storyteller makes those meanings at once more significant and less confused.

DAVID DAICHES
from *A Study of Literature*

The following report of a disaster was taken from *Life* Magazine. Read it first for story. Then as you reread it, consider the ways in which the writer brought his material into focus.

THE SOUTH AMBOY CLOCK
STOPS AT 7:26

One night last week, in the grubby little factory city of South Amboy, New Jersey, the city hall clock pointed to 7:26. Some of the 9,500 people in town were eating dinner, but along the main drag the stores were open and shoppers were out in the drizzling rain. In some of the houses, parents helped their teen-age girls struggle into their party clothes, for St. Mary's School was having its junior prom that night. Near the waterfront a Pennsylvania commuter train from Manhattan slid past the yards adjoining the railroad's docks, heading for the station. Nearby on Pier A, longshoremen were transferring the last of twelve freight cars of ammunition to a string of lighters. Standing off-shore in Raritan Bay was the Isbrandtsen Line's *Flying Clipper,* her hull still scuffed from a recent bombardment by Chinese Nationalist planes. She was to load the shells and antipersonnel mines for a voyage to Pakistan.

The city hall clock never got to 7:27, and the 467 tons of the *Flying Clipper*'s deadly cargo never got loaded. The explosives erupted into the sky above South Amboy. The concussion shattered windows over a radius of twelve miles; hundreds of people, blinking at the sound of the blast, looked at their arms and legs and saw that flying daggers of glass had stabbed them. In a Catholic church the stained glass windows dissolved over the worshipers who left their prayers to run into the streets crying that atomic war had come. The city's lights went out, a man was blown out of a barber chair and a high school boy, tying his tie before a mirror, saw his

image disintegrate as the glass flew at him. In the
wrecked and darkened business area the dazed
shoppers heard the wail of sirens, while all over
town a rain of oily mud, blasted from the bottom
of the bay, came down on them in dirty globs. Pan-
icky crowds tried to leave town and head south,
while portly Mayor John B. Leonard, who had been
dumped on the floor in front of his collapsing television set, manned a sound truck to bawl hoarse
assurances that the danger was past.

At dawn, with the cause of the explosion still
unknown, people saw that Pier A, the freight cars
and ammunition lighters had vanished. So had
twenty-two longshoremen, and four were known
dead. Three hundred and twelve were injured. In
the waterfront area, sown with live mines, search-
ers walked gingerly as they began a hopeless search
for the other victims of an explosion more devas-
tating than New Jersey's famous Black Tom disaster of World War I.

1. Read the preceding excerpts.
2. In your journal do *one* of the following:
   a. Write a journal entry in which you explain as fully as
      you can why this account of a disaster that occurred in
      1950 still has impact and interest.
   b. Write a news story about an event (sports, music—
      what you will). Tell your story so that it has impact
      and interest.
   c. Recount an incident or event just as you witnessed it.
      Then retell the episode shaping the facts so that their
      meanings are "at once more significant and less con-
      fused" than in your straight reportage.

2|4

SEEING THE FAMILIAR

See story, think essay, look for theme ideas. You'll find what you're looking for in your own experience—things worth seeing are right in your own backyard. The real problem is not that nothing happens; the real problem is finding a usable shape for the events that do happen. But before you know which shape will work or how to turn what you have observed into a usable form, you must find the material itself. One of the best ways for finding material is to keep a journal —a place for ideas—a place in which you write regularly. The discipline of regular writing sets you the writer's task of thinking about writing and looking for signs that suggest character and story. Perhaps for the first time you begin to see the familiar.

True, you are not apt to look out your window and find a group of characters enacting a story which you can simply transcribe scene by scene. Life does not order itself in such a tidy way. But you may look out and see a child, or a dog, or neighbors chatting and get your own idea for a story. Sometimes story ideas come with the morning paper (Pearl Buck found her idea for the "Old Demon" in just that way). After all, what better use for fact than to let it inform fiction? What greater challenge for taking the part and from it constructing the whole? Yes, story, essay, theme possibilities are a part of every day. You can help yourself find them by learning to look at the familiar.

Here is a classic example of how one man learned to see the things around him. Perhaps his experience will help you to see the familiar.

It was more than fifteen years ago that I entered the laboratory of Professor Agassiz and told him I had enrolled my name in the Scientific School as a student of natural history. He asked me a few questions about my object in coming, my antecedents generally, the mode in which I afterward proposed to use the knowledge I might acquire, and finally whether I wished to study any special branch. To the latter I replied that while I wished to be well grounded in all departments of zoology, I purposed to devote myself specially to insects.

"When do you wish to begin?" he asked.

"Now," I replied.

This seemed to please him, and with an energetic "Very well!" he reached from a shelf a huge jar of specimens in yellow alcohol.

"Take this fish," said he, "and look at it; we call it a haemulon; by and by I will ask you what you have seen." With that he left me, but in a moment returned with explicit instructions as to the care of the object entrusted to me.

"No man is fit to be a naturalist," said he, "who does not know how to take care of specimens. . . ."

In ten minutes I had seen all that could be seen in that fish and started in search of the professor, who had, however, left the museum; and when I returned, after lingering over some of the odd animals stored in the upper apartment, my specimen was dry all over. I dashed the fluid [alcohol] over the fish as if to resuscitate the beast from a fainting fit and looked with anxiety for a return of the normal sloppy appearance. This little excitement over, nothing was to be done but to return to a steadfast gaze at my mute companion. Half an hour passed—an hour—another hour; the fish began to look loathsome. I turned it over and around; looked it in the face—ghastly; from behind, beneath, above, sideways, at a three-quarters view—just as ghastly. I was in despair; at an early hour I concluded that lunch was necessary; so with infinite relief the fish was carefully replaced in the jar, and for an hour I was free.

On my return, I learned that Professor Agassiz had been at the museum but had gone and would not return for several hours. My fellow students were too busy to be disturbed by continued conversation. Slowly I drew forth that hideous fish and with a feeling of desperation again looked at it. I might not use a magnifying glass; instruments of all kinds were interdicted. My two hands, my two eyes, and the fish: it seemed a most limited field. I pushed my finger down its throat to feel how sharp the teeth were. I began to count the scales in the different rows, until I was convinced that that was nonsense. At last a happy thought struck me: I would draw the fish. And now with surprise I began to discover new features in the creature. Just then the professor returned.

"That is right," said he; "a pencil is one of the best of eyes. I am glad to notice, too, that you keep your specimen wet and your bottle corked."

With these encouraging words, he added: "Well, what is it like?"

He listened attentively to my brief rehearsal of the structure of parts whose names were still unknown to me: the fringed gill arches and movable operculum, the pores of the head, fleshy lips, and lidless eyes, the lateral line, the spinous fins and forked tail, the compressed and arched body. When I had finished, he waited as if expecting more, and then, with an air of disappointment:

"You have not looked very carefully; why," he continued, more earnestly, "you haven't even seen one of the most conspicuous features of the animal, which is as plainly before your eyes as the fish itself. Look again, look again!" And he left me to my misery.

I was piqued; I was mortified. Still more of that wretched fish! But now I set myself to my task with a will and discovered one new thing after another, until I saw how just the professor's criticism had been. The afternoon passed quickly, and when, toward its close, the professor inquired:

"Do you see it yet?"

"No," I replied, "I am certain I do not, but I see how little I saw before."

"That is next best," said he earnestly, "but I won't hear you now; put away your fish and go home; perhaps you will be ready with a better answer in the morning. I will examine you before you look at the fish."

This was disconcerting. Not only must I think of my fish all night, studying, without the object before me, what this unknown but most visible feature might be, but also without reviewing my discoveries, I must give an exact account of them the next day. I had a bad memory; so I walked home by the Charles River in a distracted state, with my two perplexities.

The cordial greeting from the professor the next morning was reassuring; here was a man who seemed to be quite as anxious as I that I should see for myself what he saw.

"Do you perhaps mean," I asked, "that the fish has symmetrical sides with paired organs?"

His thoroughly pleased, "Of course, of course!" repaid the wakeful hours of the previous night. After he had discoursed most happily and enthusiastically—as he always did—upon the importance of this point, I ventured to ask what I should do next.

"Oh, look at your fish!" he said and left me again to my own devices. In a little more than an hour, he returned and heard my new catalogue.

"That is good, that is good!" he repeated; "but that is not all; go on." And so for three long days he placed that fish before my eyes, forbidding me to look at anything else or to use any artificial aid. "Look, look, look" was his repeated injunction.

This was the best entomological lesson I ever had: a lesson whose influence has extended to the details of every subsequent study; a legacy the professor has left to me, as he left it to so many others, of inestimable value, which we could not buy, with which we cannot part.

The fourth day, a second fish of the same group was placed beside the first, and I was bidden to point out the resemblances and differences between the two. Another and another followed, until the entire family lay before me. . . . The whole group of haemulons was thus brought in review; and whether engaged upon the dissection of the internal organs, the preparation and examination of the bony framework, or the description of the various parts, Agassiz' training in the method of observing facts and their orderly arrangement was ever accompanied by the urgent exhortation not to be content with them.

"Facts are stupid things," he would say, "until brought into connection with some general law."

At the end of eight months, it was almost with reluctance that I left these friends and turned to insects. What I had gained by this outside experience has been of greater value than years of later investigation in my favorite groups.

SAMUEL H. SCUDDER
from "In the Laboratory with Agassiz"

Assignment 10

1. Read the chapter up to this point.
2. In your journal do *one* of the following:
   a. "This was the best entomological lesson I ever had: a lesson whose influence has extended to the details of every subsequent study." Summarize what was learned from the lesson and explain how it could extend "to the details of every subsequent study." Be specific. Draw on your own experience and observation.
   b. "That is right," said he; "a pencil is one of the best of eyes." Observe a familiar object closely. Then draw this object in your journal. Report what, if anything, you came to observe as the result of this experiment.
   c. Look at a familiar object for ten minutes. Note what you observe. Then look at the same object for another ten minutes. What more, if anything, did you observe? Be specific.

Assignment 11

The following excerpt by Anton Chekhov is an example of tight writing; much is said in a brief space. As you read the selection, note Chekov's injunctions to: (1) avoid the commonplace, (2) keep nature descriptions brief, (3) give "incidental character" to descriptions of nature, (4) be specific, (5) create a visual image, (6) make nature appear animated, (7) use metaphor, (8) show character and state of mind through action, (9) center interest on single opposites.

In my opinion descriptions of Nature should be very brief and have an incidental character. Commonplaces like: "The setting sun, bathing in the waves of the darkening sea, flooded with purple and gold," etc. . . . "The swallows, flying over the surface of the water, chirped merrily"—such commonplaces should be finished with. In descriptions of Nature one has to snatch at small details, grouping them in such a manner that after reading them one can obtain the picture on closing one's eyes.

For instance, you will get a moonlight night if you write that on the dam of the mill a fragment of broken bottle flashed like a small bright star, and there rolled by, like a ball, the black shadow of a dog, or a wolf—and so on. Nature appears animated if you do not disdain to use comparisons of its phenomena with those of human actions, etc.

The same, too, in the sphere of psychology. God defend you from generalizations. Best of all, avoid describing the psychological state of the characters; one should contrive that this is clear from their actions. One should not hunt after an abundance of characters. The center of gravity should be two: he and she.

ANTON CHEKHOV
from "Moonlight on a Broken Bottle"

1. Read the excerpt by Chekhov.
2. In your journal do *one* of the following:
   a. Consider a Chekhov story you have read. Give the title

and explain how Chekhov does or does not do what he advocates.

b. Describe a natural scene with which you are familiar. Use as many of Chekhov's points as seem appropriate to your particular piece of writing. Remember proportion; you don't need a bushel of cherries to make a cherry pie.

c. List the points at which Stephen Crane in the following paragraph uses the rules suggested by Chekhov.

A seat in his boat was not unlike a seat upon a bucking bronco, and by the same token a bronco is not much smaller. The craft pranced and reared and plunged like an animal. As each wave came, and she rose for it, she seemed like a horse making at a fence outrageously high. The manner of her scramble over these walls of water is a mystic thing, and, moreover, at the top of them were ordinarily these problems in white water, the foam racing down from the summit of each wave requiring a new leap, and a leap from the air. Then, after scornfully bumping a crest, she would slide and race and splash down a long incline, and arrive bobbing and nodding in front of the next menace.

STEPHEN CRANE
from "The Open Boat"

Assignment 12

The best descriptions are the shortest. Their point is in their effective suggestion. The reader does the rest.

STEPHEN LEACOCK
from *How to Write*

Here are two examples that illustrate the truth of Leacock's statement.

Maria was now an old woman of sixty-one and looked like a haystack on wheels. She moved with a kind of rolling motion. She had peculiar habits;

she would whistle to herself or, at table, make little pellets of bread and flick them about. She was so untidy that no one of her garments seemed to belong to any other. Her hair was white and she wore a lace cap, none too clean and set rakishly at an angle.

HUGH WALPOLE
from *Judith Paris*

The Butt Room was something like a dungeon. It was in the basement, or the bowels, of the dormitory. There were about ten smokers already there. Everyone at Devon had many public faces; in class we looked, if not exactly scholarly, at least respectably alert; on the playing fields we looked like innocent extroverts; and in the Butt Room we looked, very strongly, like criminals. The school's policy, in order to discourage smoking, was to make these rooms as depressing as possible. The windows near the ceiling were small and dirty, the old leather furniture spilled its innards, the tables were mutilated, the walls ash colored, the floor concrete. A radio with a faulty connection played loud and rasping for a while, then suddenly quiet and insinuating.

JOHN KNOWLES
from *A Separate Peace*

1. Read the preceding material.
2. In your journal do *one* of the following:
   a. Make a collection of three or four descriptive paragraphs that you find effective. Each should deal with the same subject, but each should be by a different author.
   b. Write two or three paragraphs of description. Choose any familiar topic.
   c. Write a page of observations that show "effective suggestion."

2|5

SEEING FOR YOURSELF

The previous lessons have suggested ways of observing others. This lesson will present ways of observing yourself. The techniques are not mutually exclusive but interrelated. This lesson emphasizes the need for observation that establishes personal vision and individual statement.

The following excerpt from one of Emerson's essays explains man's need to observe the highest promptings of his own mind. One must look in as well as out.

I read the other day some verses written by an eminent painter which were original and not conventional. The soul always hears an admonition in such lines, let the subject be what it may. The sentiment they instill is of more value than any thought they may contain. To believe your own thought, to believe that what is true for you in your private heart is true for all men—that is genius. Speak your latent conviction, and it shall be the universal sense; for the inmost in due time becomes the outmost, and our first thought is rendered back to us by the trumpets of the Last Judgment. Familiar as the voice of the mind is to each, the highest merit we ascribe to Moses, Plato, and Milton is that they set at naught books and traditions, and spoke not what men, but what *they* thought. A man should learn to detect and watch that gleam of light which flashes across his mind from within, more than the luster of the firmament of bards and sages. Yet he dismisses without notice his thought, because it is his. In every work of genius we recognize our own rejected thoughts; they come back to us with a certain alienated majesty. Great works of art have no more affecting lesson for us than this. They teach us to abide by our spontaneous impression with good-humored inflexibility then most when the whole cry of voices is on the other side. Else to-morrow a stranger will say with masterly good sense precisely what we have thought and felt all the time, and we shall be forced to take with shame our own opinion from another.

RALPH WALDO EMERSON
from "Self-Reliance"

In making the observations on which your thought and opinions are to be built, you should *aim at the imaginative penetration of your subject.* This is the kind of seeing the poets do best, but all men to some degree see with optics other than the eye. Here is a poem that presents this kind of observation—a seeing that gets beyond the facts and at the spirit of the thing observed.

> I like to see it lap the miles,
> And lick the valleys up,
> And stop to feed itself at tanks;
> And then, prodigious, step
>
> Around a pile of mountains,
> And, supercilious, peer
> In shanties by the sides of roads;
> And then a quarry pare
>
> To fit its sides, and crawl between,
> Complaining all the while
> In horrid, hooting stanza;
> Then chase itself downhill
>
> And neigh like Boanerges; *
> Then, punctual as a star,
> Stop—docile and omnipotent—
> At its own stable door.

EMILY DICKINSON

* **Boanerges:** "sons of thunder"; hence, any loud preacher or orator.

To observe fully you must look in as well as out. Outward vision and scientific observation, for all their clarity, are limiting. Blake expressed the idea this way:

And two fold alway—May God us keep
From single vision, and Newton's sleep.

In your observation of self and of the world, go beyond the tactual and the physical; see the metaphorical and the symbolic. Here are two examples of such writing. Each piece suggests the viewer knows himself as well as the world he looks at.

After a time, tired by his dancing apparently, he settled on the window ledge in the sun, and, the queer spectacle being at an end, I forgot about him. Then, looking up, my eye was caught by him. He was trying to resume his dancing, but seemed either so stiff or so awkward that he could only flutter to the bottom of the windowpane; and when he tried to fly across it he failed. Being intent on other matters, I watched these futile attempts for a time without thinking, unconsciously waiting for him to resume his flight, as one waits for a machine that has stopped momentarily to start again without considering the reason of its failure. After perhaps a seventh attempt he slipped from the wooden ledge and fell, fluttering his wings, on to his back on the windowsill. The helplessness of his attitude roused me. It flashed upon me that he was in difficulties; he could no longer raise himself; his legs struggled vainly. But, as I stretched out a pencil, meaning to help him to right himself, it came over me that the failure and awkwardness were the approach of death. I laid the pencil down again.

The legs agitated themselves once more. I looked as if for the enemy against which he struggled. I looked out of doors. What had happened there? Presumably it was midday, and work in the fields had stopped. Stillness and quiet had replaced the previous animation. The birds had taken themselves off to feed in the brooks. The horses stood still. Yet the power was there all the same, massed outside, indifferent, impersonal, not attending to anything in particular. Somehow it was opposed to the little hay-colored moth. It was useless to try to do anything. One could only watch the extraordinary efforts made by those tiny legs against an oncoming doom which could, had it chosen, have submerged an entire city, not merely a city, but masses of human beings; nothing, I knew, had any chance against death. Nevertheless after a pause of exhaustion the legs fluttered again. It was superb this last protest, and so frantic that he succeeded at last in righting himself. One's sympathies, of course, were all on the side of life. Also, when there was nobody to care or to know, this gigantic effort on the part of an insignificant little moth, against a power of such magnitude, to retain what no one else valued or desired to keep, moved one strangely. Again, somehow, one saw life, a pure bead. I lifted the pencil again, useless though I knew it to be. But even as I did so, the unmistakable tokens of death showed themselves. The body relaxed, and instantly grew stiff. The struggle was over. The insignificant little creature now knew death. As I looked at the dead moth, this minute wayside triumph of so great a force over so mean an antagonist filled me with wonder. Just as life had been strange a few minutes before, so death was now as strange. The moth having righted himself now lay most decently and uncomplainingly composed. Oh, yes, he seemed to say, death is stronger than I am.

VIRGINIA WOOLF
from "The Death of the Moth"

And here is the second excerpt, one by George Orwell.

As for spring, not even the narrow and gloomy streets round the Bank of England are quite able to exclude it. It comes seeping in everywhere, like one of those new poison gases which pass through all filters. The spring is commonly referred to as "a miracle," and during the past five or six years this worn-out figure of speech has taken on a new lease on life. After the sort of winters we have had to endure recently, the spring does seem miraculous, because it has become gradually harder and harder to believe that it is actually going to happen. Every February since 1940 I have found myself thinking that this time winter is going to be permanent. But Persephone, like the toads, always rises from the dead at about the same moment. Suddenly, toward the end of March, the miracle happens and the decaying slum in which I live is transfigured. Down in the square the sooty privets have turned bright green, the leaves are thickening on the chestnut trees, the daffodils are out, the wallflowers are budding, the policeman's tunic looks positively a pleasant shade of blue, the fishmonger greets his customers with a smile, and even the sparrows are quite a different color, having felt the balminess of the air and nerved themselves to take a bath, their first since last September.

GEORGE ORWELL
from "Some Thoughts
on the Common Toad"

Assignment 13

1. Read the chapter up to this point.
2. In your journal do *one* of the following:
   a. Reread Emerson's paragraph on self-reliance. From your own reading select a passage in which you feel the writer has presented his thoughts as though acting on Emerson's advice.
   b. Write a full-page journal entry in which you respond to some gleam of inward light.
   c. Comment on either or both of the other selections presented in this lesson. Speak your own mind, but look inward before you speak out.

Assignment 14

Whatever the thing we wish to say, there is but one word to express it, but one verb to give it movement, but one adjective to qualify it. We must seek till we find this noun, this verb, and this adjective, and never be content with approximations, never allow ourselves to play tricks, even happy ones, or have recourse to sleights of language to avoid a difficulty. The subtlest things may be rendered and suggested by applying the hint conveyed in Boileau's line: *"D'un mot mis en sa place enseigna le pouvoir"* ("He taught the power of a word put in the right place").

> GUY DE MAUPASSANT
> from the Preface to *Pierre et Jean*

A writer needs a personal response to his material before he can gain one from his readers. Situation has to be felt as well as seen. In theory anything in the world is fair game for a theme or a story, but in fact themes and stories are the result of impact and selective seeing—matters that reflect themselves in the writer's style, and in his shaping of material.

Although you see for yourself and feel intensely, you can't communicate those responses successfully unless you have also learned to observe words. You must train yourself to see words as well as events. Every page of clichés portrays an unobserving mind. Prose reflects personal vision. If you write in clichés, you are on your way to mind blindness, and a blind mind is apt to wreck thought and smash metaphor before hitting the first period.

One way of becoming attentive to words is to consider definitions. This approach requires you to see likeness and difference and to express them precisely. The following essay is an example of the kind of observation that reflects the importance of word choice.

If I were to describe sophistication, I should not liken it to anything deeper than a coat of paint; I believe it is a pose. The outstanding thing about a sophisticated person is his chatter, the revelation of his mentality. He can talk about things that a plainer person is ignorant of, and he can make these trivialities—for trivialities they generally are —seem truly consequential. They appear, in fact, to be consequential not to him (which sounds most astonishing) but to the person who is so abysmally out of touch with the world as to know nothing of them. The sophisticate himself has presumably seen too much, lived too hard, and experienced too many excitements to care longer for them in any but a condescending way. He is burned out, so that one could substitute him for King George IV in that famous description which denied the king any flesh and blood, reducing him to a bundle of clothes, paint, and wig. After all, there is not much to sophistication but a kind of stock knowledge concerning horses, theaters, song hits, dances, hotels, clothes, and other tinsel things. There is, of course, and one must not leave it out, an understanding of the amount of bad manners that can get by in society without causing ostracism. This paltry knowledge is borne as if it were all knowledge, with the implication that any other learning is stodgy and ridiculous. The sophisticate, even though he is weary of life, does get occasional snobbish pleasure from scorning those who do not have this particular information.

Urbanity is different. It is not just a surface icing. One cannot, for instance, bring it before one's eyes as one can bring sophistication by picturing a cocktail shaker, a pair of pearl-gray gloves, and a theater lobby. One does not think of anything material in considering urbanity, since urbanity is abstract and grows up in one as an enduring love might grow. An urbane person may have the same knowledge of places and things that a sophisticate has, but this knowledge is incidental to his sense of proportion, which is the *sine qua non* of urbanity. He could not so confuse the importance of things as to ridicule a group of people because their accent was not exactly like his, or quarrel with his landlady over the length of time he might leave his electric lights burning, or scorn a Virginia farmer because he had never heard Paderewski play— things which I think a sophisticated person might do without feeling that he had stepped out of character. I'll wager that if one placed in a small Wisconsin village of limited horizon a sophisticate from Broadway and an urbane gentleman from wherever he could be found, the sophisticate would grow irritated, scornful, and unhappy, but the urbane man would adapt himself to his environment and make himself admired by his less polished neighbors. Toleration for individual idiosyncrasies and local customs has always been characteristic of urbanity, which is essentially courteous and suave. Sophistication, however, has not enough body to it to survive any but its own rarefied atmosphere. One would expect an urbane man who had retired to the country to remain urbane, but one knows that two or three years of seclusion would take the sophistication from anyone. Sophistication, therefore, out of self-defense, is forced to be narrow. Urbanity, because it is no artificial attitude, but is completely interwoven with the character, is liberal. One might measure the relative depths of these two by reflecting that it is possible, and not infrequent, for a child to be sophisticated, but that mature persons alone can be urbane.

R. B. BAKER
from "Urbanity and Sophistication"

And now consider a paragraph of a different kind, but one that nonetheless involves word choice.

There is a glen between our house and the lake, through which winds a little brook with pools and tiny waterfalls over the great roots of trees. The glen is deep and narrow, and filled with trees; so that, in the summer, it is all a dense shadow of obscurity. Now, the foliage of the trees being almost entirely a golden yellow, instead of being full of shadow, the glen is absolutely full of sunshine, and its depths are more brilliant than the open plain of the mountain tops. The trees are sunshine, and many of the golden leaves being freshly fallen, the glen is strewn with sunshine, amid which winds and gurgles the bright, dark little brook.

NATHANIEL HAWTHORNE
from *The Heart of Hawthorne's Journals*
October 16, 1850

You may say, "Nice for 1850, but what's it got to do with today? What's the point?" Skill to see what's in your own backyard, to see and to feel it in your own way, and then to communicate your discovery in your own words—that is the point.

Reread the paragraph by Hawthorne. Notice the similarity between the first and last sentence. Study the development that permits them to be different.

Seeing the glen as "a dense shadow of obscurity" is an example of putting words together that belong together. Seeing those same depths as "more brilliant than the open plain of the mountain tops" catches something of the exaltation Hawthorne felt when fall came to the glen and turned the leaves into a reflected sunshine.

You don't have to drive a batmobile, or total the family car in order to develop an idea. Indeed, that may be quite the wrong way to go at ideas and stories. Hawthorne was able to find ideas and stories in his own backyard, in his own town—in its houses and its history.

1. Read the preceding material.
2. In your journal do *one* of the following:
   a. Write an essay in which you distinguish between any two terms that interest you.
   b. Observe two people whom you believe to be happy. Report how happiness presents itself in each case, and, insofar as you can, explain its source.

c. Report the difference you have observed between the essay and the short story. Don't turn to sources. Depend on your own observations.

Assignment 15

Don't forget to find humor. As every cartoonist shows, observation can reveal the ridiculous. Rube Goldberg, for example, has an eye for the fantastically complicated that potentially inhabits every gadget. He is an arch observer of the care with which men complicate their lives. But instead of turning these observations into a Greek tragedy, he makes us laugh at what we know is a part of ourselves. In fact, Rube Goldberg's inventions, which are impossibly complicated logical machines for achieving simple goals, are supposed to have inspired the Charlie Chaplin classic, *Modern Times,* a movie that was able to use the poignancy of man's self-defeat as the basis for comedy.

The following passage shows how keen observation can expose the ridiculous, even in ourselves.

Merely as an observer of natural phenomena, I am fascinated by my own personal appearance. This does not mean that I am *pleased* with it, mind you, or that I can even tolerate it. I simply have a morbid interest in it.

Each day I look like someone, or some*thing,* different. I never know what it is going to be until I steal a look in the glass. (Oh, I don't suppose you really could call it stealing. It belongs to me, after all.)

One day I look like Wimpy, the hamburger fancier in the Popeye the Sailor saga. Another day it may be Wallace Beery. And a third day, if I have let my mustache get out of hand, it is Bairnsfather's Old Bill. And not until I peek do I know what the show is going to be.

Some mornings, if I look in the mirror soon

enough after getting out of bed, there is no resemblance to any character at all, either in or out of fiction, and I turn quickly to look behind me, convinced that a stranger has spent the night with me and is peering over my shoulder in a sinister fashion, merely to frighten me. On such occasions, the shock of finding that I am actually possessor of the face in the mirror is sufficient to send me scurrying back to bed, completely unnerved.

All this is, of course, very depressing, and I often give off a low moan at the sight of the new day's metamorphosis, but I can't seem to resist the temptation to learn the worst. I even go out of my way to look at myself in store-window mirrors, just to see how long it will take me to recognize myself. If I happen to have on a new hat, or am walking with a limp, I sometimes pass right by my reflection without even nodding. Then I begin to think: "You must have given off *some* visual impression into that mirror. You're not a disembodied spirit yet—I hope."

And I go back and look again, and, sure enough, the strange-looking man I thought was walking just ahead of me in the reflection turns out to have been my own image all the time. It makes a fellow stop and think, I can tell you.

ROBERT BENCHLEY
from "My Face"

1. Read the remarks about humor.
2. In your journal do *one* of the following:
    a. Through essay or anecdote present some humorous observations of your own.
    b. From your reading, copy out a paragraph or two that you personally consider amusing.
    c. Write an extended entry on a topic of your own choice.

2 | Review

This business of observing can come to have the fascination of a game. The more you play, the more skillful you become. But you need to remember that most people only see what they are interested in. Newton saw his apple in a very special way, a painter sees an apple as color, form, and perhaps the subject for a still-life composition. Steinbeck saw an apple orchard as something to write about—as a way of presenting migrant laborers at work. A farmer may look at his apples as a cash crop, and you may see an apple as something to eat. The point here is that all men tend to limit their vision by one-dimensional viewing and that enlargement comes through multidimensional observation. The more you see, the more you have to say. For the end, you must, of course, bring your observation to a point of focus. But first you must observe. Do it as broadly and as searchingly as possible. Taken in this spirit, observation becomes a game of detection—a way of seeing and a way of constructing a whole from a part.

Read the following excerpt from "The Red-Headed League" by A. Conan Doyle, and you'll see just how much there may be to this game of observing.

I took a good look at the man and endeavored, after the fashion of my companion, to read the indications which might be presented by his dress or appearance.

I did not gain very much, however, by my inspection. Our visitor bore every mark of being an average commonplace British tradesman, obese, pompous, and slow. He wore rather baggy gray shepherd's check trousers, a not overclean black frock coat, unbuttoned in the front, and a drab waistcoat with a heavy brassy Albert chain, and a square, pierced bit of metal dangling down as an ornament. A frayed top hat and a faded brown overcoat with a wrinkled velvet collar lay upon a chair beside him. Altogether, look as I would, there was nothing remarkable about the man save his blazing red head, and the expression of extreme chagrin and discontent upon his features.

Sherlock Holmes's quick eye took in my occupation, and he shook his head with a smile as he noticed my questioning glances. "Beyond the obvious facts that he has at some time done manual labor, that he takes snuff, that he is a Freemason, that he has been in China, and that he has done a considerable amount of writing lately, I can deduce nothing else."

Mr. Jabez Wilson started up in his chair, with his forefinger upon the paper, but his eyes upon my companion.

"How in the name of good fortune did you know all that, Mr. Holmes?" he asked. "How did you know, for example, that I did manual labor? It's as true as gospel, for I began as a ship's carpenter."

"Your hands, my dear sir. Your right hand is quite a size larger than your left. You have worked with it, and the muscles are more developed."

"Well the snuff, then, and the Freemasonry?"

"I won't insult your intelligence by telling you how I read that, especially as, rather against the strict rules of your order, you use an arc-and-compass breast pin."

"Ah, of course, I forgot that. But the writing?"

"What else can be indicated by that right cuff so very shiny for five inches, and the left one with the smooth patch near the elbow where you rest it upon the desk?"

"Well, but China?"

"The fish that you have tattooed immediately above your right wrist could only have been done in China. I have made a small study of tattoo marks and have even contributed to the literature of the subject. That trick of staining the fishes' scales of a delicate pink is quite peculiar to China. When, in addition, I see a Chinese coin hanging from your watch chain, the matter becomes even more simple."

Mr. Jabez Wilson laughed heavily. "Well, I never!" said he. "I thought at first that you had done something clever, but I see that there was nothing in it, after all."

A. CONAN DOYLE

from "The Red-Headed League"

Before you actually do this Review assignment, read the following material, which is taken from *A Creative Approach to Writing* by Roger H. Garrison. You will find here a way of pulling together what you have learned in this unit and presenting, through a piece of your own writing, some clear observations. The final version of "Hurricane," which follows the Garrison excerpt, may serve as a model of what you will want to do.

Most of us can, by an effort of memory, re-create some scene or event we have observed. The way we re-create it is by pulling out of the fuzzy memories of the scene the facts of sight and sound that associate themselves as background. The more facts we are able to associate (make a pattern of) the more concrete the memory becomes. When a scene is finally re-created vividly, we discover that it is built up of details pulled out of the whole scene which, added together, produce a single coherent impression.

To illustrate this, I produce here another dialogue, this time between one student and the instructor, in which we worked with the problem of recalling an event and its context.

I: See if you can remember, as clearly and vividly as you can, some happening or event which impressed you very much. It doesn't matter what the event was. It could be a particularly beautiful sight or an action of some kind or a natural phenomenon like an earthquake or a heavy rainstorm. Some one impressive thing that you remember with especial vividness.

ELLEN: The thing that impressed me most was a hurricane. I was in the middle of it.

I: The New England hurricane of 1938?

ELLEN: No, this was in Bermuda. I live there. The hurricane came up all of a sudden, it seemed like. I've never seen such wind. It scared me, and I remember every detail about it.

I: In order to show you the kinds of questions you have to ask of happenings you think you remember very well, suppose we concentrate for a few minutes on this hurricane. You said you remember every detail of it. Suppose you tell me about the hurricane as you saw it. Make me see it as you did, and hear it, and feel it. If you get stuck, I'll ask you questions.

ELLEN: Well, it was a very sticky day, I remember. You know, sticky-hot and muggy. After a while I felt sort of uneasy about it, so I went and closed all the shutters because I knew it was going to blow pretty hard. Well . . . then the wind came up and the shutters banged—the wind wasn't steady at first but it came in heavy gusts—and then the lights went out. I was all by myself. It scared me, and it lasted a long time, but when it was over not much damage had been done to the house, only a lot of trees uprooted and palm branches all over the place. It was some wind. There was lots of rain, too.

I: Is that all there was to it?

ELLEN: No, but it's hard to remember exactly.

I: You didn't give any details to speak of.

ELLEN: No, I didn't, did I?

I: Let's start at the beginning. Where were you when you first began to suspect that a storm might be coming?

ELLEN: Let's see. . . . I was in the living room, I think.

I: What were you doing?

ELLEN: Reading. Sitting in father's overstuffed armchair. I remember that because from his chair you can look out the big window to the ocean.

I: What made you stop reading?

ELLEN: I don't know—the quiet, I guess. It was awfully quiet.

I: How do you know it was quiet?

ELLEN: That's a silly question. It was *quiet,* that's all. No sounds.

I: But how do you talk about quiet?

ELLEN: Oh, I see. Well, I suppose it *looked* quiet. For instance, all the flowers around the trees and the walls looked limp. There's usually a breeze that stirs them and makes sounds at the corners of the house. And the sea looked quiet, too. You know on a regular clear day when the sun shines over everything, the waves sort of dance. White caps sparkle in the sun. White on green. This time the sea didn't look like that.

I: How did it look?

ELLEN: That's hard to . . . it looked greasy; that's it, greasy. Long swells. Oh, and I couldn't hear a single bird. Which was strange because the birds are always cheeping and squeaking around in the trees and under the eaves of the house. Then later I turned on the radio, and it seemed awfully loud. Contrast with the quiet before, I guess.

I: You said the sea looked greasy—different from times when the sun shone on the white caps. Wasn't the sun shining on this day?

ELLEN: I think . . . no . . . well it was and it wasn't. I mean it was light, all right, but it wasn't like sunshine. Sort of a yellowy glare. Over everything. And, come to think of it, it was a funny thing, there weren't any shadows at all. I noticed that because I used to watch where the corner-of-the-house shadow went at different times of the day. And at this time of the afternoon it should have just about reached the flower beds—the shadow, I mean—and there wasn't any shadow at all, only the yellow light. Kind of yellow-orange.

I: You said before that you were scared. Did you feel at all scared before the hurricane struck?

ELLEN: Yes.

I: Why?

ELLEN: I don't know, exactly . . . well, yes I do. I was all alone in the house.

I: No one home at all?

ELLEN: No, just me and the two dogs.

I: Oh, two dogs. I thought you said you were alone.

ELLEN: No people, no other people, I meant.

(By this time, you should have noticed that detail after detail of the background and context of the hurricane came back to this student as her memory was probed with questions. With each detail, the picture comes clearer and clearer; she remembered not only things that she had seen directly, but things that were on the periphery of her sight—"out of the corner of her eye." She had "forgotten" them because at the time she had had no particular reason to focus her mind on them or to relate them to the whole experience.)

We went on:

I: What were the dogs doing all this time? Where were they? In the living room with you?

ELLEN: Yes, they were lying down near the chair. I remember I got up to let them out, and I had to call them. That was queer because usually when anybody makes a move to let those dogs out, they scoot out of the house and wag their tails and almost mow you down, they're so happy to get out.

I: What happened when you let them out?

ELLEN: I opened the door and—you should have seen all the bugs that were trying to get in the screen. Even little birds, flying around and knocking themselves against the screen. I had to shut the door in a hurry.

I: What did you do when you got outside?

ELLEN: It wasn't exactly outside, it was in a patio

—well, yes, of course, it was outdoors. Well, usually the dogs race for the gate and wait for me to open it so they can get out. Not this time. They stuck close to the house.

I: Anything else?

ELLEN: I looked around some. There's a road that goes past our house. It looked funny, all yellow even though it was really black macadam. I didn't see anybody. I watched the ocean again. The swells were getting heavier because I could hear the water crashing around on the shore. After I looked around some more, I went back into the house.

I: When did the hurricane come?

ELLEN: After I went in, it got darker and darker. Then the wind began. And the rain.

I: I think I have asked enough questions now to show you the idea. You can't describe anything—or talk about anything—without asking questions like these of yourself and of the scenes or actions you are describing.

HURRICANE

I was sitting in a deep armchair reading a book. There wasn't a sound anywhere. I turned a page, then looked out the window in front of me. The hills and sea looked brassy; the gray sea with pale light on the crests of the swell looked as thick as mineral oil.

After a while I began to notice sounds. The earth seemed to rumble. The waves were thundering in the caves under the island. My two dogs were nervously asleep on their sides next to me; once in a while they would jerk their heads and whimper.

The air was hot, very hot and muggy. No birds were singing. I stood up and called the dogs. I felt I had to get outside.

When I opened the patio door, masses of big frogs, birds, flies, cockroaches, and mosquitoes were clustered there, trying to get into the house. We got out quickly and shut the door. The dogs did not want to stay out. I wondered why. They usually cried to be taken out, and if I took them for an extra walk they were so happy they practically knocked me over in their joy. But now they slunk near the house. Their tongues lolled out, red and panting.

I looked at the huge flowers growing up the walls and hanging from the trees. They were tightly closed and the leaves hung limply against their stems.

There seemed to be yellow light everywhere, but there were no shadows. No shadows anywhere.

The road by the house was deserted. Not a cyclist or a carriage passed by. I was lonelier than ever outside, so I called the dogs and we went back in. The dogs immediately went to my room and both of them waited while I pulled back the skirts of my dressing table. They always went in there when they were uneasy. When I closed the skirts around them they felt snug and secure.

I went around the house and closed all the shutters. By now it had got completely dark, so I went back to the living room and turned on all the lights and listened to some boogie-woogie on the radio. Dutch courage.

Suddenly, above the jazzy blasts of trumpets and drums I heard the wind. A long gust tore viciously at the house, cracked some tiles off the roof and ripped loose a shutter and sent it crashing against the wall of the house. As abruptly as it began, there was absolute calm again.

Then, in a hard crescendo, there came a steady drum of rain. An explosion of wind shook the house to the foundations. Simultaneously, the radio commentator said, "The hurricane has reached the islands. Winds reaching velocities of 150 miles per hour are expected to——"

The radio went off, the whole house went dark, and the winds worried at the house like a dog with a bone.

ROGER H. GARRISON
from *A Creative Approach to Writing*

Review Assignment

In your journal do *one* of the following:
   a. Select a single memorable event. Ask yourself questions about it. Then write an extended entry on the topic.
   b. Write extensive observations on a topic of your own choice.
   c. Write an extended entry that shows your ability to use observation for the purpose of fiction.

UNIT 3

Imagination

To know is nothing at all;
to imagine is everything.—ANATOLE FRANCE

3|1

WHAT IS IMAGINATION?

For the purpose of this text, *imagination* means seeing things in new, fresh, or original relationships. It is playing with the observed so as to re-create reality. Imagination at one extreme includes the fantasy of delight and at the other the terrors of horror. In literature, imagination tends to present itself through metaphor and fiction. Creative manipulation of experience is the function of imagination.

The lunatic, the lover, and the poet
Are of imagination all compact.
One sees more devils than vast Hell can hold,
That is the madman. The lover, all as frantic,
Sees Helen's beauty in a brow of Egypt.
The poet's eye, in a fine frenzy rolling,
Doth glance from heaven to earth, from earth to heaven,
And as imagination bodies forth
The forms of things unknown, the poet's pen
Turns them to shapes, and gives to airy nothing
A local habitation and a name.
Such tricks hath strong imagination
That if it would but apprehend some joy,
It comprehends some bringer of that joy;
Or in the night, imagining some fear,
How easy is a bush supposed a bear!

WILLIAM SHAKESPEARE
from *A Midsummer Night's Dream*

If anyone is qualified to tell you about imagination, it's Shakespeare. Here he gives two examples of "strong imagination." The first is the case of a person who anticipates (apprehends) some joy so keenly that he reads (comprehends) the answer in the face of the bearer of that joy, as a child or a lover can read in the face of another the fulfillment or denial of his hopes. The other example of "strong imagination" is an imaginary fear at night that transforms a familiar object into a frightening one. His example is a bush transformed into a bear. Washington Irving turns his tale of "The Headless Horseman" on just this point. You'll recall that Ichabod Crane supposed a lighted pumpkin carried by a night rider to be a ghost—a headless horseman.

You have the power to anticipate joy and to read good or bad omens in the face and manner of those who bring tidings. Doubtless, you have also had your turn with night fear, when familiar sights and sounds transform themselves into a moment of uncertainty or terror.

All this is to demonstrate that there is nothing wrong with your imagination. You have a strong one. Still you may not be a lover, a poet, or a madman. They each use their imaginations in a particular way. Indeed, they are, in various ways and degrees, dominated by their imaginations.

Our concern here is with the imagination of the poet—the writer. What does Shakespeare tell about him? How does he differ from the others and the rest of us?

Shakespeare points out that all men have imaginations and respond to them. He points out, however, that the writer's response is unique. He gives form to the experiences that imagination has brought him. He not only sees airy nothing but he gives things unknown a local habitation and a name. He writes.

Your task is to start turning the forms your imagination bodies forth into words. This is perhaps an unfamiliar experience for you. People tend to conceal their dreams and fantasies (sleeping and waking) from each other and to keep their imaginations secret.

But such is not the way of the poet, the writer. His task is to find appropriate ways of sharing his vision and his dream.

Here is an anecdote that illustrates the writer's penchant for putting experience into words. In this case the writer, James Fenimore Cooper, found his imagination impulsively prompting him to a prank that created a bush-to-bear situation in reverse. But as interesting as the events themselves is that he recorded the matter in his journal and subsequently sent his close friend Samuel F. B. Morse an edited version of the same event. At the time the Coopers were staying on a little island in the Rhine. Cooper wrote in his journal:

> Here we left the carriage on the main, and crossed to the island (which is sometimes called Nonnenswerth) where an old convent is converted into a tavern. Luckily we were quite alone, not another guest happening to be in the vast buildings, which were built round a court, with the usual cloisters, forming, with the offices, a parallelogram of six by three hundred feet. The community was Benedictine, and the cells admitted of being turned into very comfortable bedrooms. We had the apartments of the Lady Abbess, which made a comfortable parlor, with a spacious bedroom. The girls were in their cells.
>
> About ten there came up a gust, and the effect was excessively fine, taken in conjunction with the peculiarities of our situation. At eleven I took a candle, and went alone into the chapel. The windows were broken, and what between the rattling of glass, the glare of lightning, images of saints, crucifixes, altars, and other appliances, I got a sensation. The convent had only been finally abandoned as such in 1820, and the chair, of stuffed velvet, with the prie-dieu of the Abbess, [was] in the gallery of the nuns, in which I had taken port. I had been walking about a quarter of an hour, enjoying all this, when the door of the gallery was slowly opened and the face of a wrinkled old woman thrust itself into the place. I groaned, and away went [the] old woman, candle, face and all. . . .

And here is the letter to his friend.

To Samuel F. B. Morse   August 15, 1832

. . . The wind begins to murmur, casements are closing, and we may have thunder next. This opinion has proved prophetic. There has arisen a sudden gust, with lightning. I take a candle and go through the corridors, in quest of a sensation. A door communicating with the gallery of the chapel is open and I enter, shutting myself in. Here was what I wanted. Images of saints, crucifixes, a dim light, rattling windows and solitude. Everything was so fresh, that the stuffed velvet chair of the Lady Abbess was near the railing, and a prie-dieu at its side. I took a seat. In a few minutes the door slowly opened, and a hag thrust her wrinkled face into the gallery. I groaned; whether it was with fear or fun, I leave you to guess, and away the old woman went, as if the devil was after her— I withdrew like a well-bred ghost that has delivered his message. . . .

> from *The Letters and Journals*
> *of James Fenimore Cooper,* Vol. II
> edited by James F. Beard

Assignment 1

1. Read the chapter up to this point.
2. In your journal do *one* of the following:
   a. Present briefly and clearly an incident of night fear—a case in which a bush becomes a bear.
   b. Look about you and imagine something—anything. Record your imaginings.
   c. If (you name the person—real, historic, or imaginary) were here, what would you say to him and he to you? Write an imaginary conversation that sounds real.

Assignment 2

The human imagination is much more capable than it gets credit for. This is why Niagara is always a disappointment when one sees it for the first time. One's imagination has long ago built a Niagara to which this one is a poor dribbling thing. The ocean "with its waves running mountain high" is always a disappointment at first sight; the imagination has constructed real mountains, whereas these when swelling at their very biggest and highest are not imposing. The Taj is a disappointment though people are ashamed to confess it. God will be a disappointment to most of us, at first. I wish I could see the Niagaras and Tajs which the human imagination has constructed; why then, bless you, I should see Atlantics pouring down out of the sky over cloud ranges, and I should see Tajs of a form so gracious and spiritual expression so divine and altogether so sublime and lovely and worshipful that—well—St. Peter's, Vesuvius, Heaven, Hell, everything that is much described is bound to be a disappointment at first experience.

MARK TWAIN
from *Mark Twain's Notebook*

1. Read the statement by Twain.
2. In your journal do *one* of the following:
   a. Recount an experience of disappointed imagination. Tell what you expected and what you received.
   b. Name an American town or city that you have never visited and then tell in some detail what you imagine it is like.
   c. Write an entry in which you explain what you think it would have been like had you been present at some historic event (you name the event).

Assignment 3

"Do not," Flaubert said to Taine, "compare the interior vision of the artist with that of the truly hallucinated man. I know both states perfectly: there is an abyss between them. In hallucination, within the meaning of the act, there is always terror, you feel your personality escaping you; you think you are going to die. In the poetic vision, on the contrary, there is joy. . . ."

ELIZABETH BOWEN
from *Collected Impressions*

Imagination liberates the mind and produces moon landings and poetry. Man is made with imagination built in, but his achievements have been greatest when imagination has gotten out—provided, of course, it has been under his control. The power of imagination is like a genie—for its master it will perform miracles—for others it will do nothing, or bring destruction.

Here you will find ways of bringing this power under your control. Then it will become a friendly genie and a glorious companion. But control rests not in magic words, spells, or numbers, but in the vocabulary of every day and in the special way of seeing that permits the extraordinary to exist in exactly the same space that is totally occupied by the ordinary. Here is an example:

The Toaster

A silver-scaled Dragon with jaws flaming red
Sits at my elbow and toasts my bread.
I hand him fat slices, and then, one by one,
He hands them back when he sees they are done.

WILLIAM JAY SMITH

Imagination creates an enlargement and vivification of reality that can be immediately experienced. Literary imagination is both seeing and saying. For example, we have all seen steam shovels and in some vague way realized they were not unlike prehistoric creatures—equipped with vast power and great snapping jaws. To see in that way is to make imagination a friendly companion. But to say the words of every day over your vision is the incantation that permits imagination to take form. Here is another example of imagination taking shape:

Steam Shovel

The dinosaurs are not all dead.
I saw one raise its iron head
To watch me walking down the road
Beyond our house today.
Its jaws were dripping with a load
Of earth and grass that it had cropped.
It must have heard me where I stopped,
Snorted white steam my way,
And stretched its long neck out to see,
And chewed, and grinned quite amiably.

CHARLES MALAM

1. Read the preceding remarks.
2. In your journal do *one* of the following:
   a. From your reading, select an imaginative paragraph or poem that you particularly like. Copy the poem or paragraph into your journal.
   b. Write an imaginative paragraph or poem of your own.
   c. Write a journal entry on the imagination of childhood.

3|2

THE VOCABULARY OF IMAGINATION

Here is a poem by Baudelaire called "The Albatross." It's about poets and the people who make fun of them. It's about the problem of being a poet or an artist of any kind in an unresponsive and nonpoetic world. Baudelaire's problem was to present power, beauty, potential, and then to diminish it so rapidly as to make it appear impotent, unwanted, and ridiculous. His problem was to present in a few lines the waste of the world through its want of imagination. The poet achieved his goal by using the language of imagination itself—metaphor and symbol. In this poem the albatross becomes both. In a few lines Baudelaire stages a mindless tragedy. Here is the drama:

L'Albatros

Souvent, pour s'amuser, les hommes d'équipage
Prennent des albatros, vastes oiseaux des mers,
Qui suivent, indolents compagnons de voyage,
Le navire glissant sur les gouffres amers.

À peine les ont-ils déposés sur les planches,
Que ces rois de l'azur, maladroits et honteux,
Laissent piteusement leurs grandes ailes blanches
Comme des avirons traîner à côté d'eux.

Ce voyageur ailé, comme il est gauche et veule!
Lui, naguère si beau, qu'il est comique et laid!
L'un agace son bec avec un brûle-gueule,
L'autre mime, en boitant, l'infirme qui volait!

Le Poète est semblable au prince des nuées
Qui hante la tempête et se rit de l'archer;
Exilé sur le sol au milieu des huées,
Ses ailes de géant l'empêchent de marcher.

The Albatross

Ofttimes, for diversion, the men of the crew
Capture albatross, vast birds of the seas
That accompany, at languid, leisurely pace,
Boats on their way through bitter straits.

Having scarce been taken aboard
These kings of the blue, awkward and shy,
Piteously their great white wings
Let droop like oars at their sides.

This wingèd voyager, how clumsy he is and weak!
He just now so lovely, how comic and ugly!
One with a stubby pipe teases his beak,
Another mimics, limping, the cripple who could fly!

The Poet resembles this prince of the clouds,
Who laughs at hunters and haunts the storms;
Exiled to the ground amid the jeering pack,
His giant wings will not let him walk.

translated by KATE FLORES

Imagination is a way of seeing and also a way of saying. When you see imaginatively, you are not limited by what exists. When you speak or write imaginatively, you don't have to be confined to words as they are—but if you don't care to invent words, then use the old ones with new power.

On the following page are two brief samples of imaginative writing. The first is from *Alice in Wonderland;* the second, from *A Clockwork Orange.* You will note that both writers invent time, place, vocabulary, and events; yet each produces a very different effect. Why? How important is tone and diction in these examples?

Jabberwocky

'Twas brillig, and the slithy toves
  Did gyre and gimble in the wabe;
All mimsy were the borogoves,
  And the mome raths outgrabe.

"Beware the Jabberwock, my son!
  The jaws that bite, the claws that catch!
Beware the Jubjub bird, and shun
  The frumious Bandersnatch!"

He took his vorpal sword in hand;
  Long time the manxome foe he sought—
So rested he by the Tumtum tree,
  And stood awhile in thought.

And, as in uffish thought he stood,
  The Jabberwock, with eyes of flame,
Came whiffling through the tulgey wood,
  And burbled as it came!

One, two! One, two! And through and through
  The vorpal blade went snicker-snack!
He left it dead, and with its head
  He went galumphing back.

"And hast thou slain the Jabberwock?
  Come to my arms, my beamish boy!
O frabjous day! Callooh, Callay!"
  He chortled in his joy.

'Twas brillig, and the slithy toves
  Did gyre and gimble in the wabe;
All mimsy were the borogoves,
  And the mome raths outgrabe.

LEWIS CARROLL

There was me, that is Alex, and my three *droogs,*
that is Pete, Georgie, and Dim, Dim being really
dim, and we sat in the Korova Milkbar making up

our *rassoodocks* what to do with the evening, a flip dark chill winter. . . . The Korova Milkbar was a milk-plus *mesto,* and you may, O my brothers, have forgotten what these mestos were like, things changing so *skorry* these days and everybody quick to forget, newspapers not being read much neither. Well, what they sold there was milk plus something else. They had no licence [*sic*] for selling liquor, but there was no law yet against *prodding* some of the new *veshches* which they used to put into the old *moloko,* so you could *peet* it with *vellocet* or *synthemesc* or *drencrom* or one or two other veshches which would give you a nice quiet *horrorshow* fifteen minutes admiring *Bog* And All His Holy Angels And Saints in your left shoe with lights bursting all over your *mozg.* Or you could peet milk with knives in it, as we used to say, and this would sharpen you up and make you ready for a bit of dirty twenty-to-one, and that was what we were peeting this evening I'm starting off the story with.

1. **droog:** friend
2. **rassoodock:** mind
3. **mesto:** place
4. **skorry:** quick, quickly
5. **prod:** to produce
6. **veshch:** thing
7. **moloko:** milk
8. **peet:** to drink
9. **vellocet:** a drug
10. **synthemesc:** a drug
11. **drencrom:** a drug
12. **horrorshow:** good, well
13. **Bog:** God
14. **mozg:** brain

ANTHONY BURGESS
from *A Clockwork Orange*

Imagination tends to present itself through metaphor and fiction.

Claude Brown was looking for a way to explain what it was like to be black and in court. His sense of not being seen or treated as a real person was strong. In the following paragraph he finds an imaginative way of presenting a part of his reaction to that day in court. You'll note that much of the emotional intensity of that experience is projected for us through metaphors.

While Dad and I were sitting there waiting for something to happen, I kept thinking about the time I saw a big black man take a little pig out of his pen at hog-killing time down South. He took the pig and tied him to a post, patted him on the back a couple of times, then picked up his ax and hit the pig in the head and killed him. The pig died without giving anybody any trouble, and the big black pig-killer was happy. In fact, everybody was happy, because we were all friends and part of the family. The only one there who didn't have a friend was the pig.

I had a feeling that something like what happened to the pig was going to happen in the courtroom and that Dad and I had already been patted on the back. I looked at the big, fat-faced judge sitting up there on the bench. He didn't look mean or anything like that, but he didn't look like he was a right-doing cat either. I even wished it was that old evil-looking lady judge who sent me to Wiltwyck sitting up there. She looked mean as hell, but I don't think I would have felt so much like that pig if she had been up there. I knew she wouldn't have been a friend of those lawyers and the people from the bus company. She looked like nobody could be her friend. And that was how it seemed that a judge should be. And she was colored too; maybe we would have been real people to her.

CLAUDE BROWN
from *Manchild in the Promised Land*

Metaphor requires imagination. Usually it is an insight, the discovery of a parallel between seemingly dissimilar things. Metaphor brings the reader the pleasure of sharing a secret and the delight of making a discovery.

One may develop his power for making metaphors by deliberate practice. One of the ways of starting such practice is to start noting how others do it and then make a try on your own. You may want to start your own collection by reading poems. Poetry is the storehouse of metaphors.

Assignment 4

1. Read the chapter up to this point.
2. In your journal do *one* of the following:
   a. Tell a story in a new language. Be sure to supply a complete key to word meanings.
   b. Write a full entry in which you examine a poem and its use of metaphor.
   c. Copy out a passage in which you feel the author has succeeded in using old words with new force.

Assignment 5

The writer lives with words. His imagination shapes them to his sentences and to his needs. The color, the contrast, the connotative values are all a part of it, and so too is the rhythm and the strength of the individual words and sentences.

One may arrange words rapidly and happily or one may weigh and pick his choices with great care. To the reader such matters are of no interest. The reader wants vicarious experience and felicity in expression, but as a student of writing you know imagination as well as practice is needed if the reader's wants are to be supplied.

Thomas Mann tells us a bit about how he uses his imagination in choosing words. He looks ahead; he pretends. He says to himself, "If I use this, then what?" As another writer might deliberate on the choice of a character, Mann picks his words with an eye to their future functions. Here is his own statement about his method.

Every morning, one step ahead, every morning, one more passage written—that has become my way of work, and it has its inner necessity. In a kind and unusually sensitive review which a critic has recently given my literary efforts. . . , he drew attention to my methods of composition, and described how I had perfected and deepened the much-used artistic device of the "leitmotif," how with me it no longer remains a mere identifying tag, a cue to remind the reader of external circumstances or to suggest a mood. On the contrary, it is used in a directly musical way, and determines the whole mode of presentation and the coloring of the style. . . .

Now this method alone is sufficient to explain my slowness. It is the result neither of anxiety nor of indolence, but of an extraordinarily keen conscientiousness in the choice of every word, the coining of every phrase, a conscientiousness which requires perfect freshness, and which, after two hours' work, prefers not to undertake an important sentence. For which sentence is important, and which not? Can one know beforehand whether a sentence, or part of a sentence, may not be called upon to serve as motif, link, symbol, citation, or association? And a sentence which must be heard twice must be fashioned accordingly. It must—I do not speak of beauty—possess a certain symbolic suggestion and level of meaning which will make it worthy to sound again in any epic future. So every bit of ground gained is also a taking-off point, every adjective, a decision. It is clear that such work is not to be produced offhand.

THOMAS MANN
from *Rede und Antwort*

Just as the imaginative use of words may produce special effects, so too may the imaginative use of sentences. For example, the last chapter of Joyce's *Ulysses* has forty-five closely printed pages with nary a punctuation mark! The flow of Mrs. Bloom's thoughts are presented in a run-on style to suggest and heighten their impulsive, illogical nature. For our own purposes here is a more manageable example of the long sentence.

. . . Climbing out now with both hands among the willows, the skim ice crinkling and tinkling against his chest, his clothes like soft cold lead which he didn't move in but seemed rather to mount into like a poncho or a tarpaulin: up the bank until he saw two feet in gum boots which were neither Edmonds' boy's nor Aleck Sander's and then the legs, the overalls rising out of them and he climbed on and stood up and saw a Negro man with an ax on his shoulder, in a heavy sheeplined coat and a broad pale felt hat such as his grandfather had used to wear, looking at him and that was when he saw Lucas Beauchamp for the first time that he remembered or rather for the first time because you didn't forget Lucas Beauchamp; gasping, shaking and only now feeling the shock of the cold water, he looked up at the face which was just watching him without pity commiseration or anything else, not even surprise: just watching him, whose owner had made no effort whatever to help him up out of the creek, had in fact ordered Aleck Sander to desist with the pole which had been the one token toward help that anybody had made—a face which in his estimation might have been under fifty or even forty except for the hat and the eyes, and inside a Negro's skin but that was all even to a boy of twelve shaking with cold and still panting from shock and exertion because what looked out of it had no pigment at all, not even the white man's lack of it, not arrogant, not even scornful: just intractable and composed.

WILLIAM FAULKNER
from *Intruder in the Dust*

1. Read the preceding material.
2. In your journal do *one* of the following:
   a. Rewrite a previous entry. As you revise it, make conscious use of Mann's technique.
   b. Write an entry based on your examination of a page or two by Thomas Mann. Discuss his use of thematic phrase.
   c. Try your hand at the imaginative use of sentence length and sentence variety. Consider the very short sentence. What are its advantages?

Assignment 6

But let us turn from these excursions into outer space, whether it be curved or not, finite or expanding, and ignoring the depressing ravages of inward time on the human frame consider the more practical matter of how to deal with our common enemy in everyday life. A suitable approach might be to begin by noting how long man has actually been present in time. It is rather deflating to our self-esteem to realize how pitifully brief is the moment during which the King of Creation has strutted on the earthly stage. In order to receive the full impact of the insignificance of man's role in the drama of evolution, let us assume, somewhat as suggested by James Ritchie, that the first flickers of life on this planet began last night at midnight and that at the present instant the clock is just starting to strike at noon. On this diagrammatically foreshortened time scale, the ascent from the ameba to vertebrate structure was not successfully accomplished until eight o'clock this morning, and no animals were fully equipped for existence on land until the reptiles emerged from the sea at half-past nine. The little birds began to fly about at quarter of eleven, but our unlovely ancestor *homo sapiens* did not make his hairy entrance until an incredibly recent moment less than two seconds ago, while *historic* man, whose career embodies all we know of human achievement or of civilization, flashed onto the stage only a small fraction of a second before the clock began its peal of noon.

KARL VOGEL, M.D.
from *What Is Time?*

This imaginative statement by Karl Vogel demonstrates the economy and power of metaphor. In your own writing you will on occasion need to present events with economy. The above passage is a good example of how it can be done.

1. Read the excerpt by Vogel.
2. In your journal do *one* of the following:
   a. Make your own statement of how long man has been present in time.
   b. Make a statement about man's total progress or lack of it.
   c. Summarize the life of a family. Write as though the summary were part of a novel or story.

33

JUST IMAGINE

Another way of developing your power of imagination is to turn a poem or a prose statement into a piece of fiction. One may find inspiration and a springboard for his imagination in the writing of others. Here is an example of imitation carried out by a student. The student followed the professional lead by saying "just suppose" and then pushing his hero in a parallel direction but with consideration for the logic and consistency of his own piece.

The model and the student's imitation of it follow.

> The nervous monotony of the schoolroom inspires a sometimes unbearable longing for something astonishing to happen, and as every boy's fundamental desire is to do something astonishing himself, so as to be the center of human interest and awe, it was natural that Penrod should discover in fancy the delightful secret of self-levitation. He found in this curious series of imaginings, during the lesson in arithmetic, that the atmosphere may be navigated as by a swimmer under water, but with infinitely greater ease and with perfect comfort in breathing. In his mind he extended his arms gracefully, at a level with his shoulders, and delicately paddled the air with his hands, which at once caused him to be drawn up out of his seat and elevated gently to a position about midway between the floor and the ceiling, where he came to an equilibrium and floated; a sensation not the less exquisite because of the screams of his fellow pupils, appalled by the miracle. Miss Spence herself was amazed and frightened, but he only smiled down carelessly upon her when she commanded him to return to earth; and then, he quietly paddled himself a little higher, leaving his toes just out of her

reach. Next he swam through a few dozen somer-
saults to show his mastery of the new art, and with
the shouting of the dumbfounded scholars ringing in
his ears, turned on his side and floated swiftly out of
the window, immediately rising above the rooftops,
while people in the street below him shrieked, and a
trolley car stopped dead in wonder.

BOOTH TARKINGTON
from *Penrod*

The sacred boredom of Sunday church is often
too overwhelming to let it pass without vast
thoughts on the fantastic possibilities of improve-
ment, and as most of us often stumble first onto the
thought that even *we* could be more inspiring,
there was nothing extraordinary in his imagining
himself in the place of that droning voice, instead
of in his back-row pew. It was quite easy, really, to
let himself slip out of his body sitting there, and
storm up the aisle prophesying hell fire and dam-
nation, while the preacher droned on, and he soon
had the feeling that every time he spoke, a thunderbolt struck violently. By this time he had torn
the robe off the preacher's back, though it was still
there to most of the rest of the congregation, and
as the humble house quaked in fear and apprehension, he damned the preacher for being boring,
and with an immediate crack and a flash, he was
consumed; and with inspired gratification the
crowd praised him, shouting and crying for mercy,
except the old ladies, but these were nonchalantly
obliterated when he gently drew his lips together
and loosed three soft puffs, hardly enough to blow
out a birthday candle. At this point even most of
the adults had begun to perceive the glory and
wonder of this supreme power, and even his own
father was begging forgiveness; but not a chance,
and spurred on by the admiring youthful section of
his audience, he arched his eyebrows, turned casually aside, and carelessly flicked a finger causing
even that sinner to meet the same fate at the next

rumble. Finally, with a slight shrug of the shoulders, he stood erect, and walked up the air, soon skipping gracefully up five feet at a time on the jagged steps of his last thunderbolt, rising unconcernedly up into the kingdom of heaven, while congregations piled out of their churches to see, and admiring ministers could do nothing but gaze in awe.

EVERARD K. MEADE

A more sophisticated way of using this basic technique will suggest itself to you if you will read the next rather difficult paragraph. Pay particular attention to the passage at the point where Thoreau begins to talk about "that devilish Iron Horse."

Now the trunks of trees on the bottom, and the old log canoe, and the dark surrounding woods are gone, and the villagers, who scarcely know where it lies, instead of going to the pond to bathe or drink, are thinking to bring its water, which should be as sacred as the Ganges at least, to the village in a pipe, to wash their dishes with!—to earn their Walden by the turning of a cock or drawing of a plug! That devilish Iron Horse, whose ear-rending neigh is heard throughout the town, has muddied the Boiling Spring with his foot, and he it is that has browsed off all the woods on Walden shore, that Trojan horse, with a thousand men in his belly, introduced by mercenary Greeks! Where is the country's champion, the Moore of Moore Hall, to meet him at the Deep Cut and thrust an avenging lance between the ribs of the bloated pest?

You will note Thoreau has a number of concerns. One of them is the machine and what it does to people. He singles out the railroad and calls it a "Trojan horse, with a thousand men in his belly, introduced by mercenary Greeks!" and then he goes on to call for a champion. His language is itself imaginative, and he makes liberal use of metaphor. But what has been said in essay form can, with imagination, be turned into fiction. Here, in fact, is a story that does it.

THE DRAGON

RAY BRADBURY

The night blew in the short grass on the moor; there was no other motion. It had been years since a single bird had flown by in the great blind shell of sky. Long ago a few small stones had simulated life when they crumbled and fell into dust. Now only the night moved in the souls of the two men bent by their lonely fire in the wilderness; darkness pumped quietly in their veins and ticked silently in their temples and their wrists.

Firelight fled up and down their wild faces and welled in their eyes in orange tatters. They listened to each other's faint, cool breathing and the lizard blink of their eyelids. At last, one man poked the fire with his sword.

"Don't, idiot; you'll give us away!"

"No matter," said the second man. "The dragon can smell us miles off anyway. God's breath, it's cold. I wish I was back at the castle."

"It's death, not sleep, we're after. . . ."

"Why? Why? The dragon never sets foot in the town!"

"Quiet, fool! He eats men traveling alone from our town to the next!"

"Let them be eaten and let us get home!"

"Wait now; listen!"

The two men froze.

They waited a long time, but there was only the shake of their horses' nervous skin like black velvet tambourines jingling the silver stirrup buckles, softly, softly.

"Ah." The second man sighed. "What a land of nightmares. Everything happens here. Someone blows out the sun; it's night. And then, and *then,* oh, listen! This dragon, they say his eyes are fire. His breath a white gas; you can see him burn across the dark lands. He runs with sulfur and thunder and kindles the grass. Sheep panic and die insane. Women deliver forth monsters. The dragon's fury is such that tower walls shake back to dust. His victims, at sunrise, are strewn hither thither on the hills. How many knights, I ask, have gone for this monster and failed, even as we shall fail?"

"Enough of that!"

"More than enough! Out here in this desolation I cannot tell what year this is!"

"Nine hundred years since the Nativity."

"No, no," whispered the second man, eyes shut. "On this moor is no Time, is only Forever. I feel if I ran back on the road the town would be gone, the people yet unborn, things changed, the castles unquarried from the rocks, the timbers still uncut from the forests; don't ask how I know; the moor knows and tells me. And here we sit alone in the land of the fire dragon, God save us!"

"Be you afraid, then gird on your armor!"

"What use? The dragon runs from nowhere; we cannot guess its home. It vanishes in fog; we know not where it goes. Aye, on with our armor, we'll die well dressed."

Half into his silver corselet, the second man stopped again and turned his head.

Across the dim country, full of night and nothingness from the heart of the moor itself, the wind sprang full of dust from clocks that used dust for telling time. There were black suns burning in the heart of this new wind and a million burnt leaves shaken from some autumn tree beyond the horizon. This wind melted landscapes, lengthened bones like white wax, made the blood roil and thicken to a muddy deposit in the brain. The wind was a thousand souls dying and all time confused and in transit. It was a fog inside of a mist inside of a darkness, and this place was no man's place and there was no year or hour at all, but only these men in a faceless emptiness of sudden frost, storm and white thunder which moved behind the great falling pane of green glass that was the lightning. A squall of rain drenched the turf; all faded away until there was unbreathing hush and the two men waiting alone with their warmth in a cool season.

"There," whispered the first man. "Oh, *there* . . ."

Miles off, rushing with a great chant and a roar —the dragon.

In silence the men buckled on their armor and mounted their horses. The midnight wilderness was split by a monstrous gushing as the dragon roared nearer, nearer; its flashing yellow glare spurted above a hill and then, fold on fold of dark body, distantly seen, therefore indistinct, flowed over that hill and plunged vanishing into a valley.

"Quick!"

They spurred their horses forward to a small hollow.

"This is where it passes!"

They seized their lances with mailed fists and blinded their horses by flipping the visors down over their eyes.

"Lord!"

"Yes, let us use his name."

On the instant, the dragon rounded a hill. Its monstrous amber eye fed on them, fired their armor in red glints and glitters. With a terrible wailing cry and a grinding rush it flung itself forward.

"Mercy!"

The lance struck under the unlidded yellow eye, buckled, tossed the man through the air. The dragon hit, spilled him over, down, ground him under. Passing, the black brunt of its shoulder smashing the remaining horse and rider a hundred feet against the side of a boulder, wailing, wailing, the dragon shrieking, the fire all about, around, under it, a pink, yellow, orange sun-fire with great soft plumes of blinding smoke.

"Did you *see* it?" cried a voice. "Just like I told you!"

"The same! The same! A knight in armor, by the Lord Harry! We *hit* him!"

"You goin' to stop?"

"Did once; found nothing. Don't like to stop on this moor. I get the willies. Got a *feel,* it has."

"But we hit *something!*"

"Gave him plenty of whistle; chap wouldn't budge!"

A steaming blast cut the mist aside.

"We'll make Stokely on time. More coal, eh, Fred?"

Another whistle shook dew from the empty sky. The night train, in fire and fury, shot through a gully, up a rise, and vanished away over cold earth toward the north, leaving black smoke and steam to dissolve in the numbed air minutes after it had passed and gone forever.

Assignment 7

1. Read the chapter up to this point.
2. In your journal do *one* of the following:
   a. Use a paragraph or a story as the springboard for an entry of your own. (State your point of departure by quoting the original.)
   b. Just imagine and record your thoughts. Then edit to give them form.
   c. Write your own dragon episode.

Assignment 8

Invention does not have to depend on the unusual. Katherine Mansfield in her *Journal* shows how interesting a writer can be by imagining things so that they are "far realer, more in detail, *richer* than life." We have all, to some extent, been given the "consolation prize"—the ability "to *live* over either scenes from real life or imaginary scenes." In your journal you may find it interesting to try your hand at such recall or invention. But first read Katherine Mansfield's statement.

It often happens to me now that when I lie down to sleep at night, instead of getting drowsy, I feel more wakeful and, lying here in bed, I begin to *live* over either scenes from real life or imaginary scenes. It's not too much to say that they are almost hallucinations: they are marvellously vivid. I lie on my right side and put my left hand up to my forehead as though I were praying. This seems to induce the state. Then, for instance, it is 10:30 P.M. on a big liner in mid-ocean. People are beginning to leave the Ladies' Cabin. Father puts his head in and asks if "one of you would care for a walk before you turn in. It's glorious up on deck." That begins it. I am *there*. Details: Father rubbing his gloves, the cold air—the *night* air, the pattern of everything, the feel of the brass stair-rail and the rubber stairs. Then the deck—the pause while the cigar is lighted, the look of all in the moonlight, the *steadying* hum of the ship, the first officer on deck, so far aloft the bells, the steward going into the smoking-room with a tray, stepping over the high, brass-bound step. . . . All these things are far realer, more in detail, *richer* than life. And I believe I could go on until . . . There's *no end* to it.

I could always do this to a certain extent; but it's only since I was really ill that this—shall we call it?—"consolation prize" has been given to me. My God! it's a marvellous thing.

from *Journal of Katherine Mansfield*

You have to use your imagination to invent, and you also have to use your imagination to reconstruct. If there is any doubt about this latter point, try your hand at putting a picture puzzle together. Intelligent reconstruction demands imagination; for example, something happened in the past, and you remember part of it. Can you reconstruct the entire event? Can you make your reconstruction realer than real? Will you be true to your memory and the facts, or will you be true to your purpose and theme?

Here is an exercise that provides a chance to develop your powers of imagination by reconstructing the past. But before you start, perhaps a few examples will help. You'll note that those ideas on observation presented in Unit 2 are relevant here. Imagination—vivid imagination, selective imagination—is but a way of putting observation to work. It is a way of working with and from the facts.

It is the smells of the school that I remember best: the sour smell of the oil they rubbed the desks with; the classroom smell of chalk dust and old pulled-down maps; the smell of fuller's earth scattered in wide arcs along the corridors, ahead of the pushbrooms that formed fat kittens out of the dirt tracked daily in by some 300 pairs of feet; the smell of a master's unlighted pipe; the smell that would periodically drift through the school late in the morning to tell us that we were going to have corned beef and cabbage for lunch; the steamy, chlorinated smell of the indoor pool; the smell of the gym, which was a mixture of wintergreen oil and sneakers.

There are sounds too—the noise of showers running; the whack of a hockey stick against the puck; the sound of a springboard—which instantly bring back the whole flavor of school days to me, along with the random pictures, etched on my brain with such clarity and poignancy at the time, that I can still see a play of sunlight on the ivy of a certain wall; an avenue of moonlight across a frozen lake; the small, pointed handwriting of the headmaster ("The following boys will please see me"); the molasses-colored varnish on my window sill; the thickening layer of stamps and address stickers on the laundry case I sent home each week.

STEPHEN BIRMINGHAM
from "New England Prep School"

Far ahead of us, four boys, looking like flags on the endless green playing fields, crossed toward the tennis courts. To the right of them the gym meditated behind its gray walls, the high, wide, oval-topped windows shining back at the sun. Beyond the gym and the fields began the woods, our, the Devon School's woods, which in my imagination were the beginning of the great northern forests. I thought that, from the Devon Woods, trees reached in an unbroken, widening corridor so far to the north that no one had ever seen the other end, somewhere up in the far unorganized tips of Canada. We seemed to be playing on the tame fringe of the last and greatest wilderness. I never found out whether this is so, and perhaps it is.

JOHN KNOWLES
from *A Separate Peace*

For some reason my most vivid memories concern examinations. Big amphitheater in Goldwin Smith; exam from 8 A.M. to 10:30; about 150 students—unwashed, unshaven young males and reasonably well-groomed young females. A general sense of tedium and disaster. Half-past eight. Little coughs, the clearing of nervous throats, coming in clusters of sound, rustling of pages. Some of the martyrs plunged in meditation, their arms locked behind their heads. I meet a dull gaze directed at me, seeing in me with hope and hate the source of forbidden knowledge. Girl in glasses comes up to my desk to ask: "Professor Kafka, do you want us to say that . . . ? Or do you want us to answer only the first part of the question?" The great fraternity of C-minus, backbone of the nation, steadily scribbling on. A rustle arising simultaneously, the majority turning a page in their blue books, good teamwork. The shaking of a cramped wrist, the failing ink, the deodorant that breaks down. When I catch eyes directed at me, they are forthwith raised to the ceiling in pious meditation. Windowpanes getting misty. Boys peeling off sweaters. Girls chewing gum in rapid cadence. Ten minutes, five, three, time's up.

from an interview with VLADIMIR NABOKOV

1. Read the preceding excerpts.
2. In your journal do *one* of the following:
   a. Re-create a past event based on your own school life.
   b. Re-create a moment in history.
   c. Invent (reconstruct from a number of disconnected memories) a character.

Assignment 9

My task which I am trying to achieve is, by the power of the written word to make you hear, to make you feel—it is, before all, to make you *see*. That—and no more, and it is everything. If I succeed, you shall find there according to your deserts: encouragement, consolation, fear, charm—all you demand—and, perhaps, also that glimpse of truth for which you have forgotten to ask.

JOSEPH CONRAD
from the Preface
to *The Nigger of the Narcissus*

Imagination, like humor, must appear spontaneous to be effective; but just as the work of the script writer lies behind the rollicking laughter of the TV comedian's anecdote, so real thought and conscious attention to the imaginative ingredients of a composition are necessary if the intended job is to get done properly.

Here is a bit of transcript from a conversation between Ray Bradbury, the dean of the science-fiction writers, and another worker in imagination, Chuck Jones, the father of Bugs Bunny. Their conversation is reported by Mary Harrington Hall.

> MHH: Remember your man in the attic, the man in "A Scent of Sarsaparilla"?
>
> BRADBURY: That's what I mean by implementation. Everything is wrong in his life, and his wife is shouting at him. He gets up in his attic and looks out the window and the year 1905 is out there, firecrackers and sunshine and all. And he looks down the stairs and his hatchet-faced wife is waiting. The only thing good is the past—outside his window. But how can I make people believe this?
>
> I worked and worked on that story. I wanted to go back in time. The attic was my time machine. But I had to prove it. So I opened all the trunks for the reader. There were the mothballs and the old clocks and the smell of machinery, and the prisms of old chandeliers that have caught all the sunlight of other days. I made a list of the things that had been put away so you could smell the attic, taste the attic, feel the old plush, and look at the time and dust put away in that old attic. If I could attack you through every one of your senses so that you believed you were there, really believed in my time machine, then you'd believe my story. Once I wrote that page of description for the senses, I proved my fantasy.

In another part of this same conversation Jones says:

> That story illustrates just what the amateur doesn't realize. When fantasy is submitted by amateurs to MGM here, it usually has something to do with outer space. And always these amateurs figure if one story element is good, four or five is better. They bury simplicity. And they confuse fantasy and distortion, which is like supposing that those distortion mirrors at the fun house are the same thing as caricature. Well, they're not.

They make people look different from what they are. They don't emphasize the thing that makes a person beautiful or ugly. All art is caricature and all art is editorial—even bad art. Bad art only proves that the artist doesn't know what he is doing.

from "The Fantasy Makers"

1. Read the preceding comments.
2. In your journal do *one* of the following:
   a. Draw a realistic setting for a piece of fantasy. Provide what Bradbury calls "implementation."
   b. Write a piece of fantasy that does not "bury simplicity."
   c. Without looking at Bradbury's story, write your version of its first paragraph.

3|4

TRAIN YOUR IMAGINATION

It seems to me very important, if a man is to get
at anything like an intelligent use of his imagination, not to let it get too much out of hand.

They are merely pretending, as we all do most
of the time, but there is this to be said, that in
imagining themselves great generals engaged in a
desperate battle out of which they are to emerge
as heroes, they are very likely missing something,
the beauty of the trained dogs at work, the fall
colors in trees on distant hills, all the living beauty
of the country in the fall. They are missing what
we all too much miss, the strangeness and wonder
of our everyday lives.

SHERWOOD ANDERSON
from *The Intent of the Artist*
edited by Augusto Centeno

Imagination is to use, to create, to experiment with. One
can do this in a controlled way as when an architect draws
his designs for a building, or in free form as when one falls
into a revery or a daydream. In both cases imagination is at
the center changing the real world in some way especially
useful or pleasant. Imagination in any form never leaves
things as they are but transforms them.

The poet uses his imagination to transform words. He
tends to use standard words but in a special way. He creates
relationships between words and ideas that cause them to
carry heightened experience or new insights. For example,
Archibald MacLeish defines a poem in words that work this
way. Here is his poem:

Ars Poetica

A poem should be palpable and mute
As a globed fruit,

Dumb
As old medallions to the thumb,

Silent as the sleeve-worn stone
Of casement ledges where the moss has grown—

A poem should be wordless
As the flight of birds.

A poem should be motionless in time
As the moon climbs,

Leaving, as the moon releases
Twig by twig the night-entangled trees,

Leaving, as the moon behind the winter leaves,
Memory by memory the mind—

A poem should be motionless in time
As the moon climbs.

A poem should be equal to:
Not true.

For all the history of grief
An empty doorway and a maple leaf.

For love
The leaning grasses and two lights above the sea—

A poem should not mean
But be.

ARCHIBALD MAC LEISH

You can train your own imagination by playing with words. Try to fit them into a creative pattern. All poetry will show you how. But don't expect a great success just at first. After all the poet is a champ whom you are observing in a winning round. His sparring matches and workouts are not so well publicized.

Here is a collection of words with which you may start:

few, to
and, and, and, the, if
revery, revery, one, one
make, clover, clover
a, a, a, alone, prairie
do, bee, bee, few
will, it
are, takes

Can you move all or part of these twenty-seven words into a verse or poem? Can you do better if you add some words of your own? Do you have an idea to center the words around?

Here is a student's response:

Revery is alone,
A one-to-one relationship—
A bee to a clover,
A wolf to a prairie,
A few to the many.

A revery alone to a revery with many;
Revery will take a man alone,
But a man can be alone with many.

JOHN HOLDEN

Here is another student's attempt:

Revery is one alone—as a bee to clover.

Here is the way Emily Dickinson made the words work:

To make a prairie it takes a clover
and one bee—
One clover, and a bee,
And revery.
The revery alone will do
If bees are few.

But in watching words work in a poem it is not enough to
say, "good," "clever," or "blah." You have to ask and answer
some real questions. You'll find key questions turn around
key words. What, for example, does the word "prairie" mean
in the Dickinson poem? The dictionary shows that in the
sense used here "prairie" means "a large area of level or rolling land . . . with generally deep, fertile soil, a cover of tall
coarse grasses and few trees."

Then too you have to decide what the poem is saying *literally* and what it is saying *imaginatively* and, finally, what it
says to you.

Literally this poem is about making a prairie from one bee
and a clover plus a revery (daydream). If there aren't many
bees to help with the job, the poet says a prairie can be constructed by revery alone.

Figuratively, the poem says a few concrete objects are
enough to form a vast construction, provided one has imagination. Then the poet comes to the central point and says
that, if need be, imagination alone can do the job.

The poem is about imagination. It says imagination tends
to feed on reality, but if hard pressed can achieve boundless
tasks by itself. Beyond this point only you can go, for in the
end—after all the preliminary understandings are arrived
at—the experience of the poem is yours.

But imagination often expresses itself not by exaggeration,
as in the Dickinson poem, but through intensity and restraint.
The following poem is an example of such a statement:

Desert Places

Snow falling and night falling fast, oh, fast
In a field I looked into going past,

And the ground almost covered smooth in snow,
But a few weeds and stubble showing last.

The woods around it have it—it is theirs.
All animals are smothered in their lairs.
I am too absent-spirited to count;
The loneliness includes me unawares.

And lonely as it is that loneliness
Will be more lonely ere it will be less—
A blanker whiteness of benighted snow
With no expression, nothing to express.

They cannot scare me with their empty spaces
Between stars—on stars where no human race is.
I have it in me so much nearer home
To scare myself with my own desert places.

ROBERT FROST

Yet another way to work with imagination is to give reality a twist. This is a kind of dangerous game in which reality is rigidly adhered to up until the last moment. Then the accepted reality is given a turn. The twist has to work, or the fiction goes smash! But if the twist works, the writer scores his point. Like an author of a murder mystery, the writer has to plan his story in such a way that the reader is both prepared for and surprised by the outcome. If at the crucial moment the tall blond girl in the black knit dress is to reach into her handbag and pull out a heavily perfumed pistol, then well in advance of that crucial event you have to see her place it there. So with the story that is to be given an imaginative twist—the parts must be assembled carefully enough so that you think you know how they are going to work. What surprises you is the twist—the way they do work. But remember, the reader has to be prepared for such distortions of reality.

Here is a story by Saki that makes use of imagination. The story that follows it was written by a student, and it too moves on a calculated, last-minute distortion. Despite the warning, see if you are not amused.

THE OPEN WINDOW

"SAKI" (H. H. MUNRO)

"My aunt will be down presently, Mr. Nuttel," said a very self-possessed young lady of fifteen; "in the meantime you must try and put up with me."

Framton Nuttel endeavored to say the correct something which should duly flatter the niece of the moment without unduly discounting the aunt that was to come. Privately he doubted more than ever whether these formal visits on a succession of total strangers would do much toward helping the nerve cure which he was supposed to be undergoing.

"I know how it will be," his sister had said when he was preparing to migrate to this rural retreat; "you will bury yourself down there and not speak to a living soul, and your nerves will be worse than ever from moping. I shall just give you letters of introduction to all the people I know there. Some of them, as far as I can remember, were quite nice."

Framton wondered whether Mrs. Sappleton, the lady to whom he was presenting one of the letters of introduction, came into the nice division.

"Do you know many of the people round here?" asked the niece, when she judged that they had had sufficient silent communion.

"Hardly a soul," said Framton. "My sister was staying here, at the rectory, you know, some four years ago, and she gave me letters of introduction to some of the people here."

He made the last statement in a tone of distinct regret.

"Then you know practically nothing about my aunt?" pursued the self-possessed young lady.

"Only her name and address," admitted the caller. He was wondering whether Mrs. Sappleton was in the married or widowed state. An undefinable something about the room seemed to suggest masculine habitation.

"Her great tragedy happened just three years ago," said the child; "that would be since your sister's time."

"Her tragedy?" asked Framton; somehow in this restful country spot tragedies seemed out of place.

"You may wonder why we keep that window wide open on an October afternoon," said the niece, indicating a large French window that opened on to a lawn.

"It is quite warm for the time of the year," said Framton; "but has that window got anything to do with the tragedy?"

"Out through that window, three years ago to a day, her husband and her two young brothers went off for their day's shooting. They never came back. In crossing the moor to their favorite snipe-shooting ground they were all three engulfed in a treacherous piece of bog. It had been that dreadful wet summer, you know, and places that were safe in other years gave way suddenly without warning. Their bodies were never recovered. That was the dreadful part of it." Here the child's voice lost its self-possessed note and became falteringly human. "Poor aunt always thinks that they will come back some day, they and the little brown spaniel that was lost with them, and walk in at that window just as they used to do. That is why the window is kept open every evening till it is quite dusk. Poor dear aunt, she has often told me how they went out, her husband with his white waterproof coat over his arm, and Ronnie, her youngest brother, singing, 'Bertie, why do you bound?' as he always did to tease her, because she said it got on her nerves. Do you know, sometimes on still, quiet evenings like this, I almost get a creepy feeling that they will all walk in through that window——"

She broke off with a little shudder. It was a relief to Framton when the aunt bustled into the room with a whirl of apologies for being late in making her appearance.

"I hope Vera has been amusing you?" she said.

"She has been very interesting," said Framton.

"I hope you don't mind the open window," said Mrs. Sappleton briskly; "my husband and brothers will be home directly from shooting, and they always come in this way. They've been out for snipe in the marshes today, so they'll make a fine mess over my poor carpets. So like you men-folk, isn't it?"

She rattled on cheerfully about the shooting and the scarcity of birds, and the prospects for duck in the winter. To Framton it was all purely horrible. He made a desperate but only partially successful effort to turn the talk on to a less ghastly topic; he was conscious that his hostess was giving him only a fragment of her attention, and her eyes were constantly straying past him to the open window and the lawn beyond. It was certainly an unfortunate coincidence that he should have paid his visit on this tragic anniversary.

"The doctors agree in ordering me complete rest, an absence of mental excitement, and avoidance of anything in the nature of violent physical exercise," announced Framton, who labored under the tolerably widespread delusion that total strangers and chance acquaintances are hungry for the least detail of one's ailments and infirmities, their cause and cure. "On the matter of diet they are not so much in agreement," he continued.

"No?" said Mrs. Sappleton, in a voice which only replaced a yawn at the last moment. Then she suddenly brightened into alert attention—but not to what Framton was saying.

"Here they are at last!" she cried. "Just in time

for tea, and don't they look as if they were muddy up to the eyes!"

Framton shivered slightly and turned toward the niece with a look intended to convey sympathetic comprehension. The child was staring out through the open window with dazed horror in her eyes. In a chill shock of nameless fear Framton swung round in his seat and looked in the same direction.

In the deepening twilight three figures were walking across the lawn toward the window; they all carried guns under their arms, and one of them was additionally burdened with a white coat hung over his shoulders. A tired brown spaniel kept close at their heels. Noiselessly they neared the house, and then a hoarse young voice chanted out of the dusk: "I said, Bertie, why do you bound?"

Framton grabbed wildly at his stick and hat; the hall door, the gravel drive, and the front gate were dimly noted stages in his headlong retreat. A cyclist coming along the road had to run into the hedge to avoid imminent collision.

"Here we are, my dear," said the bearer of the white mackintosh, coming in through the window; "fairly muddy, but most of it's dry. Who was that who bolted out as we came up?"

"A most extraordinary man, a Mr. Nuttel," said Mrs. Sappleton; "could only talk ˜bout his illnesses, and dashed off without a word of good-by or apology when you arrived. One would think he had seen a ghost."

"I expect it was the spaniel," said the niece calmly; "he told me he had a horror of dogs. He was once hunted into a cemetery somewhere on the banks of the Ganges by a pack of pariah dogs, and had to spend the night in a newly dug grave with the creatures snarling and grinning and foaming just above him. Enough to make anyone lose their nerve."

Romance at short notice was her specialty.

CAMERA OBSCURA

MICHAEL DECK

Every day after school Charles would walk home, which wasn't so very far, go in the side door, say hello to his mother who was always waiting for him, put his schoolbag in his room, which he shared with three brothers, and then run out the door to meet Ebbie, who was his best friend. There were many different things that Charles and Ebbie could do after working hard all day in the third grade. They could go to the vacant lot near Charles's house and fly a kite or play ball. They could roller-skate around the block or take turns in Charles's wagon. But their favorite pastime was to go to one of their secret places.

The best place was a special corner in Charles's garage. The garage was made of corrugated steel, painted green. Charles's father did not put the car in the garage because there was no room for it. The space was filled with bicycles, a lawn mower, an old table or two, and a workbench. The work-bench was against the back wall of a little alcove which was off to the right as you walked in. Charles's father had made the workbench himself out of two old doors. One was attached to the wall like a shelf, the other was hinged to the front edge of the other so that the two made a kind of box which you could open and crawl inside.

Under the bench it was magic. It was all dark except for a few cracks where the light leaked in. But there was a small hole in the wall of the garage where, when the sun was shining just right, the light would come through and you could see a picture of Charles's house and his backyard pro-jected on the wall. It was like your own private movie except that everything was upside down.

Every day they would go in to see if the magic was working. If it was, they stayed to watch and talk. If it was not, they went to the vacant lot or climbed the crepe myrtle which grew in Charles's backyard.

Now Charles loved to just play around, not doing anything, especially when that anything was homework. Every day, just when he and Ebbie were having the most fun, Charles's mother would call him in to do his arithmetic. To the kids in the third grade, it meant memorizing multiplication tables. Charles hated this more than anything else. When he was supposed to be studying, he just looked at the book, not seeing it, thinking of how everything looked upside down when the magic was working. His parents thought he was studying the whole time, and they couldn't figure out why he was doing poorly in arithmetic. Then one day Charles's father told him that if he failed one more arithmetic test he would be soundly spanked. That night Charles tried to study, but all he could think about was the magic in the garage.

Charles failed his test. The teacher had asked him to write out the multiplication by nine table, but all he could remember was that nine times one was nine, and the magic only worked when the sun was just right. The teacher told Charles to take the paper home to his parents. He couldn't let them find out that he had failed, so on the way home he dropped the paper into Mrs. MacMurray's flower bed and then went home to play.

The sun was out that day, and the magic was working better than it ever had before. But Charles was worried. As he and Ebbie had walked into the garage, he had looked back and seen the tattletale from across the street pick his test out of the flower bed. He knew that he would run straight to Charles's mother and show it to her. Charles sat with Ebbie looking at the picture, not seeing it, thinking of what would happen when his mother saw the test paper.

The quiet was shattered by a piercing, "Charles!" Charles wanted to hide, but he couldn't think of a place where his mother wouldn't find him. He told Ebbie to wait for him there and slowly left the garage, wishing he could escape.

Ebbie could see Charles walking upside down toward an upside-down house. He saw Charles stop, turn, face the garage and smile as though he had just seen how he could get away. Then a cloud passed in front of the sun, stopping the picture for a moment. When it came back he saw Charles coming out of the upside-down house with a glass of lemonade in his hand. Ebbie ran out to see him. When he looked out the garage door, the backyard was empty. He knocked at the back door and asked Charles's mother if she had seen him. She said that she had called him but that he had not come in.

This puzzled Ebbie because he had seen Charles come out of the house in the picture. He went back into the garage and under the workbench. Charles was not there, but Ebbie could still see him in the picture, still doing nothing but drinking his lemonade. Ebbie knew that Charles's mother would not find him. The magic was working better than it ever had before.

Assignment 10

1. Read the chapter up to this point.
2. In your journal do *one* of the following:
   a. Through an imaginative entry, see if you can catch something of "the strangeness and wonder of our everyday lives." Perhaps you can do it by presenting accepted reality and then giving it a twist.
   b. Try your hand at writing a poem.
   c. Explain what the Frost poem "Desert Places" says literally and imaginatively to you.

Assignment 11

Writing is, for most, laborious and slow. The mind travels faster than the pen; consequently, writing becomes a question of learning to make occasional wing shots, bringing down the bird of thought as it flashes by.

WILLIAM STRUNK, JR., and E. B. WHITE
from *Elements of Style*

One way to train your imagination is to take a moral or slogan that has become a cliché and by rewriting give it freshness. James Thurber did just that in a book called *Fables for Our Times*. Here is one of the fables.

THE BEAR WHO LET IT ALONE

JAMES THURBER

In the woods of the Far West there once lived a brown bear who could take it or let it alone. He would go into a bar where they sold mead, a fermented drink made of honey, and he would have just two drinks. Then he would put some money on the bar and say, "See what the bears in the back room will have," and he would go home. But finally he took to drinking by himself most of the day. He would reel home at night, kick over the umbrella stand, knock down the bridge lamps, and ram his elbows through the windows. Then he would collapse on the floor and lie there until he went to sleep. His wife was greatly distressed, and his children were very frightened.

At length the bear saw the error of his ways and began to reform. In the end he became a famous teetotaler and a persistent temperance lecturer. He would tell everybody that came to his house about the awful effects of drink, and he would boast about how strong and well he had become since he gave up touching the stuff. To demonstrate this, he would stand on his head and on his hands and he would turn cartwheels in the house, kicking over the umbrella stand, knocking down the bridge lamps, and ramming his elbows through the windows. Then he would lie down on the floor, tired by his healthful exercise, and go to sleep. His wife was greatly distressed and his children were very frightened.

Moral: You might as well fall flat on your face as lean over too far backward.

And here is a student piece in something of the same spirit:

The boy stayed outside trying to be a tree. He stood up and held out his arms trying to catch the wind and sway, but as hard as he tried he only swayed a few times because he only had two branches for wind-catching. Even when he did sway with the wind, he would only fall over because his disgusting legs were such bad roots.

"Worthwood!" his mother called. "Come in and watch television. You are too young yet for me to allow you to know that you're sad."

"I am sad and what's more I know it, Mother," said the boy. "I want to be a tree because a tree is always beautiful, and so it must always be happy. A tree is big, Mother, and it has all the wind and water it wants, and it plays in the mud with its toes, and besides it lives almost forever, and even if a tree is sad in the winter it has no mind so it can't know it is sad, and if it doesn't know that it's sad then that doesn't count, does it, Mother?"

"Come in and watch television," cried his mother, but he purposely ate some poison berries and died. They buried him in the earth in a dead tree and many years later much of his body did become part of a great oak, although most of his left eye was part of a weed. He was rather happy, but being mindless he didn't know he was happy. But then again, when he was sad he didn't know that either.

MICHAEL QUINLAN
"Tree Boy"

1. Read the preceding selections.
2. In your journal do *one* of the following or invent a project of your own:
   a. Tell a fable.
   b. Make a collection of metaphors.
   c. Turn a poem or a quotation into a story. You may not have time to complete this assignment, but do what you can in the time available.

Assignment 12

The psychologists tell us that with the ordinary man an image is less vivid than a sensation. It is an attenuated experience that serves to give information about objects of sense and in the world of sense is a guide to action. His daydreams satisfy emotional needs and fulfill desires that in the world of affairs are frustrated. But they are pale shadows of real life and at the back of his mind is the awareness that the demands of the world of sense have another validity. To the writer this is not so. The images, free ideas that throng his mind, are not guides but materials for action. They have all the vividness of sensation. His daydreams are so significant to him that it is the world of sense that is shadowy and he has to reach out for it by an effort of will. His castles in Spain are no baseless fabric, but real castles that he lives in.

W. SOMERSET MAUGHAM
from *The Summing Up*

You may remember a poem called "Dolor," which appears in the unit on observation (Unit 2, page 66). It was used there as an example of seeing the familiar from an unfamiliar point of view. The office and its routines for a moment ceased being the symbol of pride and progress and became a dangerous staleness.

This next poem, "August from My Desk," is also imaginative. Here a poet presents imagination dramatically. The speaker in the poem says, "I am drifting back to North Dakota." Do you think he was once the farm boy who drove the combine? Does another boy drive the combine this August? In the poem what is the difference between the boy and his father? What is the difference between the boy on the tractor and that boy, now a grown man, at his desk in August? How does the poem differ from revery?

August from My Desk

It is hot today, dry enough for cutting grain,
and I am drifting back to North Dakota
where butterflies are all gone brown with wheat dust.

And where some boy,
red-faced, sweating, chafed,
too young to be dying this way
steers a laborious, self-propelled combine,
and dreams of cities, and blizzards—
and airplanes.

With the white silk scarf of his sleeve
he shines and shines his goggles,
he checks his meters, checks his flaps,
screams contact at his dreamless father,
he pulls back the stick,
engines roaring,

and hurtles into the sun.

ROLAND FLINT

Here is another person who dreams of a place and a time to which he will not return. The writer is Truman Capote.

The only scenery that bores me is any that I can't imagine purchasing a part of; usually, if a place provides the slightest uplift, I instantly consider buying or building a house. The hundreds of properties I've constructed mentally! But now something serious has occurred. For the past few days we've been cruising around Rhodes, lingering a lot at the perfect little bay of Lindos. An American acquaintance who has a house above Lindos took me to see something he thinks I should own. I think so too. It is a small stone farmhouse situated inside a horseshoe-shaped cove; the beach is a sandy confection, and the water, being entirely protected, tranquil as a sapphire winking in a jeweler's window. It could be mine for three thousand dollars; an investment of another five or six would put the house in delicious order. It is a prospect that sizzles the imagination.

At night I think, yes I will, but in the morning I recall—politics, old mortality, inconvenient emo-tional commitments, the impossibilities of the Greek tongue, a trillion difficulties. Still, I ought to have the courage; I'll never again find anything quite as ideal as that.

I left the yacht at Rhodes, and this morning flew to Athens. Now at not quite midnight am sitting alone in an outdoor cafe on Constitution Square. . . .

It is very hot, and the ubiquitous white dust of Athens mists the air, coats the street and my table-top like the pale rough crust on a bilious tongue. I am remembering the stone house in the blue cove. But that is all I will ever do. Remember it.

TRUMAN CAPOTE
"Greek Paragraphs"

Another writer who used his imagination in the same way was Thoreau. His report is on the following page.

At a certain season of our life we are accustomed to consider every spot as the possible site of a house. I have thus surveyed the country on every side within a dozen miles of where I live. In imagination I have bought all the farms in succession, for all were to be bought, and I knew their price. I walked over each farmer's premises, tasted his wild apples, discoursed on husbandry with him, took his farm at his price, at any price, mortgaging it to him in my mind—even put a higher price on it; took everything but a deed of it; took his word for his deed, for I dearly love to talk; cultivated it, and him too to some extent, I trust, and withdrew when I had enjoyed it long enough, leaving him to carry it on. This experience entitled me to be regarded as a sort of real-estate broker by my friends. Wherever I sat, there I might live, and the landscape radiated from me accordingly. What is a house but a *sedes,* a seat?—better if a country seat. I discovered many a site for a house not likely to be soon improved, which some might have thought too far from the village, but to my eyes the village was too far from it. Well, there I might live, I said; and there I did live, for an hour, a summer and a winter life; saw how I could let the years run off, buffet the winter through, and see the spring come in. The future inhabitants of this region, wherever they may place their houses, may be sure that they have been anticipated. An afternoon sufficed to lay out the land into orchard, woodlot, and pasture, and to decide what fine oaks or pines should be left to stand before the door, and whence each blasted tree could be seen to the best advantage; and then I let it lie, fallow perchance, for a man is rich in proportion to the number of things which he can afford to let alone.

My imagination carried me so far that I even had the refusal of several farms—the refusal was all I wanted—but I never got my fingers burned by actual possession. The nearest that I came to actual possession was when I bought the Hollowell place, and had begun to sort my seeds, and collected materials with which to make a wheelbarrow to carry it on or off with; but before the owner gave me a deed of it, his wife—every man has such a wife—changed her mind and wished to keep it, and he offered me ten dollars to release him. Now, to speak the truth, I had but ten cents in the world, and it surpassed my arithmetic to tell, if I was that man who had ten cents, or who had a farm, or ten dollars, or all together. However, I let him keep the ten dollars and the farm too, for I had carried it far enough; or rather, to be generous, I sold him the farm for just what I gave for it, and, as he was not a rich man, made him a present of ten dollars, and still had my ten cents, and seeds, and materials for a wheelbarrow left. I found thus that I had been a rich man without any damage to my poverty. But I retained the landscape, and I have since annually carried off what it yielded without a wheelbarrow.

HENRY DAVID THOREAU
from Walden

1. Read the preceding observations.
2. In your journal do *one* of the following:
   a. Write an entry on the value of castles in Spain.
   b. Describe and discuss a place you have owned in imagination.
   c. Write about right now from your desk.

3 5

PUT YOUR IMAGINATION TO WORK

That is what the artist must do. On canvas or on printed page he must capture the thing so truly that its magnification will endure. That is the difference between journalism and literature.

A. E. HOTCHNER
from *Papa Hemingway*

MAURIAC: One cannot be a true novelist before one has attained a certain age, and that is why a young author has almost no chance of writing successfully about any other period of his life than his childhood or adolescence. A certain distance in time is absolutely necessary for a novelist, unless he is writing a journal.

INTERVIEWER: To what extent is your writing dominated by sense perceptions—hearing, sound, and sight?

MAURIAC: Very largely . . . the critics have all commented on the importance of the sense of smell in my novels. Before beginning a novel I re-create inside myself its places, its milieu, its colors and smells. I revive within myself the atmosphere of my childhood and my youth. I am my characters and their world.

from an interview with FRANÇOIS MAURIAC

You need not plan on being a novelist in order to profit from Mauriac's advice. What he says is useful to anyone interested in communicating experience through words. His method—"I re-create inside myself its places, its milieu, its colors and smells"—is a sure way of finding significant details about which to write.

Another point worth noting is the comment about perspective. Time creates an aesthetic distance that permits events to be seen in a way not possible at the moment of their occurrence. Indeed, he suggests that for certain kinds of experience such perspective may be as important as experience itself. In the next assignments, you will be working with this kind of perspective. Your focus is on vivid recollection of childhood. Follow the model offered by Alfred Kazin and then read the untitled story written by a student.

My great moment came at six, when my father returned from work, his overalls smelling faintly of turpentine and shellac, white drops of silver paint still gleaming on his chin. Hanging his overcoat in the long dark hall that led into our kitchen, he would leave in one pocket a loosely folded copy of the New York *World*; and then everything that beckoned to me from that other hemisphere of my brain beyond the East River would start up from the smell of fresh newsprint and the sight of the globe on the front page. It was a paper that carried special associations for me with Brooklyn Bridge. They published the *World* under the green dome on Park Row overlooking the bridge; the fresh salt air of New York harbor lingered for me in the smell of paint and damp newsprint in the hall. I felt that my father brought the outside straight into our house with each day's copy of the *World*.

ALFRED KAZIN
from *A Walker in the City*

Mother was standing by the stove with her apron on. She glanced at the door with the black glass window panes and formless outlines of trees in the night on the other side. And then back to us—we were sitting at the table, playing with dinner. Ed, the oldest (he was three years older than me, so he always won when we had fights), was teasing Bartlett, my little sister. He kept saying to her, "You're a cry baby," and even though she kept saying that she wasn't, she started to cry. I don't think Mother liked it when we teased Bartlett, because she always told us to stop it, and she explained to Bartlett that we only did it to make her cry; so if she wanted to get back at us, she shouldn't cry. It worked sometimes.

We went back to playing with our food (Mother had told us we shouldn't do that, but I couldn't figure out why). I built a fort with the beans—Bartlett gave me hers so that I would have enough. Mother said,

"No dessert until the plates are cleaned."

"What's for dessert?"

"Cake."

"What kind?"

"Good cake."

"I don't like it."

"Then you don't have to eat it."

"Then why do I have to eat the beans?"

"They're good for you."

"I don't like them. I won't eat them."

"Then no dessert."

I ate the beans and hated every one of them personally. But the cake was good, both of the pieces I ate. I would have eaten more, but we had to save a piece for Daddy.

Daddy always came home from work when it was dark. Mother said he worked very hard so we could have food, and clothing, and a house, and so I could go to school. I said he shouldn't work so hard so I wouldn't have to go to school. Mother laughed at that—she laughed at a lot of the things we said.

Daddy was outside the door looking in at us. He liked to do that—especially when we didn't know it. But we knew when he was there because Mother's smile opened up showing her white teeth (she brushed them when she was a little girl). When we saw her smile, we all jumped up and ran to the door to hold it closed. Daddy's face was the only thing we could see outside, and it went back and forth as he scraped his feet on the mat. He pushed the door open with all three of us behind it (he was really strong) and then he came in with his umbrella and big leather lunch box. He picked up each one of us and hugged us. We asked him, "Wha'd you bring us?" and he said, "All my love and affection." But that was not what we wanted.

Then he went over to Mother by the stove, and kissed her (we laughed and made funny noises when they kissed). He said to her, "What cha got cookin', good lookin'?" and then she laughed.

Suddenly Dad frowned. He looked at the wastepaper basket, and he said, "Whose turn is it to take out the trash?" Nobody answered, and he looked at us. I couldn't stand it when he looked at me, so I said, "Me." He just looked so I went over to the wastepaper basket, picked it up, and carried it out.

When I came back I signaled to Mother to come out of the kitchen. She came and I said,

"Are you going to tell him about it?"

"Yes."

"Why?"

"Because you have to learn right from wrong."

"But why do you have to tell him?"

"Because he's your father, you shouldn't have done it, and he'll know what to do."

"I hate you."

"Well I love you."

I was beginning to cry, so I ran away to my room. Why did she have to tell him? He was going to spank me, there was no way I could get out of it. I heard him walking toward my room, so I hid under the bed. Maybe he would think I wasn't there. Maybe he would think I ran away from home. Maybe he would think I was dead—then he'd be sorry.

He opened the door, stepped in, and stopped.

"Come out from under the bed."

I came out from under the bed. My eyes were red and the beginnings of tears made everything blurry.

"Tell me what happened," he said.

"Mother and me went downtown to Gristede's to buy some food, and there were some chocolate dollars on the floor and I picked them up."

"Go on."

"And Mother asked me where I got them when she found me eating them at home and I told her."

"Yes?"

"So we went back to Gristede's and she paid the man twenty-five cents. And I apologized. Yes I did."

"Did you find them on the floor?"

"No."

"Where?"

"I took them off the shelf."

"Do you know what that is?"

"Yes."

"Do you know what it is to say you found them on the floor when you did not?"

"Yes."

I burst into tears. I told him that I knew stealing and lying were wrong, and I said so many times that I was sorry. I asked why he had to spank me, and he only said that it must be done.

Next morning was Saturday. Ed and Bartlett went into Mom and Dad's room to wake them up. I stayed in my room because I had to let them know that I hated them. I didn't really, and I didn't want to, but I had to.

Daddy always slept with his head under the pillow, and he was hard to wake up. He had to be tickled and jumped on, and the pillow had to be taken away. Bartlett and Ed had fun that morning waking up Daddy. We could only do it on Saturday because he got up too early on the other days. I wished that I could be there too, but I couldn't.

Later Daddy came into my room. He said we

were going to have a fire and burn up the branches and leaves on the ground. He asked me if I would help him. I liked fires more than anything, so I nodded my head—I didn't say anything, I just nodded.

Outside I wordlessly dragged branches out of the woods and threw them on the fire. Daddy stood and watched me sometimes, and whenever I caught him doing that, I stuck my tongue out at him. He laughed and I almost laughed myself sometimes.

After lunch Dad asked me whether I wanted to throw the baseball or not, and I said yes. I never could figure out why he wanted to play catch, because I was always missing the ball, or overthrowing. He never got impatient like I did when I played with my little sister. Daddy and I threw the ball back and forth until I got tired and wanted to stop. Then he went into the house to help Mother do whatever she was doing, and I watched television.

After dinner Daddy cut sticks for us to roast marshmallows over the coals of the fire. I loved cooking marshmallows more than anything. He showed us how to cook them so that they would turn golden instead of catching on fire, but I couldn't do it anyway. Ed asked Daddy why Mother and he never had any fights. All the other kids' parents had fights. Daddy smiled and said that fights weren't any fun. Daddy always smiled; he was like me.

After school when I came home all the relatives were there. Mother was sitting on Uncle Robert's lap. She had a handkerchief and she was crying. Uncle Charlie and Cousin Linda were there. Linda's eyes were red too. Mother reached out her hand to me and I didn't know what to think. She said, "Your father is dead," and I still don't know what to think.

PAUL WARREN

Assignment 13

1. Read the chapter up to this point.
2. In your journal do *one* of the following:
    a. Reread the advice by Mauriac and then construct an entry in which you recapture a time from your own childhood. Before you start, re-create inside yourself the places, the milieu, the colors and smells of that time.
    b. Write on a subject of your own choice.
    c. Start a story about childhood.

Assignment 14

> We have to have the power to make real to ourselves the innerness of lives different from our own—there's nothing that matters more than this. . . .
>
> BENJAMIN DE MOTT

Sherwood Anderson suggests one way to get into other people's lives, but let him tell you in his own words how to go about it.

After you have read Anderson's statement, you may be interested in seeing a very special application of the technique he describes. Kafka makes use of it in "The Metamorphosis."

> There is something you can do. Even if you are not actually practicing writers, you can employ something of the writer's technique. When you are puzzled about your own life, as we all are most of the time, you can throw imagined figures of others against a background very like your own, put these imagined figures through situations in which you have been involved. It is a very comforting thing to do, a great relief at times, this occasionally losing sense of self, living in these imagined figures. This thing we call self is often very like a disease. It seems to sap you, take something from you, de-

stroy your relationship with others, while even occasionally losing sense of self seems to give you an understanding that you didn't have before you became absorbed.

May it not be that all the people we know are only what we imagine them to be? If, for example, you are as I was, for a good many years of my own young life, a businessman, on the whole spending my time seeking my own advantage, you lost interest, while, as opposed to this, if you lose yourself in others, life immediately becomes more interesting. A new world seems to open out before you. Your imagination becomes constantly more and more alive.

There is a profound pleasure in all of this. At least I know that when I came to it, I found it the pleasantest experience I had ever had. To be sure I do not want to discount the difficult. It is very hard to understand any other human being. It is difficult to tell truly the story of another, but it is, I think, rather a grand challenge.

SHERWOOD ANDERSON
from *The Intent of the Artist*
edited by Augusto Centeno

As Gregor Samsa awoke one morning from uneasy dreams, he found himself transformed in his bed into a gigantic insect. He was lying on his hard, as it were armor-plated, back and when he lifted his head a little he could see his domelike brown belly divided into stiff arched segments on top of which the bed quilt could hardly keep in position and was about to slide off completely. His numerous legs, which were pitifully thin compared to the rest of his bulk, waved helplessly before his eyes.

FRANZ KAFKA
from "The Metamorphosis"

1. Read the three excerpts for this assignment.
2. In your journal do *one* of the following:

a. Reread the advice by Sherwood Anderson and then construct a scene using familiar surroundings and imaginary characters.
b. Write on a subject of your own choice.
c. If you began a story about childhood for the previous assignment, complete that story.

Assignment 15

And now I was faced with another fundamental problem which every young writer must meet squarely if he is to continue. How is a man to get his writing done? How long should he work at writing, and how often? What kind of method, if any, must he find in following his work? I suddenly found myself face to face with the grim necessity of constant, daily work. And as simple as this discovery may seem to everyone, I was not prepared for it. A young writer without a public does not feel the sense of necessity, the pressure of time, as does a writer who has been published and who must now begin to think of time schedules, publishing seasons, the completion of his next book.

THOMAS WOLFE
from *The Story of a Novel*

How do you put your imagination to work? The answers that have been indicated here you will want to supplement with discoveries of your own, but here is a partial list for a start.

1. By just supposing.
2. By trying to make your story truer than if it had really happened.
3. By letting theme and purpose order fact and event.
4. By creating characters with lives of their own.
5. By inviting recall of things seen and unseen and by combining disconnected memories and impressions.
6. By trusting your own imagination and your own words.

But remember that as a writer what you see must be put in words before it can take form; otherwise, you are like the foolish photographer who never gets around to developing his film. Here is need and use for your journal. Preserve the picture that shapes itself before you. Write down what you have seen and felt and thought. Have enough confidence in the rightness of your own mind to trust its promptings. It is so and only so that you can put your imagination to work.

> . . . one begins a piece of writing by asking himself what kind of treatment is natural to the subject and what kind of effect he wants to work on the reader.
>
> ROBERT PENN WARREN
> from *Fundamentals of Good Writing*

1. Read the preceding comments.
2. In your journal do *one* of the following:
   a. What follows is taken from De Maupassant's "The Necklace." You will note that the fourth paragraph has been omitted. You are to construct it. In doing so, retain the author's tone and style. You may find it helpful to first state in a single sentence what the writer is trying to do in each of the paragraphs that has been presented.

   [1] She was one of those pretty and charming girls who are sometimes, as if by a mistake of destiny, born in a family of clerks. She had no dowry, no expectations, no means of being known, understood, loved, wedded by any rich and distinguished man; and she let herself be married to a little clerk at the Ministry of Public Instruction.

   [2] She was dressed plainly because she could not dress well, but she was as unhappy as though she had really fallen from her proper station, since with women there is neither caste nor rank; and beauty, grace, and charm act instead of family and birth. Natural fineness, instinct for what is elegant, suppleness of wit, are the sole hierarchy, and make from women of the people the equals of the very greatest ladies.

[3] She suffered ceaselessly, feeling herself born for all the delicacies and all the luxuries. She suffered from the poverty of her dwelling, from the wretched look of the walls, from the worn-out chairs, from the ugliness of the curtains. All those things, of which another woman of her rank would never even have been conscious, tortured her and made her angry. The sight of the little Breton peasant who did her humble housework aroused in her regrets which were despairing, and distracted dreams. She thought of the silent antechambers hung with Oriental tapestry, lit by tall bronze candelabra, and of the two great footmen in knee breeches who sleep in the big armchairs, made drowsy by the heavy warmth of the hot-air stove. She thought of the long salons fitted up with ancient silk, of the delicate furniture carrying priceless curiosities, and of the coquettish perfumed boudoirs made for talks at five o'clock with intimate friends, with men famous and sought after, whom all women envy and whose attention they all desire.

* * * * *

[5] She had no dresses, no jewels, nothing. And she loved nothing but that; she felt made for that. She would so have liked to please, to be envied, to be charming, to be sought after.

from "The Necklace"

b. Write on a subject of your own choice.
c. Copy out a paragraph or two in which you feel the writer has put his imagination to work. Then see if you can list some of the ways that he has managed to do it.

3 | Review

Here are two quotations that may start you on your own story. The review exercise will give you an opportunity to write and to use your imagination.

> Hawthorne died on May 18, 1864, in the mountains of New Hampshire. His death was tranquil and it was mysterious, because it occurred in his sleep. Nothing keeps us from imagining that he died while dreaming, and we can even invent the story that he dreamed—the last of an infinite series —and the manner in which death completed or erased it. Perhaps I shall write it some day; I shall try to redeem this deficient and too digressive essay with an acceptable story.
>
> JORGE LUIS BORGES
> from *Other Inquisitions*

> If a man could pass through Paradise in a dream, and have a flower presented to him as a pledge that his soul had really been there, and if he found that flower in his hand when he awoke—Ay!—and what then?
>
> SAMUEL TAYLOR COLERIDGE

You will soon be asked to do some imaginative writing, but first you may enjoy looking at the work of another student.

A SURE THING

GARY JOHNSON

The atmosphere of superficial happiness pervaded the entire fairground in various forms: the smell of popcorn, roasted nuts, and cotton candy;

the eager tugging of parents' arms by their tireless children; and even the brightly colored waste-paper trampled into the grass. Beneath and above the roar of the crowd and the piercing shouts of barkers and concession-stand salesmen flowed the droning of a calliope. People moved in all directions, meandering from tent to tent, stuffing their mouths with popcorn as they walked. Their blank, smiling faces drifted aimlessly, irradiated by the color and gaiety of the fair.

In quite a different part of the fair two men were busily at work. They were in a stable, and, except for twenty or thirty horses, they were alone. The din from the people outside drifted in and died quickly in the soft dirt floor. The only other sound was an occasional whinny or snort from a horse. The two men were crouched over a leather bag, their faces knit in concentration. They were dressed similarly, both covered with dark denim. Each wore a pair of large, thick-heeled black boots, and each had his hair slicked back over his head. Their builds were complementary, one being short and stocky, the other tall and gangly. Presently they arose and cautiously approached one of the horses, the stocky one speaking in a deep Southern drawl:

"You hold her steady, now, while ah give her the shot," he whispered in the relative silence.

"Sho' thing, Sam," said the other hesitantly. He timidly drew up to the horse, speaking to it in a trembling voice, his hand outstretched. "That's a good horse," he said. "You jes' calm down and take it easy an' ev'thin's gonna be awright." The horse looked at the strange figure approaching him and drew back on its halter. The man finally got his hand on the horse's forehead and began petting the animal, speaking to it now in a low hushed tone that a man might use in seducing a woman.

"Heck, ah didn't say to make love to the beast, Bert," said Sam, looking at his companion impatiently.

"Sho' thing, Sam," responded Bert and shut up.

"Okay, heah goes," said the other. He slowly walked toward the horse's rear, while the horse eyed him suspiciously. He brought the needle up to the horse's buttock and jabbed. The horse whinnied and responded with a quick jerk, its hind leg catching Sam in the shin. He immediately grabbed his leg and began hopping about the stable, cursing, his thick pouting lips pressed into a contorted grimace, "Ahhh, Ohhh, Goshdarnit-anyway, Ohhh, Owww."

Bert looked on dumbfoundedly not knowing what to do. "Jes' don't stand theah, Goshdarnit," Sam yelled at him, still hopping on one foot.

"Well I didn't kick ya," he mumbled defensively. This only made him madder, and a new string of curses filled the stable.

The horses had begun milling uneasily about the stable when Bert said suddenly, "Sam, look!" Sam stopped hopping and turned to see the dark silhouette of a man disappear from the stable entrance. "D'ya s'pose he saw what we were doin'?"

"Aw, heck," replied Sam disgustedly, "he's prob'ly jes' a stable hand wanderin' 'round. Come on, le's get out a' heah an' make some money."

"Sho' thing, Sam," replied Bert.

The two men walked out into the bright morning sunlight, squinting uneasily at first and Sam limping slightly. They strolled along toward the betting booth, appearing to admire the surrounding pageantry with everyone else. They made their bets, using all the money they had earned, borrowed, and stolen. There was an hour or two before the race so they walked on through the fair.

"She's gonna run like the wind, ain't she, Sam?" said Bert after a while.

"She darn well better," said Sam pensively.

They had wandered about for half an hour when they came to a small tent bearing a sign which read, "Fortunes." Sam stopped. "Duck in heah a sec'," he shouted above the din. "Gonna have mah fohtune told me," he added with an ironic chuckle to himself. His lanky comrade followed him.

Inside was relative dark and quiet. A man knelt before a velvet-covered table on which rested a glass sphere. He was draped in a white silk robe, and on his head sat a ridiculous-looking white turban. He grinned broadly when he saw the two men enter, his small, deep-set eyes darting about anxiously.

"You tell fohtunes?" Sam demanded imposingly, his tall shadow peering out from behind.

"Indeed I do," he replied still grinning. He seemed to know something the other two didn't.

"Well," said Sam, "s'pose you do jes' that foh me an' mah chum heah." They approached the man and sat down opposite him. "How much you charge us?"

"I charge fifty cents," said the fortune teller. Sam reached into his pocket and flipped a coin onto the table.

"Ah want to know what's in stoah foh me an' mah chum today," he chuckled, elbowing his companion in the side. The other was giggling excitedly.

The fortune teller put the coin in a tray and turned to the glass globe on the table. He routinely placed his fingers on the globe and closed his eyes. The other two grinned at him smugly.

The fortune teller's face took on a strange expression as he seemingly drifted off into another world. He had been this way for a few minutes when Sam abruptly snapped his fingers in front of his face saying, "Hey, mistah, don't you fall asleep on us now." The fortune teller opened his eyes in annoyance.

"If you don't mind," he said irritably, "this requires a great deal of concentration."

"Sho' thing, fella," apologized Sam. "Jes' don't want you sleepin' on the job, that's all." He elbowed his companion in the side again, and they both chuckled.

The fortune teller ignored this last comment and closed his eyes again. In a few minutes his head began to sway back and forth as though he were in a swoon. "Ah, yes," he began. "Swami is beginning to receive the galactic impulses. The world beyond is intimating with Swami's id. Images are swimming in Swami's mind. They are coming to the surface now." He pressed his fingers to his temples. "Ah, yes, the images are becoming clear now. Swami sees two men—one fat, one skinny. They resemble yourselves. They appear to be counting something. . . ." The men glanced at each other uneasily. "Ah, what's this? Swami sees something else now. It's white and eerie. It looks like . . . yes it is, it's an apparition of some sort, and it's riding a horse. Oh, this is terrible! It's riding after the two men. It's making a weird shrieking noise." The men were now spellbound. "The two men are running away, but the apparition is too fast for them. This is terrible. Oh! Oh!" At this point the fortune teller opened his eyes and put his hand to his heart, sighing heavily. "I'm sorry," he gasped, "but I just can't go on."

The two men were silent. The grins had disappeared from their faces. Bert was sitting still, his mouth agape and his eyes opened wide. Sam had turned pale, but he hadn't lost his composure. "That's a lotta bull," he said defensively. "You're full a' bull. This whole deal's full a' bull."

"I'm sorry," said the fortune teller emphatically, "but I only told you the images that came to my mind. I can do nothing about what the future holds in store for you."

"Oh, s'at so?" reasserted Sam. "Well ah sho' ain't gonna stay heah an' listen to that kind a' stuff. Come on, le's get out a' heah." The two men got up. "Sho' is a waste of fifty cents," he added with finality. They left, the tall one last, his lips trembling.

They had wandered around for a while when the tall one said plaintively, "I don't like what he said,

Sam. I think he was tellin' the truth. I'm scared, Sam."

"You actually believe in that stuff?" he said. "How in heck can somethin' like that come true anyway? There ain't no such a thing as fortune tellin'. It was jes' coincidence that he was talkin' 'bout horses and such runnin' after us. Jes' coincidence I'm tellin' ya."

"Yeah," said Bert, "but I got a funny feelin' 'bout this thing. I know somethin's gonna happen, Sam. I've had a funny feelin' about this whole deal. Le's back out before it's too late. It's evil what we're doin', it ain't right," he concluded with all the deliberation he could muster.

"Aw bull," replied Sam. "Anyway it's too late now." The men started over toward the racetrack.

Half an hour later the race was over. Nothing surprising had happened, at least not surprising to the two men. The drugged horse had won easily against heavy odds, and the two men collected their small fortunes from the betting booth with no questions asked. Their earlier anxieties were allayed by the sudden realization that they were now fairly rich. Each bought a cheap cigar and smoked it in royal satisfaction, blowing smoke into the faces of the less fortunate.

But their newly found elation was short-lived, for in a short while it was announced that the winning horse had been drugged and that the authorities were searching for the ones responsible. Hearing this, the two men left the fairground as inconspicuously as possible and made off for the nearby woods.

They had been walking a while when Bert stopped and spun around. "I got a feelin' some-one's followin' us, Sam," he said suspiciously. Sam looked back, but it was growing dark and he could discern nothing. "You an' your feelin's," he retorted in exasperation. "I s'pose next you'll be tellin' me ya see ghosts."

The other shuddered at the thought. "Don't even say that," he shrilled.

"Come on, le's go before we get caught," urged Sam. Bert followed obediently.

They kept walking until they felt safe from anyone who might still be searching for them.

It was dark by the time they stopped and rested. Thin light from half a moon filtered down through the still branches of the trees above. The only sound other than the monotone of the crickets came from the two partners. Sam opened the leather bag and poured out its green contents. "Goshdarn," he said, running his fingers through the crisp bills. "Ah ain't felt this good in a long time. Think ah'll hightail it on down to Mobile and live it up a while. New clothes, a car, one a' them convertible jobs like them rich fellas drive all the time. Make me a new man. Why ah might even get me a good-lookin' wife an' settle down in some high-class area. How 'bout you?"

"Oh, I s'pose I'll do the same," said Bert thoughtfully. Then suddenly, "Sam, I hear somethin'. Off in the trees. Ya hear?"

"Ah don't heah nothin', darnit. It's jes' your imagination. You're gonna worry yourself crazy if ya don't relax." He stretched out on the soft leaf-covered ground, resting his head against a log. "Don't know 'bout you, but ah'm gonna get some rest. It's been a long day."

Bert lay down and closed his eyes, but he was a long time in getting to sleep. He awoke periodically, imagining sounds in the darkness. Drowsiness finally overcame him, though, and he too dozed off.

They had both been sleeping soundly for a good time when Bert awoke again. This time he woke Sam. "Sam, I hear somethin'. I'm sure of it," he said shakily.

"You wake me up jes' foh that?" groaned Sam. "I hear things, too, but I don't go wakin' you up all the time now, do I? Go back to sleep and don't bother me no moh."

"But I heard somethin'. It woke me up," he continued.

"Why don't you jes . . ." Sam stopped in the middle of his sentence. They listened for a moment.

"Ya hear it. D'ya hear it!" whispered Bert desperately. From off in the distance came a faint rumbling like a horse's hoofbeats. "It's nothin'," said Sam nervously. Both men were still. The rumbling grew louder, and presently a soft, deep moaning could be heard.

Bert clutched Sam's arm in terror. Sam's face was white and his eyes wide open. "What in Hades' name is that?" he breathed.

"It's comin' after us!" the other bawled hysterically. "The ghost, it's comin' after us, it's comin' after us!" He was holding Sam's arm and rocking back and forth.

Sam's mouth was open, but he made no reply. He just sat, his eyes frozen to the darkness where the noise was coming from.

They could now hear the thrashing of leaves and the breaking of branches as it approached. The deep moan suddenly burst into a piercing wail that unglued the men. They bolted up and sprinted in the opposite direction, Bert in the lead, howling like a banshee. The pounding of hooves and the thrashing through the brush grew louder. Sam looked back and saw a white figure mounted on a large black horse, galloping after them at full tilt not a hundred yards behind. Seeing this, his pace doubled, and he overtook Bert.

Before the apparition could overtake them they came to a river. Without a moment's hesitation they both jumped in and began thrashing toward the opposite shore. The apparition came to a stop before the river and watched the two men reach the other side and take off again into the woods.

The apparition stayed there a while before returning to the place where the two men had left the bag of money. He dismounted and removed the white silk robe he had been wearing. He picked up the money-laden bag, and a broad grin spread across his quite unghostlike face. He couldn't have been more pleased with the prediction he had made.

Review Assignment

In your journal do *one* of the following:
  a. Write a piece of science fiction.
  b. Write a poem.
  c. Write a story with a surprise ending.

UNIT 4

---◆---

Reflection

Composition is, for the most part,
an effort of slow diligence and
steady perseverance, to which the mind
is dragged by resolution,
or necessity.—SAMUEL JOHNSON

41

SOME GUIDES TO REFLECTION

Writing can never be achieved by learning what to avoid and what to leave out. There must be something put in before you can leave anything out. Writing comes from having something to say and trying hard to say it.

STEPHEN LEACOCK
from *How to Write*

This unit brings into focus your previous work. Observation and imagination supply the facts and ideas that make reflection possible. No observation, no imagination, then no reflection. Writing—all kinds of writing—calls for reflection. Indeed, much that is bad in writing is simply caused by a lack of it. Stories need depth and that can come only from thought. The inability to reflect is what makes parrots such unsatisfactory conversationalists. They have thought of nothing. Thinking powers writing and lends character and color to your page. Hence this unit.

Reflection here means contemplation, introspection, thinking over, studying, pondering, seeing cause and effect, abstracting, generalizing, synthesizing, finding logical relations, and making value judgments. Reflection makes use of insight and employs order and logic—the parents of analysis. Reflection is synonymous with thought.

If you would reflect, start with observation, insight, or imagination. Then put your idea or impression into statement form. As you write, explore, examine, contemplate, introspect, think over what you have seen or shared or thought. Present your thinking so that there is order and clarity in all you say. Express your ideas with interest, but keep the focus on idea. Write in such a way that others may follow your thought and understand your conclusion, whether or not they agree.

Here are some examples that may prompt you to your own independent reflection:

You are aware that the fundamental law followed by the human brain is the *law of the association of ideas*. A recollection, an idea, an image, does not start up singly in our memory; that "image" (this is the term used by philosophers) is always introduced by a preceding image, and never fails to draw a third after it. The imagination is like a moving-picture that never stops. Day and night, it reels off its long succession of photographs; they come fast or slow, sometimes clear-cut, sometimes blurred, but never is there the slightest gap.

The force that moves this chain of images is purely mechanical. It is independent of reflection. Often, indeed, the feebler the thought, the more vivid the image. When we are half-asleep or worn out by illness—that is, under conditions when our will falters, or our reasoning powers grow weak—imagination holds more sway over us: instead of guiding it, we are led, carried along by it; we no longer desire, we no longer reason, we drift. What we call waking is nothing but the reason or the will reasserting its rights and saying to the mechanical, subconscious part of our being: "Halt! I resume command!" Clearly, this mechanical force acts quite differently from reflection. Reflection everywhere introduces order and logic; it establishes a rational connection between images. The peculiar quality of a dream is its absurdity, its incoherence; images are associated with one another almost haphazardly, by any insignificant, accessory detail, rarely by the essential parts. Even when wide awake, if we are the least absent-minded, or are talking by fits and starts, we are sometimes astonished at the distance we have traveled over the stepping stones of four or five ideas.

JULIEN BEZARD
from *My Class in Composition*

Julien Bezard has indeed thought about thought. He has no new facts, but he has an idea and he examines it for us. The next writer has an idea too, though of a different kind. What both writers share is an interest in examining relationships; they have the power to abstract and to formulate principle. Benjamin Franklin demonstrates this ability by reflecting on a youthful experience.

. . . I am charmed with your description of Paradise, and with your plan of living there; and I approve much of your conclusion, that, in the meantime, we should draw all the good we can from this world. In my opinion we might all draw more good from it than we do, and suffer less evil, if we would take care not to give too much for whistles. For to me it seems that most of the unhappy people we meet with are become so by neglect of that caution.

You ask what I mean? You love stories, and will excuse my telling one of myself.

When I was a child of seven years old, my friends, on a holiday, filled my pocket with coppers. I went directly to a shop where they sold toys for children; and being charmed with the sound of a whistle, that I met by the way in the hands of another boy, I voluntarily offered and gave all my money for one. I then came home, and went whistling all over the house, much pleased with my whistle, but disturbing all the family. My brothers, and sisters, and cousins, understanding the bargain I had made, told me I have given four times as much for it as it was worth; put me in mind what good things I might have bought with the rest of the money; and laughed at me so much for my folly, that I cried with vexation; and the reflection gave me more chagrin than the whistle gave me pleasure.

This, however, was afterward of use to me, the impression continuing on my mind; so that often, when I was tempted to buy some unnecessary thing, I said to myself, "Don't give too much for the whistle," and I saved my money.

As I grew up, came into the world, and observed the actions of men, I thought I met with many, very many, who gave too much for the whistle.

When I saw one too ambitious of court favor, sacrificing his time in attendance on levees, his repose, his liberty, his virtue, and perhaps his friends, to attain it, I have said to myself, "This man gives too much for his whistle."

When I saw another fond of popularity, constantly employing himself in political bustles, neglecting his own affairs, and ruining them by that neglect, "He pays, indeed," said I, "too much for his whistle. . . ."

. . . In short, I conceive that great part of the miseries of mankind are brought upon them by the false estimates they have made of the value of things, and by their giving too much for their whistle. . . .

BENJAMIN FRANKLIN
from "The Whistle"

We have been considering essays of ideas. Now we turn to a somewhat formalized expression of idea called the epigram. The purpose of the epigram is to hold within a sentence an antithesis or witty thought. Epigrams call for shrewd observation, keenness of mind, and clarity of expression. Here is a collection from the pen of a master:

No preacher is listened to but Time, which gives us the same train and turn of thought that elder people have in vain tried to put into our heads before.

When a true genius appears in the world, you may know him by this sign, that the dunces are all in confederacy against him.

I have known some men possessed of good qualities which were very serviceable to others, but useless to themselves—like a sundial on the front of a house, to inform the neighbors and passengers, but not the owner within.

The stoical scheme of supplying our wants by lopping off our desires is like cutting off our feet when we want shoes.

Ill company is like a dog, who dirts those most whom he loves best.

Most sorts of diversion in men, children, and other animals, are an imitation of fighting.

Men of great parts are often unfortunate in the management of public business, because they are apt to go out of the common road by the quickness of their imagination. This I once said to my Lord Bolingbroke, and desired he would observe that the clerks in his office used a sort of ivory knife with a blunt edge to divide a sheet of paper, which never failed to cut it even, only requiring a steady hand: whereas if they should make use of a sharp penknife the sharpness would make it go often out of the crease and disfigure the paper.

I must complain the cards are ill shuffled, till I have a good hand.

Elephants are always drawn smaller than life, but a flea always larger.

JONATHAN SWIFT
from "Thoughts on Various Subjects, Moral and Diverting"

Assignment 1

1. Read the chapter up to this point.
2. In your journal do *one* of the following:
   a. Give your understanding of these terms: (1) idea, (2) epigram, (3) value judgment, (4) synthesis. You may look them up if you wish.
   b. Write a reflective entry on a subject of your own choice. You may wish to start by recounting a youthful experience and explaining what you learned from it. In any case, if you begin with the specific, move to

a general statement; and if you begin with a general
statement, move to the specific.

c. Write some epigrams.

Assignment 2

A man was cleaning the attic of an old house in
New England and he found a box which was full
of tiny pieces of string. On the lid of the box there
was an inscription in an old hand: "String Too
Short to Be Saved. . . !"

Here is a statement of fact, an observation made without
comment. Still the event is memorable. Indeed the author
uses the inscription as the title for an entire book. What do
you think such a book might be about? Why is the phrase
"String Too Short to Be Saved" regional? Why memorable?
Does it prompt you to any reflections? Following is an excerpt from the book itself. The excerpt comments on the life
and death of Washington Woodward, and the author gives
us one of his own reflections about the man and his life. The
book talks about this character in considerable detail. In
one of its chapters we learn that Washington Woodward was
a hermit and an eccentric who near the end of his time had
an acute illness and a resulting mental derangement in which
he had a vision of white hogs.

As you read the excerpt ask yourself, Is the author right?
Was Washington Woodward's life irrelevant, or does the
very fact that the author wrote about him, and that we now
consider him, suggest that life is never irrelevant—especially
when it can be said "He worked hard all his life at being
himself . . ."?

Does death make life irrelevant? Is a life of principle the
best life? What are the best principles? How do you know?
These and questions like them are proper ones to ask if you
would develop your powers of reflecting. But here is the excerpt. See what you make of it.

He died in a state nursing home. My grandfather
and I went to see him a month before he died, and

his cheeks were flushed above the white beard, and his eyes shone while he performed his monologue. He joked with us and showed us the sores on his legs. He displayed me to his nurses and to the silent old men in the room with him. It was a little like all the other times I had met him, yet seeing him ready to die I was all the more impressed by the waste of him—the energy, the ingenuity, the strength to do what he wanted—as he lay frail and bearded in a nightgown provided by the legislature. The waste that he hated, I thought, was through him like blood in his veins. He had saved nails and wasted life. He had lived alone, but if he was a hermit he was neither religious nor philosophical. His fanaticisms, which might have been creative, were as petulant as his break from the church. I felt that he was intelligent, or it would not have mattered, but I had no evidence to support my conviction. His only vision was a delusion of white hogs. He worked hard all his life at being himself, but there were no principles to examine when his life was over. It was as if there had been a moral skeleton which had lacked the flesh of the intellect and the blood of experience. The life which he could recall totally was not worth recalling.

Standing beside him in the nursing home, I saw ahead for one moment into the residue, five years from then, of Washington Woodward's life: the shack has caved in and his straightened nails have rusted into the dirt of Ragged Mountain; though the rocks stay where he moved them, no one knows how they got there; his animals are dead, and their descendants have made bad connections; his apple trees produce small and sour fruit; the best-built hayracks rot under rotting sheds; in New Hampshire the frost tumbles the cleverest wall; those who knew him best are dead or dying, and his gestures have assumed the final waste of irrelevance.

DONALD HALL
from *String Too Short to Be Saved*

This short excerpt summarizes the topic of this chapter:

> In its loosest sense, thinking signifies everything
> that, as we say, is "in our heads" or that "goes
> through our minds. . . ." In this sense, silly folk
> and dullards think. . . . Active, persistent, and
> careful consideration of any belief or supposed
> form of knowledge in the light of the grounds that
> support it, and the further conclusions to which it
> tends, constitutes reflective thought.
>
> JOHN DEWEY
> from *How We Think*

1. Read the material for this assignment.
2. In your journal do *one* of the following:
   a. Write your reaction, your thoughts, your reflections
   on the excerpt about Washington Woodward from
   String Too Short to Be Saved, or comment on any of
   the questions raised by it.
   b. If you wish, state a problem that you have thought
   about, and then give some of your own thoughts
   about it.
   c. Copy out a thought passage from a short story or essay.
   Pick a selection you personally find interesting.

Assignment 3

Here are some guides to reflection freely adapted from
the rules set out by the French philosopher Descartes.

1. *Consider matters in which you are interested.*
2. *Move from the known to the unknown.* As you
   move, avoid great leaps, or better—take them,
   but then look back and consider the intervening
   ground.
3. *Seek to prove nothing. Feel free to examine all.*
   The entire world is the province of the mind.
4. *Entertain a variety of hypotheses in order to explore all possibilities.* Get into the habit of sup-

posing, making hypotheses, and drawing distinctions. Put your thoughts into words.

5. *Don't argue; examine.*
6. *Don't be pretentious.* Say only what you honestly see, feel, or think.
7. *Remember the importance of being able to laugh at man and his works.* This includes you.

These seven rules may be of help to you in your own search for ideas. In any case, do search! You'll find ideas invigorate both conversation and writing. You'll interest yourself and be of greater interest to others if you make a habit of entertaining ideas. Don't be pretentious about your interest; you don't have to ring a bell or create a mystical silence in order to talk about a book or to present an observation, but what you must do is go beyond the surface of events —beyond the weather, your diet, and the neighborhood news. Any one of these topics may, of course, serve as a point of departure provided ideas are added. Here is an example of how the thing can be done. The example is taken from the beginning of the short story "They Grind Exceeding Small" by Ben Ames Williams.

> I telephoned down the hill to Hazen Kinch. "Hazen," I asked, "are you going to town today?"
>
> "Yes, yes," he said abruptly in his quick, harsh fashion. "Of course I'm going to town."
>
> "I've a matter of business," I suggested.
>
> "Come along," he invited brusquely. "Come along."
>
> There was not another man within forty miles to whom he would have given that invitation.
>
> "I'll be down in ten minutes," I promised him. . . . Bitterly cold and steadily cold, and deep snow lay upon the hills, blue-white in the distance. The evergreens were blue-black blotches on this whiteness. The birches, almost indistinguishable, were like trees in camouflage. To me the hills are never so grand as in this winter coat they wear. It is easy to believe that a brooding God dwells upon them. I wondered as I plowed my way down to

Hazen Kinch's farm whether God did indeed dwell among these hills; and I wondered what he thought of Hazen Kinch.

This was no new matter of thought with me. I had given some thought to Hazen in the past. I was interested in the man and in that which should come to him. He was, it seemed to me, a problem in fundamental ethics; he was, as matters stood, a demonstration of the essential uprightness of things as they are. The biologist would have called him a sport, a deviation from type, a violation of all the proper laws of life. That such a man should live and grow great and prosper was not fitting; in a well-regulated world it should not be. Yet Hazen Kinch did live; he had grown—in his small way— great; and, by our lights, he had prospered. Therefore I watched him. There was about the man the fascination which clothes a tight-rope walker above Niagara; an aeronaut in the midst of the nose dive. The spectator stares with half-caught breath, afraid to see and afraid to miss seeing the ultimate catastrophe. Sometimes I wondered whether Hazen Kinch suspected this attitude on my part. It was not impossible. There was a cynical courage in the man; it might have amused him. Certainly I was the only man who had in any degree his confidence.

BEN AMES WILLIAMS
from "They Grind Exceeding Small"

Here we see how reflection gives to detail a significance that does not attach to naked fact—although that is what the story starts with. Events, people, and the weather have interest, but that interest is heightened and extended when ideas take over and point to significance. Williams's entire story moves from the thought implicit in its title—a title taken from the following line of "Retribution," written by the seventeenth-century German poet Friedrich von Logau.

Though the mills of God grind slowly,
    yet they grind exceeding small.

There is idea! In the story itself the idea is dramatized to the point of impact.

> To be really creative, ideas have to be worked up and then "put over," so that they become a part of man's social heritage.
>
> JAMES HARVEY ROBINSON
> from *The Mind in the Making*

This assignment provides practice in presenting thought. You may wish to construct epigrams or move one step closer to the short story by writing dialogue. In any case, the point of this assignment is to provide practice in working up ideas and "putting them over."

1. Read the material for this assignment.
2. In your journal do *one* of the following:
   a. Reflect on and write about an aspect of the past six weeks.
   b. Write some epigrams.
   c. Present a character who might be workable in a short story. Your character may be similar to the one presented in the excerpt from *String Too Short to Be Saved*. Show the character presenting ideas or show how he, himself, suggests ideas and prompts reflection.

4|2

WATCH THE
OTHER FELLOW THINK

One of the best ways to learn is to observe the experts. In this chapter you will watch professional writers expand a thought into a sentence, a sentence into a paragraph, and a paragraph into an essay.

Analytical observation on your part will show you how this writing is done and in turn will help you structure and develop your own work. In this chapter, practice will be directed to writing a paraphrase, summary, précis, and outline. Each of these forms will permit you to demonstrate your skill in following another's thought. At the same time you will gain practice in economy of expression, clarity, and the control of sentence structure. But a word of caution before you start. The word is *persist!* This kind of reading and writing demands close attention and its rewards are not apparent until you have done it long enough and well enough to acquire facility.

The information on note-taking and outlining is designed to assist you in managing ideas as they appear in extended works. This lesson then is but an introduction that suggests ways in which you may learn from the experts. Once started, remember to persist.

Now for some definitions and examples.

Paraphrase

Definition: A paraphrase is the restatement of ideas so that their meaning becomes absolutely clear. Writing a paraphrase usually requires simplification of vocabulary and expansion of statement. The goal is not compression but clarity. In an unambiguous way you are demonstrating your ability to follow the thoughts of another and to express them in your own words when you paraphrase.

Example: "The Love Song of J. Alfred Prufrock" by T. S. Eliot

> Let us go then, you and I,
> When the evening is spread out against the sky
> Like a patient etherized upon a table;
> Let us go, through certain half-deserted streets. . . .

The speaker, J. Alfred Prufrock, invites the "you" of the poem to go with him at the close of the day—not any day but one that has a fatally relaxed quality—a quality that parallels that of someone under anesthetic on an operating table. The evening chosen will be hushed and quiet, and yet its peace will possess an artificial quality. By extension the speaker implies that both city and nature are in harmonious suspension, as if living were carried on by both in a suspended and artificial state. Thus the statement appears as a submerged metaphor of the speaker's own attitude toward life and nature.

Summary

Definition: A summary is a brief statement covering the main points at issue.

Example: On the Road by Jack Kerouac

Narrative of young men giving up all responsibility and slumming around the country. The style shows Joycean influence and also reminds one of Salinger. Good characterization. A Beat Bible.

Précis

Definition: A précis is a brief original expression of ideas contained in a longer piece. The aim of the précis is to give in condensed form the thought and general effect of the original. Thoughts must be presented in the order in which they stand in the longer piece. A précis is usually a quarter to a third as long as the statement from which it comes.

A Model for Précis:

> I have read *Oliver Twist* in obedience to the opinions of so many intelligent people as have praised it. The author has an acute eye for cos-

tume; he sees the expression of dress, of form, of gait, of personal deformities; of furniture, of the outside and inside of houses; but his eye rests always on surfaces; he has no insight into character.

RALPH WALDO EMERSON

Examples: (Each of these statements is an example of a précis. There is no "right answer"; though it is clear that economy, clarity, coherence, and order are required in all cases.)

1. The literate applaud *Oliver Twist,* but I discover Dickens a master of surface rather than soul.
2. Dickens sees only man and his exterior; never man himself.
3. Dickens depicts man's surface but never his soul.
4. Dickens sees surface not soul.

And now we come to "outlining," a major technique for presenting and following ideas—a way of marshaling evidence in the order of its importance and at the same time of summarizing large amounts of material. Particularly in the reading and writing of history and literature is an understanding of outlining important.

Outline

Definition: An outline is a composition in skeletal form that presents logical steps for reaching stated goals.

The whole subject of outlining may strike you as gratuitous or fatuous. If so, your response is probably conditioned by overexposure to the subject; "outlining" is often overtaught and oversold. But despite the fact that many people start outlining at grade four, it is unusual to find someone who has acquired skill in outlining before grade fourteen. Too often outlining gets an early write-off as another exaggerated "good thing."

The value of outlining depends on its utility for you. Can you make it work—not just go through the motions? More than one student when required to outline and then write a composition has found it expedient to reverse the process.

The reason for this reversal may in part be explained by this comment:

> Regarding outlines, it is clear that two persons, with access to the same data, would not make the same outline or write the same article. Outlines clarify your ideas perhaps, but you must govern the outline, not let the outline govern you. I have never found that good outliners were good writers.
>
> Possibly the strangest phenomenon in the process of writing is the fashion in which the writing creates itself, so to speak. Any writer will tell you that when he sits down to write, he generally hasn't much notion of what he is going to say. He doesn't know beforehand what is going to come out of the end of his pen or pencil or from the keys of his typewriter. The act of writing begets writing. As Anatole France once said, "We think with words." The flow of words produces thoughts. The thoughts are nonexistent until they are clothed in language.
>
> MAX J. HERZBERG
> from "It's No Fun to Write"

Although outlining is a clear and effective way of photographing structure, turning an outline into writing may be as difficult as making the objects in a photograph return to nature. An outline looks good—neat and ordered—but its real value for you depends on your ability to write from it.

In reading, however, the outline is of undisputed service. Nothing reveals with greater economy and clarity your grasp of what you have read. Outlines made from reading help you see how the experts expand and support thought. Mortimer J. Adler in the chapter called "Seeing the Skeleton" from *How to Read a Book* gives a detailed account of how outlining relates to reading.

But whether outlining from reading or for writing, you'll find the two-step outline the most practical device for exposing the relative importance of ideas. Just in case you've forgotten how it goes (despite your early training) here is a brief review of the form.

The Two-Step Outline and How It Works

I. Main topic
Thesis statement
   A. Subtopic
      1. Detail of first importance
      2. Detail of second importance
   B. Subtopic
      1. Detail of first importance
      2. Detail of second importance
II. Main topic
   A. Subtopic
      1. Detail of first importance
      2. Detail of second importance
   B. Subtopic
      1. Detail of first importance
      2. Detail of second importance

Example:

I. *Main topic*—Watch the other fellow think
Thesis statement—Paraphrasing, summarizing, preparing a précis, and outlining require skill in following the thoughts of others and in presenting your understanding of those thoughts.
   A. *Subtopic*—Paraphrase
      1. Definition
      2. Example
   B. *Subtopic*—Summary
      1. Definition
      2. Example
II. *Main topic*—Additional ways of watching and recording thought
   A. *Subtopic*—Précis
      1. Definition
      2. Example
   B. *Subtopic*—Outline
      1. Definition
      2. Example

In following the thoughts of others, the cardinal rule for readers is think as you go, summarize, and then outline. If this rule is followed, you need not look at the text while out-lining but rather can depend on what you gained from your reading. But that is a counsel of perfection and asking a bit much; even so reading notes—except for direct quotations—should be made from memory rather than from the text.

Now a few final precepts that may help you as you make your own notes and watch the other fellow think.

1. Be brief. Remember you are taking notes and not repro-ducing the text.
2. Be clear. Don't crowd the page; write on only one side of the paper.
3. Be orderly. Keep together the things that belong together.
4. Be meticulous. Use utmost care in recording sources, quotations, figures, formulas, definitions.
5. Be thoughtful. Distinguish between fact and opinion.

Reading without subsequent reflection is ridicu-lous; it is a proof of folly and of vanity. Further, it is a sign of undue self-esteem to suppose that we can grasp the full import of an author's message at a single reading. I would not say that every book worth reading once is worth reading twice over. But I would say that no book of great and estab-lished reputation is read till it is read at least twice. You can easily test the truth of this by read-ing again any classic.

ARNOLD BENNETT
from *Things That Have Interested Me*

Assignment 4

1. Read the chapter up to this point.
2. In your journal do *one* of the following:
   a. Make a brief summary of this chapter or select a passage from your reading and write a précis of it.
   b. Outline a short story with which you are familiar, or write a summary of it.

c. Select a passage of prose or poetry that presents some difficulty, copy out the passage, and make a paraphrase of it.

Assignment 5

You may have wondered why you fail to carry over into your writing the vigor and ease of your ordinary conversation. The probability is that when your work is criticized as stiff and formal, on the one hand, or as tame and colorless, on the other, you are in your writing simply not being fair to yourself. You have associated with the term "composition" ideas of unreal dignity or owlishness. One often detects this tone in the letters of practical men who do not write much. Or you have been so disturbed by the notion that you must be clear, correct, and concise, and must diligently herd the "sacred cows of Composition"— unity, coherence, and emphasis—that your writing has lost all the native hue of resolution; all the joy has gone out of it; and it has become flaccid, pale, tame. All writing done without joy—or love, or hate, or pride, or other quality of earnestness—is like that. In your conversation you were not thinking of rules; you were enjoying yourself. In your writing you were miserable; and the misery shows just as plainly in the one as the joy in the other.

ROBERT M. GAY
from *Fact, Fancy, and Opinion*

1. Read the preceding excerpt.
2. In your journal do *one* of the following:
   a. Write a summary of Chapter 5 from *The Elements of Style,* or pick any writing you think particularly important and summarize it.
   b. Write a paraphrase of lines from Shakespeare, or from a poem or book you are reading.

c. Write a précis of the following passage. Make your statement about one fourth the length of the original but omit no essential parts.

About the simplest and most completely controlled methods of learning to write are transcription and writing from dictation. Let us take these as an example. Suppose you made a resolution (and kept it) to copy carefully every day twenty lines of good prose, after having read them aloud slowly and expressively two or three times; while you were transcribing, keeping your attention concentrated upon the values and placing of the words, noting the relations among the words, and asking yourself the reason for the choice and placing of all important words. Suppose, moreover, you resolved to learn by heart some lines of first-rate prose or verse every week. And finally suppose you planned to take down from dictation a complete paragraph once or twice a week—a paragraph read to you by someone who knew how to break up the sentences into their natural and rhetorical phrasing. Can there be any doubt that by the end of a year you would have learned more about the craft of writing than you have ever learned in an equal time by following rules?

ROBERT M. GAY
from *Reading and Writing*

Assignment 6

In your journal do *one* of the following:
  a. Copy out a passage from a short story and then make a précis of it.
  b. Copy carefully a short poem that you like. Then make a paraphrase of it.
  c. Outline or summarize a plan for a short story of your own.

4|3

START THINKING

What is to be said here may, at first, strike you as a repetition of the previous lesson. Not so. There the concern was that you sharpen your ability to follow the ideas of others. The ability to understand and clearly report the thoughts of another is an admirable first step not only in clarity, but also in reflection. For you see how the job of reflection is done when carried out properly. But marshaling your own thoughts is another matter.

In this lesson you will be concerned with your own thoughts, ways to test them, and ways to make them grow. One of the best ways to move forward with your thinking is to find out what other people and other cultures have said on a subject. This is a tradition within which all artists work. They expand their own thoughts by exposing their minds and imaginations to the cultural imagination of the world. This is but another way of saying that one way to start thinking is to expose yourself to the world of ideas. Reading will give you something to bounce your own ideas against. It is assumed that in your subsequent writing you will take care to acknowledge the other fellow's thought.

Reading and discussion are both good ways to start thinking. If you have ever been in an argument, you know how the reasoning of another can force you to the clearest statement of which you are capable; in the heat of a discussion you have probably found yourself presenting good reasons that had never occurred to you before. One way to do your own thinking is to test your ideas against the ideas of others—and a good way to do that is to read and discuss reading. But before you start, set down whatever you have for ideas on your subject. List your concepts. Then read and discuss and see what happens to your ideas and your idea inventory. Don't be driven by every wind; take responsibility for your own ideas, but remember Robinson's observations:

We are incredibly heedless in the formation of
our beliefs, but find ourselves filled with an illicit
passion for them when anyone proposes to rob us
of their companionship. It is obviously not the
ideas themselves that are dear to us, but our self-
esteem, which is threatened.

JAMES HARVEY ROBINSON
from *The Mind in the Making*

Another good way to start thinking is to start writing. A
great deal of evidence suggests that we catch ideas with our
pens. Here is some evidence:

> There is a paradox in this matter of knowing and
> telling, however, which is of first importance. For
> a reason hard to understand, we do not seem to
> have a full grasp on experience itself until we have
> symbolized it in some fashion; we do not know
> until we have *told*. The telling may be done, of
> course, by many kinds of symbols—words spoken
> or written, musical notes, paints brushed on can-
> vas, and so on. But whatever the kind of symbol,
> it appears to be true that we do not really know
> our experiences until we have expressed them. Yet
> it is also certainly true that when we express, we
> express *something;* that is to say, we do not use
> words at random when we begin to write about an
> experience but instead seem to be directed by our
> unexpressed consciousness of the experience to
> choose certain words and ignore others.

HAROLD C. MARTIN
from *The Logic and
Rhetoric of Exposition*

And here is a more personal statement about the effect of
writing on thinking:

> My own method is to give no thought whatever
> to the form of what I am writing. I put down my
> ideas as they present themselves pell mell to my
> mind, fanciful, extravagant, sentimental, bawdy,

irreverent, irrelevant, they are all equally welcome. In going over my work, however, I am prepared to spend a great deal of care in endeavoring to find the just word or an adequate balance for any particular paragraph. I have noticed that when I am writing at my best I experience a peculiar physical sensation. I first became aware of this peculiarity at school as a boy of twelve when we were given an essay to write on the Pied Piper. I have never been able to think a subject through before writing. I daresay I should do much better if it were my nature to adopt such a method. I consider the greatest difficulty to be overcome by immature, untrained writers is lack of confidence. They are too self-conscious. When once the pen is in the hand it is important to forget about the opinion of others and to write away after your own fashion with careless, proud indifference.

"Letter to Warner Taylor"
from *Types and Times in the Essay*
selected and arranged by Warner Taylor

One of the key ways to start thinking is to make "think time." We are all apt to lose the point of what we are doing in the sheer doing of it. Develop your powers of reflection by reflecting. Then share your thoughts with your readers. The journal is an ideal place.

We all have daily fires to put out. Most of us are too busy doing to think. Thinking takes time, so make time. Here are some rules for reflection:

1. *Make reflection a personal must.* Build "think time" into your daily schedule; give it priority.
2. *Explore "areas of agreement."* Look for spots where your own personal interests fit with the general pattern of your work or assignments.
3. *Focus your interest.* Start with a single topic; you can't think about "everything" at once.
4. *Collect data.* Books, experience, observation, and conversation are the prime suppliers.
5. *Get specific.* Give examples; make distinctions.
6. *Keep a record of your thoughts.*

That's about as far as rules will take us—which may be no place at all. In the end you have to do your own thinking in your own way. Your next journal entry is a chance to demonstrate how well you do it. Here are some check points that will help you see how well you or any writer succeeds.

1. Is there a generalization?
2. Is the generalization true?
3. Is the generalization worth making?
4. Is the generalization supported?
5. Is the total expression felicitous?

Assignment 7

1. Allow ten minutes to reread and consider the material presented in this chapter.
2. In your journal do *one* of the following:
   a. Reread the rules given in this chapter. Then pay particular attention to them as you write on a subject with which you are thoroughly familiar.
   b. Read one of your previous journal entries. Then write a short paragraph exploring your own method of "catching ideas."
   c. Practice automatic writing (writing freely done with a noncritical mind) for three to five minutes just to see what ideas can be caught with your pen. Then revise the automatic writing. Take care to find the just word and to establish coherence and balance in your paragraph.

Assignment 8

That there are no really brand-new ideas is a fact every psychologist knows. Creative thinking is just another name for finding new idea-combinations.

How do you hit upon new combinations? The recipe is obvious: Have a large number of ideas and experiences on hand; put them together; stir vigorously. Or, more concretely: Have a well-stocked mind; and, as William James put it, "get your mind whirling and see what happens."

RUDOLF FLESCH
from *The Art of Readable Writing*

1. Read the preceding excerpt.
2. In your journal do *one* of the following:
   a. Present some pet idea or philosophy of yours—one that you have had in mind for some time. Write for half an hour on this subject about which you have strong feelings or beliefs.
   b. Think back on your own experience with your journal. How has it helped you? What could you do to improve as a writer?
   c. "Remember the importance of being able to laugh at man and his works." Recall or create a humorous situation, and then present it in your journal.

Assignment 9

. . . the truth of fiction involves such matters as the following: (1) the consistency and comprehensibility of character; (2) the motivation and credibility of action; and (3) the acceptability of the total meaning. As for the method of fiction, it should also be evident, even at this point, that these three matters, character, action, and theme, are intimately bound up together.

CLEANTH BROOKS and ROBERT PENN WARREN
from *Understanding Fiction*

As we move toward our ultimate goal of becoming creative writers—of telling our own story in our own way—we do well to consider the interrelation of plot, character, and theme. Let's start with character. In a story, events (plot) must modify character. The hero at the start is never the same as the hero at the end. A white horse may go unchanged through a great many adventures, but his rider should be intelligent and sensitive enough to register change. Story starts with conflict that produces change. If the events related are not important enough to have an impact on the central character, there is little chance they will affect an intelligent reader. Hence the need to develop an understanding of the relation between character and plot. Both have to be credible—not just possible but believable. One way of managing the kind of practice we've been talking about is by considering idea or theme and its relation to character and event. Hawthorne used his journal for just this purpose, as Newton Arvin explains:

> The difference, after all, between Hawthorne and any of those other writers of journals is the only too manifest difference between a philosopher or an essayist and a teller of tales. Not general ideas for their own sake, or personal experience on its own level, but dramatic conceptions, the fruit of imaginative revery, or observations of the external world, men and women no less than inanimate nature—these are the central substance of Hawthorne's journals. Much, no doubt, might be made of them taken merely by themselves; their real interest yields itself only to the reader who keeps in mind the figure of the prose romancer behind them. Here one can observe, almost without obstacle, the restless play of Hawthorne's imagination over the strange data of the moral world, entertaining one possibility after another, returning again and again to characteristic conceptions, and betraying always the special temper of his mind. Here in the journals, not always easily recognizable, are the original statements of the organizing ideas in tale after tale as we are now familiar with them in *Twice-Told Tales* or the *Mosses* or the *Snow Image;* here is that extraordinary series of notes, beginning as early as 1836, in which the complicated unity of *The Scarlet Letter* grad-

ually asserts itself; here is the leading dramatic note of *The Blithedale Romance*, stated some sixteen years before the book was undertaken. . . .

from *The Heart of Hawthorne's Journals*

A single excerpt from the *Journal* of October 14, 1837, will suggest how idea can be made to shape theme, event, and character. This journal entry is Hawthorne's seminal idea for his story "The Birthmark."

A person to be in the possession of something as perfect as mortal man has a right to demand; he tries to make it better, and ruins it entirely.

To see how such a notation may structure story, read "The Birthmark." As you read, consider the way in which character, action, and theme are interrelated.

Here are exercises that may further your own skill as a teller of tales.

In your journal do *one* of the following:
   a. Take a short story and find its theme. Reflect on the story and its theme. Then comment on its value as story and idea.
   b. List your ideas on any topic. Then do such reading and discussing of the topic as time permits. List the new ideas or information acquired.
   c. Recall an experience in your life that required reflection; for example, recall the period before an examination.
       (1) Report what went on in your mind.
       (2) Report what went on in your emotions.
       (3) Write a piece that imaginatively combines points 1 and 2 above.

44

SOME THINGS TO THINK ABOUT

The world is so full of a number of things I'm
sure we should all be as happy as kings and you
know how happy they are.

FRANKLIN PIERCE ADAMS
from *The Poetry Cure*

The number of things and the points of view one may
take toward them guarantee that one will never run out of
subject matter. The notion of not having anything to write
about is absurd. Clearly there is enough to write about even
if you limit yourself to a discussion of the stars—one by one
—or kings, or days, or anything.

The writer's problem—if he has one, and he usually does
—is not subject matter but personal interest. The writer's
first responsibility is to interest his reader, and his best chance
of doing that is to be interested himself. No less a writer
than E. B. White gives us this advice: "Even in evil times, a
writer should cultivate only what naturally absorbs his fancy,
whether it be freedom or cinch bugs, and should write in the
way that comes easy."

Thinking can't be done in a vacuum. You'll need some
facts, impressions, and ideas to get you started. Presumably
you already have a large and growing supply of those good
things. The problem you will be considering here is what to
do with them.

First, look for similarities. What are the likenesses between
any two objects? Second, what are the differences between
any two objects? Third, how can these objects that are related or unrelated be joined in such a way as to create a
unique relationship—one never before established? As you
start reflecting about any matter you will at some point become aware of ironies that exist when you relate it to other

objects. For example, there may be nothing at first ironic in the idea of a sandwich. But if you are now hungry and have money in your pocket but can't get a sandwich, you may find that situation ironic. Irony exists in many forms, any one of which may be useful to you as you think on your subject. For irony gives depth; of necessity it reveals aspects of a matter that are not apparent on the surface. And that is what reflection aims at; seeing into matters more fully, more imaginatively, and more creatively than when looking only at the surface or, similarly, when seeing events in isolation.

These are some proper or at least possible steps that you may take when starting to reflect, but remember that when you write about your reflections, the key word is *coherence*. Reflection may be as random as chaos, but your reportage of it must be clear and hence orderly. But here our focus is on stimulating thought. The first rule is to give your ideas freedom. Explore before you pin down. Live with ideas rather than demand instant solution—but pick solutions! An example will illustrate.

> In October 1833 the great English scientist William Henry Fox Talbot sat "on the lovely shores of the Lake of Como," reflecting on the "inimitable beauty" before him. "It was during these thoughts that the idea occurred to me," he wrote later, "how charming it would be if it were possible to cause these natural images to imprint themselves durably and remain fixed upon the paper."
>
> In January of 1834, Talbot returned to England and went to work in his laboratory. The remembrance of Como's beauty drove him on, as did the knowledge that the Frenchman, Louis Daguerre, was working in the same direction. The two men today share the honor of inventing photography, but Como shares with no other spot the honor of having inspired it.
>
> FRANC SHOR
> from "Lombardy's Lakes, Blue Jewels in Italy's Crown"

Of course there is no formula for invention, but to the receptive mind nature does suggest analogies and metaphor. As Talbot's experience suggests, insights can't be forced, but they can be responded to. Some measure of inventive response is sure to be ours if we keep ideas and then associations free. As suggested earlier, one way of finding insight is to take any two seemingly unrelated objects or terms, and then look at the ways in which they are similar. For example, suppose we start with a pair of terms that are seeming opposites—"reflections" and "first impressions" should serve our purposes. We might begin our exploration by asking, "How are these two terms related?" In reply we might say, "Both are in English, both are on this same page, both use some of the same letters"—all of which doesn't seem to get us anywhere. Still it is a way of avoiding the stereotype and of getting started.

In this process of looking for likeness, it may occur to us that "first impressions" can be the cause of prejudice—prejudice that dominates subsequent "thought" and kills reflection. It has happened! Then, too, both "reflection" and formation of "first impressions" happen in time, and both acts require people. We are, of course, not seeking to prove anything. We are just playing around, loosening up our minds by thinking about ways in which these expressions are alike.

For step two, we ask "How do these two terms differ?" "First impressions" suggests a quick and immediate act whereas "reflection" suggests a slow and deliberate process. "First impressions" requires little or no support, but "reflection" suggests examined thought.

And now we come to step three—a bit hurriedly to be sure, but it's always a rough step or a long leap to three. Here our goal is to relate the term to objects, words, and ideas in such a way as to show or suggest fresh relationships. Perhaps a poem will illustrate the point. Remember "Richard Cory"? The poem dramatizes the discrepancy created by the man's appearance and way of life, and his final act. The poem "gives us something to think about." We are forced to reflect on the difference between "first impressions" and the insight that is the fruit of reflection.

Here is the poem. It may prompt you to reflect on the difference between appearance and reality.

Richard Cory

Whenever Richard Cory went downtown,
We people on the pavement looked at him:
He was a gentleman from sole to crown,
Clean favored, and imperially slim.

And he was always quietly arrayed,
And he was always human when he talked;
But still he fluttered pulses when he said,
"Good morning," and he glittered when he walked.

And he was rich—yes, richer than a king—
And admirably schooled in every grace:
In fine, we thought that he was everything
To make us wish that we were in his place.

So on we worked, and waited for the light,
And went without the meat, and cursed the bread;
And Richard Cory, one calm summer night,
Went home and put a bullet through his head.

EDWIN ARLINGTON ROBINSON

This poem shows one way that observation and imagination can combine with reflection to produce new entities or insights. That these activities are not isolated—except to facilitate study—is illustrated by our own experience as well as that of the scientist at Lake Como.

When you start on this business of reflecting, you never know where you are going. Let your mind be free.

Here is the testimony of the writer John Gunther, who explains how he preserves and associates ideas:

> Above all, I would repeat to anybody interested in journalism, "Write it down!" . . . So—write down at once what you want to remember and

write it down *in full*. . . . At last, when work on
the notes is finished, when sources have been
checked and essential reading has been done, it is
time to write. . . . The key to sustained writing
is concentration, saturation, and the trick is to
get your subconscious to work for you. I write
while I sleep. The hard job is to build up the
charge that carries you through. Once an illustri-
ous writer, engaged busily on an article, mentioned
to me casually, but with astonishment, that she
had become so excited about her project that she
found herself writing down notes and phrases
wherever she went—in taxis, on menus at lunches,
and so on. I listened with incredulity. Any time I
am well along on a book I do the same thing, and
have done so for many years. It astounded me that
she had never had this experience before. If, while
working, I do not reach out for odd bits of paper
several times a day, no matter where I am, and
scribble on them, I know that my work is not
going well. Usually, too, I keep a pad on the bed
table. The most germinal of all creative periods is,
in my experience, the hour at night that comes
after a spurt of work is finished. . . . Another
important factor is pace. For me the way to achieve
pace is to cut, cut, cut. In the most extraordinary
way, which I cannot explain, part of what you cut
from a book stays with it. Of course, there can be
such a thing as too much cutting; this rubs the
bloom off. Also paragraphing is of the utmost importance. Sometimes it is effective to combine two
different themes in the same paragraph; I know no
device better calculated to keep the reader's nose
to the page. Punctuation counts for a good deal as
well. My favorite punctuation mark is the semi-
colon; it gives the reader a bit of breath, but does
not destroy continuity. My favorite words are adjectives. One device is to put adjectives together in
an unexpected sequence. For instance, say about
somebody that he is "a coarse, brilliant man." But

the effect of this is ruined if you insert an "and" or a "but" between "coarse" and "brilliant." Even the most insignificant words or phrases can assist or destroy cadence and euphony. There can be a vast difference between "et cetera" and "and so forth" at the end of a sentence. . . .

I write almost everything, if I have time, three times. This is a curse. I fiddle and faddle. It is my ill fortune never to be able to write a good first draft; I happen, alas, to be one of those luckless creatures who can never get anything right on the initial attempt. First I do an insanely hurried rough draft. I can typewrite ten pages, say 2000 words, in about three hours. Then this must be revised—often rewritten. My experience is that revision takes just as long as the original writing, perhaps longer. If it takes me three hours to write a section of a chapter, it will take me three hours or more to revise it. Sometimes hardly a word of the original script survives. . . .

Perhaps the reader will ask what, in the last analysis, determines *what* I write. I try to report facts as I see them and to tell the truth, but truth is an elusive concept. I think it was Frank Lloyd Wright who once said, "The truth is more important than the facts." I would hesitate to recommend this maxim unreservedly to a school of journalism, but surely what Mr. Wright meant is clear—that selection of facts can be as important as the facts themselves. . . .

Why do I write? I suppose the best answer to this is that basically I write for myself, to satisfy my own multiple curiosities. In other words, my work has been a kind of exercise in self-education at the public's expense. I myself am a fairly good average guinea pig, and if something interests me I am reasonably sure it will interest the general reader too.

JOHN GUNTHER
from *A Fragment of Autobiography*

In other words, literature not only leads us toward the regaining of identity, but it also separates this state from its opposite, the world we don't like and want to get away from. The tone literature takes toward this world is not a moralizing tone, but the tone we call ironic. The effect of irony is to enable us to see over the head of a situation—we have irony in a play, for example, when we know more about what's going on than the characters do —and so to detach us, at least in imagination, from the world we'd prefer not to be involved with.

NORTHROP FRYE
from The Educated Imagination

Assignment 10

1. Read the chapter up to this point.
2. In your journal do *one* of the following:
   a. Outline the three steps presented here and then show that they do or do not apply to the poem or any short précis of reflection.
   b. Write a poem or a journal entry that presents the difference between appearance and reality.
   c. Write on a subject of your own choice, or start an anthology of hypotheses; use ideas that develop outside class. Jot them down and then try them out in conversations and journal entries.

Assignment 11

Here is a journal entry by Thoreau and a poem by a modern poet. You'll note there are several similarities.

I saw a small hawk fly along under the hillside and light on the ground, its breast and belly pure downy white. It was a very handsome bird. Though they are not fitted to walk much on the ground,

but to soar, yet its feet, which are but claws to seize
its prey and hold to its perch, are handsome append-
ages, and it is a very interesting sight on the
ground. Yet there is a certain unfitness in so fair a
breast, so pure white, made to breast nothing less
pure than the sky or clouds, coming so nearly in
contact with the earth. Never bespattered with the
mud of earth. That was the impression made on me
—of a very pure breast, accustomed to float on the
sky, in contact with the earth. It stood quite still,
watching me, as if it was not easy for it to walk.

from *The Journal*
of Henry David Thoreau, Vol. IV

The Gull

Riding the wind, in planetary sweep
The gull wheels on the radius of a wing;
Ocean and air, concourse of height and deep,
Acclaim the exultant orbit of their king.

Precise he lands, defter than any dancer,
Red legs, red eye, white body, whiter than foam;
No loveliest yacht so light to lean and answer,
No soul so white in its celestial home.

O Attic joy, O grace made visible,
Beauty and joy embodied into bird!
Malice, or truth—which is it pricks your spell
With sarcasm of the loathsome and absurd?

Those lacquered feathers, sleek to wind and wave,
Or downy to the softly fingering breeze,
Are an infested jungle, a living grave,
The haunt of lice, mites, parasites, and fleas.

Filth feeds that savage beauty; when head, beak, eyes
Plunge in the putrid whale, or, harsh as sin,
Are stretched agape, with cannibalistic cries,
To tear the wounded body of his kin.

O beauty born of death, to death returning,
You are our Middle Earth, nor Heaven nor Hell;
You are ourselves, our turning globe still turning,
The fractured light in which we have to dwell.

Here truth is ever tangent. Therefore, gull,
Gorged with the stinking offal that you eat,
Rise in the light, infested, beautiful,
In fragmentary loveliness complete.

MICHAEL THWAITES

1. Read the pieces by Thoreau and Thwaites.
2. In your journal do *one* of the following:
   a. Explain what the poet has done to enhance the value of his bird-watching; for example, discuss his use of contrast and idea.
   b. Get at the poet's idea of the gull by writing a paraphrase or a précis of the poem.
   c. Copy a reflective passage of prose or poetry. Then write a précis of it.

Assignment 12

Reflection has too often been associated with black gowns and stern faces. But reflections can be amusing:

OBSERVER: INTERPRETATIONS ON A TUFFET

WASHINGTON, March 24—Little Miss Muffet, as everyone knows, sat on a tuffet eating her curds and whey when along came a spider who sat down beside her and frightened Miss Muffet away. While everyone knows it, the significance of the event had never been analyzed until a conference of thinkers recently brought their special insights to bear upon it. Following are excerpts from the transcript of their discussion:

Sociologist: We are clearly dealing with a proto-typical illustration of a highly tensile social structure's tendency to dis- or perhaps even de-structure itself under the pressures created when optimum minimums do not obtain among the disadvantaged. Miss Muffet is nutritionally underprivileged, as evidenced by the subminimal diet of curds and whey upon which she is forced to subsist, while the spider's cultural disadvantage is evidenced by such phenomena as legs exceeding standard norms, odd mating habits and so forth.

In this instance, spider expectations lead the culturally disadvantaged to assert demands to share the tuffet with the nutritionally underprivileged. Due to a communications failure, Miss Muffet assumes without evidence that the spider will not be satisfied to share her tuffet, but will also insist on eating her curds and whey. Thus, the failure to preestablish selectively optimum norm structures leads to . . .

Militarist: Second-strike capability, sir! That's what was lacking. If Miss Muffet had developed a second-strike capability instead of squandering her resources on curds and whey, no spider on earth would have dared launch a first strike capable of carrying him right to the heart of her tuffet. I am confident that Miss Muffet had adequate notice from experts that she could not afford both curds and whey and at the same time support an early-spider-warning system. Yet curds alone were not good enough for Miss Muffet. She had to have whey, too. Tuffet security must be the first responsibility of every diner. . . .

Book Reviewer: Written on several levels, this searing sensitive exploration of the arachnid heart illuminates the agony and splendor of Jewish family life with a candor that is at once breathtaking in its simplicity and soul-shattering in its implied ambiguity. Some will doubtless be shocked to see such subjects as tuffets and whey discussed without flinching, but hereafter writers too timid to call a tuffet a tuffet will no longer . . .

Editorial Writer: Why has the Government not seen fit to tell the public all it knows about the so-called curds-and-whey affair? It is not enough to suggest that this was merely a random incident involving a lonely spider and a young diner. In today's world, poised as it is on the knife edge of . . .

Psychiatrist: Little Miss Muffet is, of course, neither little, nor a miss. These are obviously the self she has created in her own fantasies to escape the reality that she is a gross divorcee whose superego makes it impossible for her to sustain a normal relationship with any man, symbolized by the spider, who, of course, has no existence outside her fantasies. She may, in fact, be a man with deeply repressed Oedipal impulses who sees in the spider the father he would like to kill, and very well may some day unless he admits that what he believes to be a tuffet is, in fact, probably the dining-room chandelier and that the whey he thinks he is eating is in fact, probably . . .

Flower Child: This beautiful kid is on a bad trip. Like . . .

Student Demonstrators: Little Miss Muffet, tuffets, curds, whey, and spiders are what's wrong with education today. They're irrelevant. Tuffets are irrelevant. Curds are irrelevant. Whey is irrelevant. Meaningful experience! How can you have relevance without meaningful experience? And how can there ever be meaningful experience without understanding? With understanding and meaningfulness and relevance, there can be love and good and deep seriousness and education today will be freed of slavery and Little Miss Muffet, and life will become meaningful.

Child: This is about a little girl who gets scared by a spider.

(The child was sent home when the conference

broke for lunch. It was agreed that the child was too immature to add anything to the sum of human understanding and should not come back until he had grown up.)

RUSSELL BAKER

from *The New York Times,* March 25, 1969

Not all reflections are intrinsically funny, but imagination can sharpen and enliven them, as you will see by reading this excerpt from *The Book:*

For there is a growing apprehension that existence is a rat-race in a trap: living organisms, including people, are merely tubes which put things in at one end and let them out at the other, which both keeps them doing it and in the long run wears them out. So to keep the farce going, the tubes find ways of making new tubes, which also put things in at one end and let them out at the other. At the input end they even develop ganglia of nerves called brains, with eyes and ears, so that they can more easily scrounge around for things to swallow. As and when they get enough to eat, they use up their surplus energy by wiggling in complicated patterns, making all sorts of noises by blowing air in and out of the input hole, and gathering together in groups to fight with other groups. In time, the tubes grow such an abundance of attached appliances that they are hardly recognizable as mere tubes, and they manage to do this in a staggering variety of forms. There is a vague rule not to eat tubes of your own form, but in general there is serious competition as to who is going to be the top type of tube. All this seems marvelously futile, and yet, when you begin to think about it, it begins to be more marvelous than futile. Indeed, it seems extremely odd.

ALAN WATTS

from *The Book*

Still there are times when a serious subject responds best to a thoroughly serious tone.

In the evolution of scientific thought, one fact has become impressively clear: there is no mystery of the physical world which does not point to a mystery beyond itself. All highroads of the intellect, all byways of theory and conjecture lead ultimately to an abyss that human ingenuity can never span. For man is enchained by the very condition of his being, his finiteness and involvement in nature. The farther he extends his horizons, the more vividly he recognizes the fact that as the physicist Neils Bohr puts it, "we are both spectators and actors in the great drama of existence." Man is thus his own greatest mystery. He does not understand the vast veiled universe into which he has been cast for the reason that he does not understand himself. He comprehends but little of his organic processes and even less of his unique capacity to perceive the world about him, to reason and to dream. Least of all does he understand his noblest and most mysterious faculty: the ability to transcend himself and perceive himself in the act of perception.

LINCOLN BARNETT
from *The Universe and Dr. Einstein*

Perhaps one of the best devices for developing your power as a writer is to practice humor. Nothing, save poetry, puts such a premium on the right word in the right place. If you can recall the agony of listening to a joke badly told, you already know how important pace, event, and conclusion are to story. Use this journal exercise to sharpen your own narrative skill. Start by playing with humor.

1. Read the three preceding observations.
2. In your journal do *one* of the following:
    a. Find a short passage of serious thought. Express the

same idea in a humorous vein. Read some selections by Mark Twain if you need help.

b. Write a humorous scene for a short story. Don't concern yourself with plot—simply present characters in action. Make it funny but avoid slapstick.

c. Start a short story based on irony of first impressions.

4|5

GIVE YOUR IDEAS SHAPE

The concept of form is one of the most difficult of literary ideas. Yet in fact it is most simple. Here shape means exactly what it means in geometry or at the shoemaker's. A box has a standard number of sides and that is its shape, or form. You may build your boxes for matches or dynamite, but basically the form remains, whether platonic or pine; the idea of box is simply a variation on a theme. Some may look boxier than others, but within a very wide range we are comfortable in calling numerous objects boxlike.

Poetry has a thousand variations, but as a form it is as easy to recognize as a box. So too with all literary forms: short story, essay, novel, etc. The broad limits of each form are defined for us in a hundred different places. No particular short story, or particular poem, has to fit the particular definition exactly, but as *box* carries a sense of tangible shape, so too do literary forms. Get to know the shape and feel of each of these terms: poetry, short story, essay, novel.

Here is some specific advice by the author of a great many novels, Anthony Trollope. What he has to say about novel-writing may be applied, with a little judicious judgment, to many of your attempts to give ideas shape.

> The writer of stories must please, or he will be nothing. And he must teach whether he wish to teach or no. . . . A good novel should be both [realistic and sensational], and both in the highest degree. If a novel fail in either, there is a failure in art. Let those readers who believe that they do not like sensational scenes in novels think of some of those passages from our great novelists which have charmed them most. . . . As in poetry, so in prose, he who can deal adequately with tragic elements is a greater artist and reaches a higher aim

than the writer whose efforts never carry him above the milk walks of everyday life. . . . I have from the first felt sure that the writer, when he sits down to commence his novel, should do so, not because he has to tell a story, but because he has a story to tell. The novelist's first novel will generally have sprung from the right cause. Some series of events, or some development of character, will have presented itself to his imagination—and this he feels so strongly that he thinks he can present his picture in strong and agreeable language to others. He sits down and tells his story because he has a story to tell; as you, my friend, when you have heard something which has at once tickled your fancy or moved your pathos, will hurry to tell it to the first person you meet. . . . But many young fail also, because they endeavor to tell stories when they have none to tell. And this comes from idleness rather than from innate incapacity. The mind has not been sufficiently at work when the tale has been commenced, nor is it kept sufficiently at work as the tale is continued. I have never troubled myself much about the construction of plots, and am not now insisting specially on thoroughness in a branch of work in which I myself have not been very thorough. I am not sure that the construction of a perfected plot has been at any period within my power. But the novelist has other aims than the elucidation of his plot. He desires to make his readers so intimately acquainted with his characters that the creatures of his brain should be to them speaking, moving, living, human creatures. This he can never do unless he knows those fictitious personages himself, and he can never know them unless he can live with them in the full reality of established intimacy. They must be with him as he lies down to sleep, and as he wakes from his dreams. He must learn to hate them and to love them. He must argue with them, quarrel with them, forgive them, and even submit to them. He must know of them whether they be cold-blooded or passionate, whether true or false, and how far true, and how far false. The depth and the breadth, and the narrowness and the shallowness of each should be clear to him. And, as here, in our outer world, we know that men and women change—become worse or better as temptation or conscience may guide them —so should these creations of his change, and every change should be noted by him. On the last day of each month recorded, every person in his novel should be a month older than on the first. If the would-be novelist has aptitudes that way, all this will come to him without much struggling; but if it does not come, I think he can only make novels of wood. . . . It is the first necessity of his position that he make himself pleasant. To do this, much more is necessary than to write correctly. He may indeed be pleasant without being correct, as I think can be proved by the works of more than one distinguished novelist. But he must be intelligible—intelligible without trouble; and he must be harmonious. . . . The novel-writer who sticks to novel-writing as his profession will certainly find that this burden of length is incumbent on him. How shall he carry his burden to the end? How shall he cover his space? . . . Though the novel which you have to write must be long, let it be all one. And this exclusion of episodes should be carried down into the smallest details. Every sentence and every word used should tend to the telling of the story. "But," the young novelist will say, "with so many pages before me to be filled, how shall I succeed if I thus confine myself; how am I to know beforehand what space this story of mine will require? There must be the three volumes, or the certain number of magazine pages which I have contracted to supply. If I may not be discursive should occasion require, how shall I complete my task? The painter suits the size of his canvas to his subject, and must I in my art stretch my subject to my canvas?" This undoubtedly must be done by the novelist; and, if he will learn his business, may be done without injury to his effect. He may not paint different pictures on the same canvas, which he will do if he allows himself to wander away to matters outside his own story; but by studying proportion in his work, he may teach himself so to tell his story that it shall naturally fall into the required length. Though his story should be all one, yet it may have many parts. Though the plot itself may require but few characters, it may be so enlarged as to find its full development in many. There may be subsidiary plots, which shall all tend to the elucidation of the main story, and which will take their places as part of one and the same work—as there may be many figures on a canvas which shall not to the spectator seem to form themselves into separate pictures. There is no portion of a novelist's work in which this fault of episodes is so common as in the dialogue. It is so easy to make any two persons talk on any casual subject with which the writer presumes himself to be conversant! Literature, philosophy, politics, or sport, may thus be handled in a loosely discursive style; and the writer, while indulging himself and filling his pages, is apt to think that he is pleasing his reader. I think he can make no greater mistake. The dialogue is generally the most agreeable part of a novel; but it is only so as long as it tends in some way to the telling of the main story. It need not seem to be confined to that, but it should always have a tendency in that direction. . . . And the dialogue, on which the modern novelist in consulting the taste of his probable readers must depend most, has to be constrained also by other rules. The writer may tell much of his story in conversations, but he may only do so by putting such words into the mouths of his personages as persons so situated would probably use. He is not allowed for the sake of his tale to make his characters give utterance to long speeches, such as are not customarily heard from men and women. The ordinary talk of ordinary people is carried on in short, sharp, expressive sentences, which very frequently are never completed—the language of which even among educated people is often incorrect. The novel-writer in constructing his dialogue must so steer between absolute accuracy of language—which would give to his conversation an air of pedantry, and the slovenly inaccuracy of ordinary talkers, which if closely followed would offend by an appearance of grimace as to produce upon the ear of his readers a sense of reality. If he be quite real he will seem to attempt to be funny. If he be quite correct he will seem to be unreal. And above all, let the speeches be short. No character should utter much above a dozen words at a breath—unless the writer can justify to himself a longer flood of speech by the specialty of the occasion. In all this, human nature must be the novel-writer's guide. . . . But in following human nature he must remember that he does so with a pen in his hand, and that the reader who will appreciate human nature will also demand artistic ability and literary aptitude. The young novelist will probably ask, or more probably bethink himself, how he is to acquire that knowledge of human nature which will tell him with accuracy what men and women would say in this or that position. He must acquire it as the compositor, who is to print his words, has learned the art of distributing his type—by constant and intelligent practice. Unless it be given to him to listen and to observe—so to carry away, as it were, the manners of people in his memory, as to be able to say to himself with assurance that these words might have been said in a given position, and that those other words could not have been said, I do not think that in these days he can succeed as a novelist. And then let him beware of creating tedium! . . . I know no guard against this so likely to be effective as the feeling of the writer himself.

from *The Autobiography of Anthony Trollope*

Assignment 13

1. Read the chapter up to this point.
2. In your journal do *one* of the following:
   a. Outline or summarize the points made in the Trollope reading.
   b. Apply the points made in the Trollope essay to a particular short story. Explain how the author of the story puts them to use.
   c. Make your reader intimately acquainted with a character.

Assignment 14

Between Stevenson and Poe I confess I can hardly imagine a stranger or more puzzling parallel. I leave aside, in deference to such aesthetic critics, everything except aesthetic criticism. I say nothing of secondary matters like morality and philosophy and a whole outlook on life. I toss aside such trifles as belief, doubt, despair, pessimism, piety, faith, hope, and charity. Considering art simply as a method of calling up certain visions or adumbrating certain atmospheres, it seems to me that no two great artists could possibly be more unlike each other than Stevenson and Poe. The atmospheres they tried to create were quite opposite; the technical tricks by which they tried to create them were quite opposite. It was the purpose of Poe to suggest not merely horror but hopelessness. It was the whole point of Stevenson that he never did suggest hopelessness even when he suggested horror. Or, to put the matter another way, he always suggested a fight, even when it was a hopeless fight. The two brothers of the house of Durrisdeer go down fighting to the last. The people of the house of Usher never begin fighting even from the first. I find it difficult to believe, even in fact of the text, that Dr. Jekyll and Mr. Hyde will not go on fighting, if it were only fighting in hell. But when the other gentleman had his rather one-sided conversation with the raven, that raven did not croak over a battlefield.

As I have said I did not mean merely the matter of moral atmosphere, but of purely artistic atmosphere. Stevenson's technical method is lean, wiry, taut, and alert. If he seems too much to be picking his words, to be watchful of his style, it is because he is above all things very wide-awake. It is the whole point and pleasure and beauty of the poetry of Poe that he is half-asleep. Consider those dreamy melodies, those drowsy repetitions, like everlasting echoes of an endless snore. And compare them with the short-lined, sharply worded verses of "R.L.S.," generally rather too bald and angular to be quite good poetry. Poe was above all things luxuriant. He loved, in the literal sense of the phrase, the luxury of woe. He was at home on rich but somber cushions "That the lamp-light gloated o'er"; but it was not only the lamp-light that gloated. I defy anyone to find one sentence in all the collected works of Robert Louis Stevenson in which it can be said that he gloated. It might be said that he sometimes tasted too fastidiously or that he sometimes snapped up too sharply. But he never wallowed in purple seas of woe; and it was the whole point of Stevenson that the seas were infinite and unfathomable. Poe's people are not people who have been made unhappy, like Henry Durie or Robert Herrick, or who have made themselves unhappy, like Dr. Jekyll or Markheim; they are people who never could conceivably have been happy. They are unhappy before they are unfortunate. They are tragic before their tragedy begins. With Poe the mood was the fundamental thing; and it was a mood of incurable melancholy. It was, of course, the essence of the Stevensonian spirit that the melancholy was not incurable even if the misfortune was incurable.

But I am not speaking for the moment of such ethical motives, but merely of artistic methods and artistic effects. And this vigilance, and alertness and spirit of choice is in the very style of Stevenson. It is also in the very imagery of Stevenson. He loved above all things what was clean-cut and clearly colored; nothing could be less like the magnificent monochrome of the other writer's dark libraries and dim corridors. The things that Stevenson liked were things like the chip of hard wood hacked out of the wooden sign of the Admiral Ben Bow by the cutlass of Billy Bones the buccaneer. They were things like the crutch of the horrible cripple, that went flashing in the tropical sun sped on its errand of death. In short, the things he loved were almost always solid and were generally self-evident in the sun. Even when they were not, as in the duel scene of *The Master of Ballantrae,* the starlight seems as hard as the steel and the candle-flames as steady as the swords. Surely nothing could have so little of the dark halls and drowsy odors in which the brains of the other heroes brilliantly decayed. Stevenson afterward regretted the exaggeration which had made Mrs. Durie wipe the sword blade by driving it into the frozen soil. But it was a truly Stevensonian exaggeration, for it was an exaggeration of what was hard and acute. He was always working with a sharp blade on a hard ground.

This fact appears in his real failure as well as his real success. Where he failed, as compared with the great Victorian novelists, was in being too severe with himself and with his characters. He described a character in a few strokes where the

Victorians described him in a hundred little touches. The strokes were artistically exactly right —almost too right. For while the few strokes only give the impression of being right, the many touches give the impression of being real. Long John Silver's crutch always comes in at the right moment, and is almost too solid to be true. The Colonel's bamboo cane comes in quite casually in Thackeray's novel, and we cannot remember how many times it has been mentioned; but we are all the more sure that there really was a cane and that there really was a Colonel. There is no gossip about Stevenson's characters as there is about Thackeray's characters. There is no overflowing of trivial things, or, better still, of irrelevant things. There is no halo of hearsay or indirect impressions. Stevenson was relentlessly relevant; he limited himself to words so perfect and so few that his figures were really too clear to be convincing. He knew this well himself, being an admirable critic.

On the moral side the meaning of his position seems also to be entirely missed. Yet it is symbolized in the same imagery of sunbeams and sword blades. Death in Stevenson is brighter than life in Poe. And the point of his position in history is that he came at the precise moment when he could resist a pessimistic spirit, even in accepting parts of a pessimistic philosophy. Living in that Victorian phase, he accepted the struggle for life as described in terms of natural selection but declared himself ready to enjoy the struggle like a struggle of pirates and picturesque sailors. When opinion was passing through its most depressing phase, Stevenson, like the men who did not differ except in opinions, refused altogether to despair except in opinion. He resolved to keep the mood militant and sanguine whatever the theories might be. That fine essay, "Pulvis et Umbra," which was so much misunderstood, was truly the defiance of an optimistic man to a pessimistic world, even if it were a pessimistic universe. I am the last person alive to think it a true and complete view of the universe. But, in order to appreciate it, one must appreciate the period through which the world was passing—the decadent darkness of the "nineties." I for one remember it very well, for it surrounded my boyhood and early youth, and my first literary impulse was to fight against it. But there are many of my own age to testify with me that they would hardly have been able to fight against it, or even live through it, but for the spirit and the genius of Robert Louis Stevenson.

G. K. CHESTERTON
from *Generally Speaking*

Why does Chesterton's essay succeed as a piece of reflection?

1. Chesterton gives us a supported personal judgment.
2. Chesterton involves his reader as well as himself. The reader feels rewarded—instructed—not preached at.
3. Chesterton shows insight and understanding of his material. He expresses his ideas in clear and balanced sentences: "Death in Stevenson is brighter than life in Poe."
4. Ideas are marshaled and controlled by a major hypothesis or point of view that, in effect, organizes the entire essay.
5. Individual sentences and the entire essay carry a tone of balance and thought; for example, "That fine essay, 'Pulvis et Umbra,' which was so much misunderstood, was truly the defiance of an optimistic man to a pessimistic world, even if it were a pessimistic universe."

1. Read the Chesterton essay.
2. In your journal do *one* of the following:
   a. If you do not think Chesterton's essay is a successful piece of reflection, find a selection that you think does succeed and explain what makes it work. If you find additional reasons for feeling Chesterton does or does not succeed in his composition, state and explain them.
   b. Write on an author. In your essay incorporate as many of the points listed above as seem practical.
   c. Discuss the ideas of a short story; be sure to make clear why you feel and think as you do about the story.

Assignment 15

You will develop your powers of reflection if you get in the habit of attending to those moments that bring you insight. James Joyce made use of this technique by recording what he referred to as "epiphanies"—moments of discovery and revelation. Some of these entities he later made use of in his stories.

In religion, the Feast of Epiphany occurs on the sixth of January (the twelfth day of Christmas). Derived from a Greek word meaning "a showing forth," Epiphany celebrates the coming of the Magi to Christ, whose holiness "showed forth."

Joyce gave the term metaphorical extension. His special use of the word is explained by Dorothy Van Ghent in *The English Novel.*

> Those moments in the dialectical process when a synthesis is achieved, when certain phrases or sensations or complex experiences suddenly cohere in a larger whole and a meaning shines from the whole, Joyce—who introduced the word into literary currency—called "epiphanies." They are "showings-forth" of the nature of reality. . . . The epiphany is an image, sensuously apprehended and emotionally vibrant, which communicates instantaneously the meaning of experience. It may contain a revelation of a person's character, brief and fleeting, occurring by virtue of some physical trait in the person . . . as in the spectacle of Miss Havisham * leaning on her crutch beside the rotten bridecake, or of Jaggers * flourishing his white handkerchief and biting his great forefinger. . . . Or the epiphany may be a kind of "still life" with which are associated deep and complex layers of experience and emotion. . . .
>
> . . . The "new office" of the image is to communicate to others the significant character of a complete and harmonious body of experience. The

* Miss Havisham and Jaggers are characters in Charles Dickens's novel *Great Expectations.*

artist is a midwife of epiphanies. Joyce's doctrine of the epiphany assumes that reality does have wholeness and harmony—even as Stephen * as a child premises these, and with the same trustfulness —and that it will radiantly show forth its character and its meaning to the prepared consciousness. . . .

As a guide to reflection, one could hardly do better than record his own moments of clearest insight. As a first step, you may wish to make rough notes to yourself that will act as guides to memory. The moments of epiphany may be sudden and unexplained—yet none the less true and clear. Still, to present such moments in journal or story may be difficult. A writer is usually obliged to go beyond reportage and to inquire into the way events shaped themselves. Presenting epiphanies prompts reflection.

1. Read the comments for this assignment.
2. In your journal do *one* of the following:
   a. Record an epiphany from personal experience.
   b. Copy into your journal an epiphany taken from your reading. Give your source accurately.
   c. Construct a story incident that presents a character in a moment of discovery. Be sure to *show;* don't tell.

---

* Stephen Dedalus is the main character in *A Portrait of the Artist as a Young Man.*

4 | Review

The Department, a novel by Gerald Warner Brace, deals with an English faculty of a Boston College. The novel is presented in the form of notes or journal entries that recall personalities and experiences from the teaching years of the narrator, "Robert Sanderling, doctor of philosophy, professor of English, sixty-odd years old, not really a celebrity, but a man of some culture. . . ." His random reflections compose a story and include his personal observations and interior responses to life: personal, professional, and absurd.

The novel is reflective and ironic. In the course of his musings Professor Robert Sanderling makes this deadly accurate observation about writing:

> When I try to formulate ideas, as thinking men do, I end up with embarrassing clichés. Ideas themselves are almost never new, but style can be new, and relevance and appropriate drama can give old ideas new life.

This is wisdom that has come out of a lifetime of teaching. We do move toward the cliché—if not in our thought, at least in our writing and speaking. Ideas always look best just before they are formulated. Still, ideas must be dealt with. In our dealings with them we do well to remember Sanderling's words: "Ideas themselves are almost never new, but style can be new, and relevance and appropriate drama can give old ideas new life."

By way of example, here is a reflection that Sanderling makes on his life.

> What some of my feelings settled down to was simply guilt, or regret. Life had come, offered itself, and gone, and I had rejected—not all but much of it. I think almost all men feel this way, and I am sure it is never very clear to anyone what exactly it is that we reject—or accept.

Is it that mysterious veiled bride "Opportunity" that Conrad evokes in *Lord Jim?* Anyway, I did regret. I had simply done too little, had been lazy and passive, had succumbed to a too easy routine. I had written one mediocre book early in life and had never summoned up will or energy to do another—unless these rather random reflections can be considered "another."

Emerson worked with the same idea though he knew it had been old when Plato was a boy. But Emerson gave the idea new life through appropriate drama and his own style. Here is how Emerson formulated his thoughts and avoided the cliché.

Days

Daughters of Time, the hypocritic Days,
Muffled and dumb like barefoot dervishes,
And marching single in an endless file,
Bring diadems and fagots in their hands.
To each they offer gifts after his will,
Bread, kingdoms, stars, and sky that holds them all.
I, in my pleachèd garden, watched the pomp,
Forgot my morning wishes, hastily
Took a few herbs and apples, and the Day
Turned and departed silent. I, too late,
Under her solemn fillet saw the scorn.

RALPH WALDO EMERSON

Review Assignment

Now, in your journal, try your skill at reflection by doing *one* of the following:

a. Choose one of the numbered statements below, taken from *The Department.* What can you do with the given idea? Where can you take it and your reader?

1. "She was actually quite a sharp and competent scholar, and little by little she grew up, as we say—which

means that she was able to examine and criticize her own illusions."

2. "Aunt Martha's white house was a fine specimen of Vermont classic, built actually by Uncle Dan's grandfather, about 1810. Even to me it has seemed that our New England origins belong to a time infinitely remote. In my boyhood everything was said to be a hundred years old, houses, furniture, all properties: I can hear people saying it over and over. Oh, it's been there for a hundred years. And to a child that's the same as forever. To think of one of the old houses as actually having been built by someone's remembered grandfather was almost an impossibility. The very look of the houses removed them from time. To me as I grew up, and even now, what we call a colonial house belongs to the infinity of history, like a medieval church or even an ancient temple. Uncle Dan's grandfather belonged, so far as my imagination went, with the Caesars. The house itself could never have been 'new': even in 1810, 'a hundred years ago,' it must have appeared somehow as a venerable classic."

b. Select an idea from a book you have read and develop it. Be sure to write out the parent statement and to give its source accurately.
c. Formulate an idea about which you have done some thinking. State your core idea briefly; then write your reflections on it.

UNIT 5

Develop Your Powers of Perception

Forceless, reasonless action disrupts plot. The term "creation of character" (or characters) is misleading. Characters preexist. They are found. They reveal themselves slowly to the novelist's perception—as might fellow-travelers seated opposite one in a very dimly lit railway carriage.

The novelist's perceptions of his character take place in the course of the actual writing of the novel. *To an extent, the novelist is in the same position as his reader. But his perceptions should be always just in advance.*

The ideal way of presenting character is to invite perception.—ELIZABETH BOWEN

5|1

PERCEPTION

A journal is an instrument of expression, and central to that expression is perception. You must know in order to tell. But how does knowing get done? Through the senses—of course; but more than that, in knowing there is often a mystery and a medley of forces that elude explanation or examination, and yet the totality—the combination of sense and instincts—may result in a certitude and a knowing. Let's call this phenomenon—however produced—perception. And even though this ability may defy definition and watertight compartmentalization, let's admit that, like personality, everyone has it to a greater or lesser degree.

Throughout this book you have been working with approaches to perception: observation, imagination, reflection. Now you move to that final stage in which the parts are put together; central to that combining is perception—the instinct for seeing into a matter and for relating subjects in new and unexpected ways.

Perception contributes to the unity of your writing and provides a sustaining force that carries both reader and writer toward the center of experience and idea. Perception seeks a union between sensory experience and meaning. Perception goes beyond seeing—it fuses instinct and intellect. For the writer, perception is a search for characters and a search for symbols that will dramatize action and idea. Perhaps an example will help. Here are a few excerpts from Richard Wright's *How "Bigger" Was Born.* They may give you some idea of how perception shapes itself into story. Wright is talking about his central character in *Native Son.*

> So, at the outset, I say frankly that there are phases of *Native Son* which I shall make no attempt to account for. There are meanings in my book of which I was not aware until they literally spilled

out upon the paper. I shall sketch the outline of how I *consciously* came into possession of the materials that went into *Native Son,* but there will be many things I shall omit, not because I want to, but simply because I don't know them.

The birth of Bigger Thomas goes back to my childhood, and there was not just one Bigger, but many of them, more than I could count and more than you suspect. But let me start with the first Bigger, whom I shall call Bigger No. 1.

When I was a bareheaded, barefoot kid in Jackson, Mississippi, there was a boy who terrorized me and all of the boys I played with. If we were playing games, he would saunter up and snatch from us our balls, bats, spinning tops, and marbles. We would stand around pouting, sniffling, trying to keep back our tears, begging for our playthings. But Bigger would refuse. We never demanded that he give them back; we were afraid, and Bigger was bad. We had seen him clout boys when he was angry and we did not want to run that risk. We never recovered our toys unless we flattered him and made him feel that he was superior to us. Then, perhaps, if he felt like it, he condescended, threw them at us and then gave each of us a swift kick in the bargain, just to make us feel his utter contempt.

That was the way Bigger No. 1 lived. His life was a continuous challenge to others. At all times he *took* his way, right or wrong, and those who contradicted him had him to fight. And never was he happier than when he had someone cornered and at his mercy; it seemed that the deepest meaning of his squalid life was in him at such times.

I don't know what the fate of Bigger No. 1 was. His swaggering personality is swallowed up somewhere in the amnesia of my childhood. But I suspect that his end was violent. Anyway, he left a marked impression upon me; maybe it was because I longed secretly to be like him and was afraid. I don't know.

If I had known only one Bigger I would not have written *Native Son*. Let me call the next one Bigger No. 2; he was about seventeen and tougher than the first Bigger. Since I, too, had grown older, I was a little less afraid of him. And the hardness of this Bigger No. 2 was not directed toward me or the other Negroes, but toward the whites who ruled the South. He bought clothes and food on credit and would not pay for them. He lived in the dingy shacks of the white landlords and refused to pay rent. Of course, he had no money, but neither did we. We did without the necessities of life and starved ourselves, but he never would. When we asked him why he acted as he did, he would tell us (as though we were little children in a kindergarten) that the white folks had everything and he had nothing. Further, he would tell us that we were fools not to get what we wanted while we were alive in this world. We would listen and silently agree. We longed to believe and act as he did, but we were afraid. We were Southern Negroes and we were hungry and we wanted to live, but we were more willing to tighten our belts than risk conflict. Bigger No. 2 wanted to live and he did; he was in prison the last time I heard from him.

There was Bigger No. 3, whom the white folks called a "bad nigger. . . ."

And then there was Bigger No. 4, whose only law was death. . . .

Then there was Bigger No. 5, who always rode the Jim Crow streetcars without paying and sat wherever he pleased. . . .

The Bigger Thomases were the only Negroes I know of who consistently violated the Jim Crow laws of the South and got away with it, at least for a sweet brief spell. Eventually, the whites who restricted their lives made them pay a terrible price. They were shot, hanged, maimed, lynched, and generally hounded until they were either dead or their spirits broken. . . .

But why did Bigger revolt? No explanation based

upon a hard and fast rule of conduct can be given. But there were always two factors psychologically dominant in his personality. First, through some quirk of circumstance, he had become estranged from the religion and the folk culture of his race. Second, he was trying to react to and answer the call of the dominant civilization whose glitter came to him through the newspapers, magazines, radios, movies, and the mere imposing sight and sound of daily American life. In many respects his emergence as a distinct type was inevitable.

As I grew older, I became familiar with the Bigger Thomas conditioning and its numerous shadings no matter where I saw it in Negro life. It was not, as I have already said, as blatant or extreme as in the originals; but it was there, nevertheless, like an undeveloped negative. . . .

It was not until I went to live in Chicago that I first thought seriously of writing of Bigger Thomas. Two items of my experience combined to make me aware of Bigger as a meaningful and prophetic symbol. First, being free of the daily pressure of the Dixie environment, I was able to come into possession of my own feelings. Second, my contact with the labor movement and its ideology made me see Bigger clearly and feel what he meant.

I made the discovery that Bigger Thomas was not black all the time; he was white, too, and there were literally millions of him, everywhere. The extension of my sense of the personality of Bigger was the pivot of my life; it altered the complexion of my existence. . . .

As my mind extended in this general and abstract manner, it was fed with even more vivid and concrete examples of the lives of Bigger Thomas. The urban environment of Chicago, affording a more stimulating life, made the Negro Bigger Thomases react more violently than even in the South. More than ever I began to see and understand the environmental factors which made for this extreme conduct. It was not that Chicago segregated Negroes more than the South, but that Chicago had more to offer, that Chicago's physical aspect—noisy, crowded, filled with the sense of power and fulfillment—did so much more to dazzle the mind with a taunting sense of possible achievement that the segregation it did impose brought forth from Bigger a reaction more obstreperous than in the South.

So the concrete picture and the abstract linkages of relationships fed each other, each making the other more meaningful and affording my emotions an opportunity to react to them with success and understanding. The process was like a swinging pendulum, each to and fro motion throwing up its tiny bit of meaning and significance, each stroke helping to develop the dim negative which had been implanted in my mind in the South. . . .

Let me give examples of how I began to develop the dim negative of Bigger. I met white writers who talked of their responses, who told me how whites reacted to this lurid American scene. And, as they talked, I'd translate what they said in terms of Bigger's life. But what was more important still, I read their novels. Here for the first time, I found ways and techniques of gauging meaningfully the effects of American civilization upon the personalities of people. I took these techniques, these ways of seeing and feeling, and twisted them, bent them, adapted them, until they became *my* ways of apprehending the locked-in life of the Black Belt areas. This association with white writers was the life preserver of my hope to depict Negro life in fiction, for my race possessed no fictional works dealing with such problems, had no background in such sharp and critical testing of experience, no novels that went with a deep and fearless will down to the dark roots of life.

Here are examples of how I culled information relating to Bigger from my reading:

There is in me a memory of reading an interesting pamphlet telling of the friendship of Gorky and Lenin in exile. The booklet told of how Lenin and Gorky were walking down a London street. Lenin turned to Gorky and, pointing, said: "Here is *their* Big Ben." "There is *their* Westminster Abbey." "There is *their* library." And at once, while reading that passage, my mind stopped, teased, challenged with the effort to remember, to associate widely disparate but meaningful experiences in my life. For a moment nothing would come, but I remained convinced that I had heard the meaning of those words sometime, somewhere before. Then, with a sudden glow of satisfaction of having gained a little more knowledge about the world in which I lived, I'd end up by saying: "That's Bigger, That's the Bigger Thomas reaction."

I remember reading a passage in a book dealing with old Russia which said: "We must be ready to make endless sacrifices if we are to be able to overthrow the Czar." And again I'd say to myself: "I've heard that somewhere, sometime before." And again I'd hear Bigger Thomas, far away and long ago, telling some white man who was trying to impose upon him: "I'll kill you and go to hell and pay for it." While living in America I heard from faraway Russia the bitter accents of tragic calculation of how much human life and suffering it would cost a man to live as a man in a world that denied him the right to live with dignity. Actions and feelings of men ten thousand miles from home helped me to understand the moods and impulses of those walking the streets of Chicago and Dixie.

Above and beyond all this, there was that American part of Bigger which is the heritage of us all, that part of him which we get from our seeing and hearing, from school, from the hopes and dreams of our friends; that part of him which the common people of America never talk of but take for granted. Among millions of people the deepest convictions of life are never discussed openly; they are felt, implied, hinted at tacitly and obliquely in their hopes and fears. We live by idealism that makes us believe that the Constitution is a good document of government, that the Bill of Rights is a good legal and humane principle to safeguard our civil liberties, that every man and woman should have the opportunity to realize himself, to seek his own individual fate and goal, his own peculiar and untranslatable destiny. I don't say that Bigger knew this in the terms in which I'm speaking of it; I don't say that any such thought ever entered his head. His emotional and intellectual life was never that articulate. But he knew it emotionally, intuitively, for his emotions and his desires were developed, and he caught it, as most of us do, from the mental and emotional climate of our time. Bigger had all of this in him, dammed up, buried, implied, and I had to develop it in fictional form.

Now, after all of this, when I sat down to the typewriter, I could not work; I could not think of a good opening scene for the book. I had definitely in mind the kind of emotion I wanted to evoke in the reader in that first scene, but I could not think of the type of concrete event that would convey the motif of the entire scheme of the book, that would sound, in varied form, the note that was to be re-sounded throughout its length, that would intro-duce to the reader just what kind of an organism Bigger's was and the environment that was bearing hourly upon it. Twenty or thirty times I tried and failed; then I argued that if I could not write the opening scene, I'd start with the scene that fol-lowed. I did. The actual writing of the book began with the scene in the pool room.

Now, for the writing. During the years in which I had met all of those Bigger Thomases, those varieties of Bigger Thomases, I had not consciously gathered material to write of them; I had not kept a notebook record of their sayings and doings. Their actions had simply made impressions upon my sensibilities as I lived from day to day, impressions which crystallized and coagulated into clusters and configurations of memory, attitudes, moods, ideas. And these subjective states, in turn, were automatically stored away somewhere in me. I was not even aware of the process. But, excited over the book which I had set myself to write, under the stress of emotion, these things came surging up, tangled, fused, knotted, entertaining me by the sheer variety and potency of their meaning and suggestiveness.

With the whole theme in mind, in an attitude almost akin to prayer, I gave myself up to the story. In an effort to capture some phase of Bigger's life that would not come to me readily, I'd jot down as much of it as I could. Then I'd read it over and over, adding each time a word, a phrase, a sentence until I felt that I had caught all the shadings of reality I felt dimly were there. With each of these rereadings and rewritings it seemed that I'd gather in facts and facets that tried to run away. It was an act of concentration, of trying to hold within one's center of attention all of that bewildering array of facts which science, politics, experience, memory, and imagination were urging upon me. And, then, while writing, a new and thrilling relationship would spring up under the drive of emotion, coalescing and telescoping alien facts into a known and felt truth. That was the deep fun of the job: to feel within my body that I was pushing out to new areas of feeling, strange landmarks of emotion tramping upon foreign soil, compounding new relationships of perceptions, making new and —until that very split second of time!—unheard-of and unfelt effects with words. It had a buoying and tonic impact upon me; my senses would strain and seek for more and more of such relationships; my temperature would rise as I worked. That is writing as I feel it, a kind of significant living.

RICHARD WRIGHT
from *How "Bigger" Was Born*

Assignment 1

1. Read the chapter up to this point.
2. In your journal do *one* of the following:
   a. From your own experience, *find* a character (or characters) that "preexist" and give them expression.
   b. Elizabeth Bowen reminds us that "to an extent, the novelist is in the same position as his reader." As a reader, see how far your perceptions will carry a story you have been reading. First, read a few pages in a story or novel. Then from your sense of character and situation, write out the next scene. Once you have done your writing, see how the author treated the same problem. Summarize your findings.
   c. Write on a topic of your own choice.

Assignment 2

Upon the fact in nature the imagination must constantly feed in order that the imaginative life remain significant.

SHERWOOD ANDERSON
from *Sherwood Anderson's Notebook*

Perception is heightened by daily writing. Whatever you observe is better understood when commented on; both seeing and saying are sharpened by statement. Journal writing invites statement, idea, discrimination, and at the same time provides the discipline of regularity. Hawthorne found it so; Emerson and Thoreau demonstrated the utility of the method, and in our own day Galbraith's *Ambassador's Journal* is not the last work to show accomplishment that may come in this way. In part the accomplishment comes from finding ways of expressing essential meanings. For example, a person may say, "It's a dull evening," but a poet may apprehend the same quality of suspended time and catch its feeling in particular words. If the poet is T. S. Eliot, he may say:

Let us go then, you and I,
When the evening is spread out against the sky
Like a patient etherized upon a table.

The perceptions of the poet realize the experience and identify the parts that organize its uniqueness. The person who
says "It's a nice day; a nice car; a nice child" may also be
perceptive, but for lack of expression these perceptions stay
undeveloped and locked in. Such a person is not unpercep-
tive, but untrained, and as long as he remains untrained he
is unable to identify, particularize, or fully experience either
sensation or psychic responses.

By studying the work of others, you can with practice
train yourself to find words for your own feelings. Here is an
example that may be of some immediate help in demonstrating how you can articulate the observed if you but trust
yourself to speak of common experiences with honesty and
without pretension. This example is taken from Marcel
Proust's *Remembrance of Things Past.* The occasion is no
more than the taking of a cup of tea.

> . . . I raised to my lips a spoonful of the tea in
> which I had soaked a morsel of the cake. No sooner
> had the warm liquid, and the crumbs with it,
> touched my palate than a shudder ran through my
> whole body, and I stopped, intent upon the ex-
> traordinary changes that were taking place. An
> exquisite pleasure had invaded my senses, but indi-
> vidual, detached, with no suggestion of its origin.
> And at once the vicissitudes of life had become in-
> different to me, its disasters innocuous, its brevity
> illusory—this new sensation having had on me the
> effect which love has of filling me with a precious
> essence; or rather this essence was not in me, it was
> myself. I had ceased now to feel mediocre, acci-
> dental, mortal. Whence could it have come to me,
> this all-powerful joy? I was conscious that it was
> connected with the taste of tea and cake, but that
> it infinitely transcended those savors, could not,
> indeed, be of the same nature as theirs. Whence did
> it come? What did it signify? How could I seize
> upon and define it?

I drink a second mouthful, in which I find nothing more than in the first, a third, which gives me rather less than the second. It is time to stop; the potion is losing its magic. It is plain that the object of my quest, the truth, lies not in the cup but in myself. The tea has called up in me, but does not itself understand, and can only repeat indefinitely with a gradual loss of strength, the same testimony; which I, too, cannot interpret, though I hope at least to be able to call upon the tea for it again and to find it there presently, intact and at my disposal, for my final enlightenment. I put down my cup and examine my own mind. It is for it to discover the truth. But how? What an abyss of uncertainty whenever the mind feels that some part of it has strayed beyond its own borders; when it, the seeker, is at once the dark region through which it must go seeking, where all its equipment will avail it nothing. Seek? More than that: create. It is face to face with something which does not so far exist, to which it alone can give reality and substance, which it alone can bring into the light of day.

And I begin again to ask myself what it could have been, this unremembered state which brought with it no logical proof of its existence, but only the sense that it was a happy, that it was a real state in whose presence other states of consciousness melted and vanished. I decide to attempt to make it reappear. I retrace my thoughts to the moment at which I drank the first spoonful of tea. I find again the same state, illumined by no fresh light. I compel my mind to make one further effort, to follow and recapture once again the fleeting sensation. And that nothing may interrupt it in its course I shut out every obstacle, every extraneous idea, I stop my ears and inhibit all attention to the sounds which come from the next room. And then, feeling that my mind is growing fatigued without having any success to report, I compel it for a change to enjoy that distraction which I have just denied it, to think of other things, to rest and refresh itself before the supreme attempt. And then for the second time I clear an empty space in front of it. I place in position before my mind's eye the still recent taste of that first mouthful, and I feel something start within me, something that leaves its resting place and attempts to rise, something that has been embedded like an anchor at a great depth; I do not know yet what it is, but I can feel it mounting slowly; I can measure the resistance, I can hear the echo of great spaces traversed.

Undoubtedly what is thus palpitating in the depths of my being must be the image, the visual memory which, being linked to that taste, has tried to follow it into my conscious mind. But its struggles are too far off, too much confused; scarcely can I perceive the colorless reflection in which are blended the uncapturable whirling medley of radiant hues, and I cannot distinguish its form, cannot invite it, as the one possible interpreter, to translate to me the evidence of its contemporary, its inseparable paramour, the taste of cake soaked in tea; cannot ask it to inform me what special circumstance is in question, of what period in my past life.

MARCEL PROUST
from *Remembrance of Things Past*

1. Read the material for this assignment.
2. In your journal do *one* of the following:
   a. Present memories and perceptions of your own that cluster about a single simple event.
   b. Return to your journal notes, and in a full entry develop some of your earlier perceptions.
   c. Write on a topic of your own choice.

Assignment 3

Perception may present itself through the essay quite as well as through story or novel. Indeed the essay has the advantage of an immediate intimacy and directness. The following passage demonstrates how arresting a single perception may be. Here Cox is concerned with a phenomenon he has termed "the vampire cult of The Girl." You will note in this excerpt that abstraction has been particularized and made concrete. The writer is dealing with an idea—saying something about it in his own special way of looking, thinking, and saying.

Like every idol she is ultimately a creation of our own hands and cannot save us. The values she represents as ultimate satisfactions—mechanical comfort, sexual success, unencumbered leisure—have no ultimacy. They lead only to endless upward mobility, competitive consumption, and anxious cynicism. The devilish social insecurities from which she promises to deliver us are, alas, still there, even after we have purified our breaths, our skins, and our armpits by applying her sacred oils. She is a merciless goddess who draws us farther and farther into the net of accelerated ordeals of obeisance. As the queen of commodities in an expanding economy, the fulfillment she promises must always remain just beyond the tips of our fingers.

HARVEY COX
from *The Secular City*

1. Read the material for this assignment.
2. In your journal do *one* of the following:
   a. Write an essay of ideas.
   b. Write a humorous editorial.
   c. Write on a related topic of your own choice.

5|2

SENSITIVITY

Sensitivity means bothering to notice and bothering to respond. It is not just seeing objects, but seeing them in relation to each other, and seeing them with an appreciation for beauty, pattern, and design. Sensitivity contributes to perception by adding significance to the observed. Facts alone are neither sensitive nor perceptive. As currently constituted, computers are not perceptive—although their programmers may be.

You can develop sensitivity by exploring feelings. For a time, don't judge but observe other people. Seek to understand their lives. For example, read *Durango Street* by Frank Bonham or another novel or story that depicts a neighborhood and its feelings. Then examine your own feelings about your own neighborhood.

Sensitivity aids perception. Hepzibah in *The House of the Seven Gables* appears as a lone, mean creature always encircled by a scowl, but the author, and we through him, come to realize that her scowling is the result of poor vision, not bad temper. Sensitivity brings insights and frequently a fusion of the known with the unexpected. Steinbeck in *The Red Pony* presents feelings through the behavior of Joey. As you read that or another story of comparable quality, see if you can find points within the story where perception is shown by the writer or one of his characters. Look for additional ways of seeing life as others see it. One of the best exercises for this sort of thing is to play with differing points of view. How, for example, would a conversation go between a father and son when the boy is ten, fifteen, or twenty-five? How would the boy's and father's points of view change? First take the role of the boy and then of the father. This kind of role-playing will help you immerse yourself in the life and thoughts of another person and, to the degree that you succeed, increase your sensitivity and perception.

Assignment 4

1. Read the chapter up to this point.
2. In your journal do *one* of the following:
   a. Write out an experience with role-playing. Create the different parts and present believable responses.
   b. Examine and write down your own feelings about a topic of special interest to you.
   c. Examine a story and explain how the writer has presented perception through character.

Assignment 5

> The poet's job is not to tell you what happened,
> but what happens: not what did take place, but the
> kind of thing that always does take place.
> NORTHROP FRYE
> from *The Educated Imagination*

The following poem, written by a young poet, presents a sensitive projection into the life of another person. In the process of telling us about the clerk, the poet manages what Northrop Frye calls "the poet's job." As you read the poem consider how the job gets done. In particular, consider how the writer has in some way made special "the kind of thing that always does take place."

The Clerk Retires

Fog infects the entrance of the house,
suffocates the lights like summer flies.
Sick, he breathes the pallid city dawn,
trembles like an ancient closet-moth,
incapable and blind.

                    Now he rubs
the smoothness of his hands, listens
to the knock of heat in walls, and chants:

I have fingered forty years of letters,
written picture postcards in the summers;
now I'll sing; I'll do many things.

Then he closed the shades, and dressed,
washed his hands again, and left, fresh
as a turned collar. Avoiding ice,
he took the alley, followed by dogs,
and went downtown.

In the subway, the breast of a shop-girl
touched him. He could feel it, there,
against his arm. It was the first time
in years. He felt sick, then, standing
in an overcoat and rubbers.

At the cafeteria, the same strangers sat
four to a table, quiet, as if in separate grief.
He had a good seat. He could see, in the window,
the paper garden. Flowers leaned in the glare,
painfully, awkwardly, like ghosts of his mother.

Nine o'clock,
but there was no work that day. He walked.
The traffic drenched his feet with cold.
He went to the lunch-place, too early;
without the others, they never knew his face.
Stiff, ashamed, a small man at the edge of a chair,
he ate another breakfast.

The reading room was warm. He slept,
in magazines and papers, all day.
Time to go home, the guard said.
He woke, feverish, still
in his overcoat and rubbers.
He went to the washroom.
The icy water was too wonderful.
He died there.

MILTON KESSLER

1. Read the material for this assignment.
2. In your journal do *one* of the following:
    a. Examine a poem or story and explain how it does or does not meet the requirements suggested by Frye.
    b. Through imaginative and sensitive projection, present a person who is very different from yourself.
    c. Write on a topic involving sensitivity in perception.

Assignment 6

Sensitivity suggests an ability to adjust rapidly to even minimal changes. We tend to think of this capacity as an impulse for responding to the given—and so it is—but the given may allow for subtraction as well as addition. For example, it may be both perceptive and inventive to respond to a character in life by seeing him not only as he is, but also as he might be. Stevenson puts the case clearly in these words.

> And then I had an idea for John Silver from which I promised myself funds of entertainment: to take an admired friend of mine . . . to deprive him of all his finer qualities and higher graces of temperament, to leave him with nothing but his strength, his courage, his quickness, and his magnificent geniality, and to try to express these in terms of the culture of a raw tarpaulin. Such psychical surgery is, I think, a common way of "making character"; perhaps it is, indeed, the only way. We can put in the quaint figure that spoke a hundred words with us yesterday by the wayside; but do we know him? Our friend, with his infinite variety and flexibility, we know—but can we put him in? Upon the first we must engraft secondary and imaginary qualities, possibly all wrong; from the second, knife in hand, we must cut away and deduct the needless arborescence of his nature; but the trunk and the few branches that remain we may at least be fairly sure of.
>
> ROBERT LOUIS STEVENSON

1. Read the material for the assignment.
2. In your journal do *one* of the following:
   a. Describe a character as he exists. Present both his physical and his psychic being. Then describe the same character as he might appear with a few Stevensonian adjustments.
   b. Childhood has an innocence that is perceptive. Capture something of that time and those insights by listening to the talk of children, or by returning in memory to your own childhood. In a full entry, report on this activity.
   c. Present a set of free associations occasioned by listening to music.

5|3

FOCUS

The most important thing in a work of art is that
it should have a kind of focus; i.e., there should be
some place where all the rays meet or from which
they issue. And this focus must not be able to be
completely explained in words. This indeed is one
of the significant facts about a true work of art—
that its content in its entirety can be expressed only
by itself.

A. B. GOLDENWEIZER
from *Talks with Tolstoi*

Global viewing is a blur. If you try to see everything, you
see nothing. You can verify the truth of that statement by
visiting a large museum or by going to another kind of contemporary museum—the large department store. What do
you see if you try to see everything there? What do you miss?
Try this same exercise in reverse. Go to your museum and
look at one area only. What do you see? What do you miss?
True, in a sense you can't have it both ways. Intense seeing
precludes the large smear of impressions; the merry-go-
round blur does not occur when the viewer stands still.

Perception requires intensity—intensity of response as
well as intensity of observation. Dickens is reported to have
been able to walk down a street and fully record all its objects—down to the wording on shop signs—although it is less
evident he was able to observe and record nuances of human
feeling with anything approaching such accuracy. But there
were other writers—James, Fitzgerald, Joyce—who, as you
know, caught emotion and recorded it with fidelity and insight.

The good poem, the good story, and the good theme all
have a point in common: each requires focus. The writer
can set the lens in any way he approves, but having set it he

must maintain his vision or idea. If he does not start with focus and the perspective it provides, a writer must in one way or another arrive at it, for focus brings perceptions under control and establishes a center about which ideas and impressions may revolve without becoming tangential. Once established, focus lessens the element of chance and increases the importance of decision.

Assignment 7

1. Read the chapter up to this point.
2. In your journal do *one* of the following:
   a. Discuss the focus of a story you know well. In the course of your discussion, identify the "place where all the rays meet or from which they issue."
   b. Point of view may be thought of as one element of focus. By examining a particular story or poem, show how point of view influences perception.
   c. Present a moment of perception as it occurred in life or was presented in a story. Rewrite the incident, giving it a sharply altered focus. As you change focus, what else do you change? Explain.

Assignment 8

The true subject is a topic brought to focus.
    CLEANETH BROOKS and
    ROBERT PENN WARREN
    from *Fundamentals of Good Writing*

Focus is another word for concentration. In life it is the skill of closely centered attention that so often makes for success. In literature it is a narrowing of range that collects interest and suggests life. Maugham comes to the point in the following paragraph.

It is a psychological trait in human nature that interest is established in the persons whom the playwright introduces at the beginning of his play so firmly that if the interest is then switched off to other persons who enter upon the scene later, a sense of disappointment ensues. The astute dramatist presents his subject as early as possible, and if for theatrical effectiveness he does not introduce his principal characters till later, the conversation of the persons on the stage at the rising of the curtain concentrates the attention of the audience on them so that the delay in their appearance increases the expectation. No one followed this practice more scrupulously than that very competent dramatist, William Shakespeare.

W. SOMERSET MAUGHAM
from *The Summing Up*

1. Read the material for this assignment.
2. In your journal do *one* of the following:
   a. Show from your own experience how an idea or attitude shaped itself and came into focus.
   b. Show how a familiar object acquired, through accident or perception, a new significance.
   c. Do some stream-of-consciousness writing. Then re-order the same material by imposing focus.

Assignment 9

Narrowing or "focusing down" can be as important as any single aspect of composition. The following comments by C. L. Sulzberger, *The New York Times* foreign affairs columnist, illustrates the point. Sulzberger is reviewing *Very Lovely People,* a book by Ludovic Kennedy (British television commentator and author). He speaks favorably of much of Kennedy's work, but failure in "focusing down" costs Kennedy heavily, as you will see from the following comments taken from the close of the review.

I particularly enjoyed Kennedy's descriptions of his visit to the Sixth Fleet, his stay in Saudi Arabia and his brief tour of South Vietnam. He writes with wit and takes pains to describe the unabashed goodness of many of his characters. Nevertheless, despite patches of lucidity, elegance and humor and despite frequently vivid dialogue, this book doesn't quite come off. I have a feeling the author was such a thorough reporter that he ended up with a mountain of material impossible to reduce in orderly arrangement.

He must have traveled with a tape recorder—or he must be a shorthand expert—to take down in such detail so many interminable conversations and such needlessly long excerpts from broadcasts of the U.S. Armed Forces Network which are, as everyone (including Kennedy) knows, aimed at the L'il Abner I.Q. of the average G.I.

I appreciated the effort by this author, so clearly a good friend of the United States, to explain what Americans are doing in the world. He has succeeded to a considerable degree—if one has the patience to persist. But apart from the fact that it is much too drawn-out, *Very Lovely People* lacks a summing up, even by inference. I particularly missed this because it is clear that the author has an engaging, bright mind and it would have been worth pondering his conclusions.

C. L. SULZBERGER
from *The New York Times Book Review*

The portion of Sulzberger's essay you have just read also illustrates the place of focus within a critical review. As demonstrated, the critic must be aware of the value of the parts as well as the value of the whole. Training in such perception prompts a writer, whatever his subject, to aim at balance, and to carry on a kind of esthetic accounting that scrutinizes detail—the kind of detail that is adequate to the job and not excessive or irrelevant. For the new writer in particular, the need is for ample detail but supportive detail always. Focus seeks the true center from which a work departs and to which it must return.

One way of gaining skill at focus is to practice formulating thesis statements about material you have read and then to establish topic sentences for each of its paragraphs. The goal here is to gather within a single sentence as many of the author's perceptions as possible. Clearly, much must be implied and all must be condensed, but the exercise is a certain way of making you more observant about the ways in which focus is established and maintained.

This same kind of perception may of course be practiced in reverse. First you attempt to formulate a thesis statement that implicitly covers all you wish to say. Then turn to constructing topic sentences for each of the projected parts. This exercise is a kind of outlining that puts a premium on order and focus.

1. Read the comments on focus.
2. In your journal do *one* of the following:
   a. Present an edited and focused version of a tape recording that you have made of an actual conversation.
   b. Write an entry on a topic of your own choice. This entry should be controlled by a thesis statement and supported by three properly footnoted comments.
   c. With clear focus, comment on a political speech or current issue; or put into your own words a thesis statement and topic sentences that cover an article you have recently read.

5|4

EMPATHY

The isolated fact that cannot be related to a large
or universal significance is merely observed, not
perceived. . . .

WILLIAM VAN O'CONNOR
from *Sense and Sensibility in Modern Poetry*

em·pa·thy / 'em-pə-thē / *n* **1**: the imaginative projection of a subjective state into an object so that
the object appears to be infused with it **2**: the
capacity for participating in another's feelings or
ideas—*Webster's Seventh New Collegiate Dictionary.*

Empathy is a word worth defining and knowing, for the
concept is important in writing. Maugham, for example,
said:

> But the point of the writer is that he is not one
> man but many. It is because he is many that he
> can create many, and the measure of his greatness
> is the number of selves that he comprises. When
> he fashions a character that does not carry con-
> viction it is because there is in himself nothing of
> that person; he has had to fall back on observa-
> tion, and so has only described, not begotten. The
> writer does not feel with; he feels in. It is not sym-
> pathy that he has; that too often results in senti-
> mentality; he has what the psychologists call
> empathy. It is because Shakespeare had this to so
> great a degree that he was at once the most living
> and the least sentimental of authors.
>
> W. SOMERSET MAUGHAM
> from *The Summing Up*

There is, of course, nothing new about investing the inanimate with human feelings or a personal identity; the Greeks were good at it. When a bush moved, they were as aware as we that the wind moved also, but they invested both the wind and the bush with spirit, personality, and powers. They in fact projected the unseen from the seen much as we say "a train is coming" when we hear no more than a whistle or see no more than a gate go down at a crossing. The train, to be sure, is not there, but from the seen we project the unseen. Unless we are poetically inclined, we are not, however, apt to think of the train in personal terms. We prefer to be scientific. But a railroad buff may refer to it as Old 98, and the engineer may recognize a particular personality in the machinery much as a horseman responds to the personality of his mount. Empathy, then, is a way of responding, of feeling, and of seeing—a way that conditions experience and personalizes the otherwise impersonal. The childhood story of the little train that said "I think I can, I think I can" is one example, and Emily Dickinson's poem (page 95) "I Like to See It Lap the Miles" another. On the other hand, empathy may not involve objects but people and so intensify our feeling for the personal and human by permitting us to place ourselves—through imagination—in the place of others. News shots of the starving and suffering may for a moment bring feelings of identity with the victims even though they be in distant lands or of a different age or culture; for a moment we experience their experience—or think we do. That too is empathy.

For the writer, empathy is not only a way of perceiving but also a way of organizing and intensifying what he has perceived. Through empathy a writer is able to interest and involve readers; for a moment they are the hero. Doubtless you remember TV shows, movies, and novels in which the presentation permitted you to participate in the feelings and ideas of others, or perhaps as a child you yourself endowed a doll, a pencil, or a baseball bat with special and individual powers.

In writing, empathy is more apt to intensify itself for the reader if feelings or objects are turned into symbols; further interest and significance is achieved if these same symbols are allied with folklore or myth. For example, Ray Bradbury in his story "The Dragon" (page 137) is able to give a railroad train mythic proportions. Empathy, like myth itself, draws together a multiplicity of sensory impressions and stimulates our interpretative mechanisms. The empathic experience promotes a feeling of unity and consequently invites us to seek out and establish other unities even though we are dealing with seemingly disparate objects. By discovering a center behind objects and events that at first appear unrelated, we are prompted to organize and to abstract. Thus even though empathy is primarily emotional and projectional, its end result tends to organize, unify, and promote abstraction.

If artistic creation requires that a writer filter experience through his own perceptions, it is not surprising to discover that creation can be fueled by the assimilation of objects and experience that first appear outside oneself. Coleridge made an interesting comment on how this process worked for him:

> "From my very childhood, I have been accustomed to abstract and, as it were, unrealize whatever of more than common interest my eyes dwelt on, and then by a sort of transfusion and transmission of my consciousness to identify myself with the object." And Lowes, in a painstaking study of the materials Coleridge had immersed himself in during the years prior to his writing "The Ancient Mariner," was able to trace to these sources every word and phrase of the poem's most vivid stanzas. . . . This is not, of course, to detract a grain from Coleridge's achievement; it is only a recognition and demonstration of the sensory components on which imagination operates.
>
> quoted in *The Creative Process*
> by Brewster Ghiselin

Assignment 10

1. Read the chapter up to this point.
2. In your journal do *one* of the following:
   a. Attempt to identify yourself with an object by using

the method described by Coleridge. Report on your experiment.

b. Comment on an author's use of empathy in a particular story or poem.

c. Give your own thoughts on empathy and perception. Insofar as you can, illustrate your discussion by reference to your reading. For example, you may wish to show how an author has fused different sets of empathic projections to create a new character. *See Theodore Dreiser: His World and His Novels* by Richard Lehan for an explanation of how Dreiser used his sister Emma and his brother Paul to create the character Carrie Meeber.

Assignment 11

I want to re-create a child's world, not of fairies and giants but of colors more clear than they are to adults, of tastes more sharp and of queer heart-breaking feelings that overwhelm children in a moment. . . . I want to put down the way "afternoon" felt. . . .

JOHN STEINBECK

Empathy permits Steinbeck and many another writer to realize deeply felt moments—moments unified by a perception that brings together the forces of observation, imagination, and reflection. For example, in "The Great Mountains" (Part 2 of "The Red Pony") Steinbeck is able to capture an afternoon from childhood, capture it so completely that you find yourself being Jody. You find that the absurdity of Jody's pushing the clouds along is not absurd, but important and a part of the texture of that afternoon.

Then he lay on his back in the grass and looked up at the dumpling summer clouds. By closing one eye and destroying perspective he brought them down within reach so that he could put up his fingers and stroke them. He helped the gentle wind push them down the sky; it seemed to him that they went faster for his help. One fat white cloud he helped clear to the mountain rims and pressed it firmly over, out of sight. Jody wondered what it was seeing, then. He sat up the better to look at the great mountains where they went piling back, growing darker and more savage until they finished with one jagged ridge, high up against the west. Curious secret mountains; he thought of the little he knew about them.

JOHN STEINBECK
from "The Red Pony"

Empathy is a reaching out of feeling and understanding that permits insight. Because you have been a child yourself you know what it is to be lonely, or surprised, or happy in the ways peculiar to children. Because other people are shaped by influences that influence you, you must understand yourself if you are to understand them. As you better understand yourself and others, you are better able to empathize and to write about your own feelings as well as theirs. Robert W. White treats empathy with psychological perspective in his book *Lives in Progress*. He says:

There are times, however, when a growth trend moves ahead by sudden jumps. Such occasions correspond to the "learning by insight" first emphasized by the Gestalt school of psychologists, a good example of cognitive learning. The other person is perceived first in one way, then in an entirely different way, the change representing a sudden reorganization of the perceptual field. Hartley Hale's attitude toward his eldest daughter seems to have undergone one of these abrupt reorganizations. He felt nothing but irritation at the child's disobedience until he suddenly realized how much it resembled his own stubborn independence at a like age. He thenceforth grasped the inner meaning of the little girl's behavior and became much better able to treat her with an appropriate amount of patience. Hale's learning exhibited *empathy* which in this connection means experiencing the same feelings as another person through having been in the same situation oneself. He realized why his daughter rebelled because he had "been there" himself. In a study of nursery school children Lois Murphy showed that empathy was very much influenced by personal past experience. A child who had once had a broken arm, for instance, would display special solicitude when another child arrived with an arm in a sling. The capacity to produce new behavior in social situations is thus favorably affected by having a large *empathic range,* a rich store of experiences which can be used as a basis for understanding the meaning of another person's behavior. Sometimes a person can use the tragedies in his own life as a means of understanding other people's tragedies.

ROBERT W. WHITE
from *Lives in Progress*

For the writer and artist the most important part of seeing is not visual recognition, but empathic understanding. It is an understanding that permits and encourages visual transformation—the shift from object to symbol. No one knows just how this comes about or why some people are so much better at making it happen than others. Certainly instinct and openness are a large part of it, but a large part is also practice. People who see best in this way do so daily and not as a stunt for a composition. Empathic understanding prompts a way of thinking, a way of feeling, and ultimately a way of saying. For the writer, seeing involves esthetics. The writer, like the creative photographer, seeks to present those aspects of reality that speak for all reality, and so liberate an inner voice to which we may all respond.

1. Consider the comments on empathy.
2. In your journal do *one* of the following:
   a. Recount an incident from childhood.
   b. Recount an incident in which empathy plays a significant part.

c. Recount an incident in which you first saw a person in one way and then through empathy saw him in quite another way.

Assignment 12

For in the beginning of literature is the myth, and in the end as well.

JORGE LUIS BORGES
from *Labyrinths*

Myth: Anonymous stories having their roots in the primitive folk beliefs of races or nations and presenting supernatural episodes as a means of interpreting natural events in an effort to make concrete and particular a special perception of man or a cosmic view. Myths differ from legends in that they have less of historical background and more of the supernatural; they differ from the fable in that they are less concerned with moral didacticism and are the product of a racial group rather than the creation of an individual. Every country and literature has its mythology; the best known to English readers being the Greek, Roman, and Norse. But the mythology of all groups takes shape around certain common themes; they all attempt to explain the creation, divinity, and religion, to guess at the meaning of existence and death, to account for natural phenomena, and to chronicle the adventures of racial heroes.

They also have a startlingly similar group of motifs, characters, and actions, as a number of students of myth and religion, particularly Sir James Frazer, have pointed out. Although there was a time when myth was a virtual synonym for error, notably in the Neoclassic Period, the tendency today is to see myths as dramatic or narrative embodiments of a people's perception of the deepest truths. Various modern writers have insisted on the necessity of myth as a material with which the artist works, and in varying ways and degrees have appropriated the old myths or created new ones as necessary substances to give order and a frame of meaning to their personal perceptions and images; notable among such "mythmakers" have been William Blake, W. B. Yeats, T. S. Eliot (particularly in *The Waste Land*), James Joyce, and Wallace Stevens.

Since the introduction of Jung's concept of the "racial unconscious" . . . and of Ernst Cassirer's theories of language and myth, contemporary critics have found in the myth a useful device for examining literature. There is a type of imagination, Philip Wheelwright insists, that can properly be called "the Archetypal Imagination, which sees the particular object as embodying and adumbrating suggestions of universality." The possessors of such imagination arrange their works in archetypal patterns, and present us with narratives which stir us as "something at once familiar and strange." They thus give concrete expression to something deep and primitive in us all. Thus those critics— and they are many—who approach literature as myth see in it vestiges of primordial ritual and ceremony, or the repository of racial memories, or a structure of unconsciously held value systems, or an expression of the general beliefs of a race, social class, or nation, or a unique embodiment of a cosmic view. One significant difference should be noted, however; myth in its traditional sense is an anonymous, nonliterary, essentially religious formulation of the cosmic view of a people who approach its formulations not as representations of truth but as truth itself; myth in the sophisticated literary sense in which it is currently used is the intelligible and often self-conscious use of such primitive methods to express something deeply felt by the individual artist which will, he hopes, prove to have universal responses.

WILLIAM FLINT THRALL, ADDISON HIBBARD,
and C. HUGH HOLMAN
from *A Handbook to Literature*

1. Read the excerpt on myth.
2. In your journal do *one* of the following:
   a. Discuss the statement by Borges given above. For example, summarize what you discover from additional reading (give source) about the place of myth in early literature, or examine a story or poem with which you are familiar and show how myth has been used to project individual and universal feelings.
   b. Myth is an enduring expression of empathy. Agree or disagree. Discuss.
   c. Write on a topic of your own choice.

5|5

EXPERIENCE

There is evidence that every person has creative
abilities that can be developed.

HERBERT A. OTTO

Here is a poem by James Dickey called "A Screened Porch
in the Country." As you read the poem you will note that
"point of view" is more than a stereotyped term, and that
summer evenings, screened porches, little bugs, and little
words are experiences that can filter into a man's mind and
emerge as statements about a reality perceptively experienced. The poem itself is an experience. Like all good poems,
it catches something of the mystery of created things and their
interrelatedness. The poem sits upon the page, like the people
on the screened porch, making its own golden shadow.

A Screened Porch in the Country

All of them are sitting
Inside a lamp of coarse wire
And being in all directions
Shed upon darkness,
Their bodies softening to shadow, until
They come to rest out in the yard
In a kind of blurred golden country
In which they more deeply lie
Than if they were being created
Of heavenly light.

Where they are floating beyond
Themselves, in peace,
Where they have laid down
Their souls and not known it,

The smallest creatures,
As every night they do,
Come to the edge of them
And sing, if they can,
Or, if they can't, simply shine
Their eyes back, sitting on haunches,

Pulsating and thinking of music.
Occasionally, something weightless
Touches the screen
With its body, dies,
Or is unmurmuringly hurt,
But mainly nothing happens
Except that a family continues
To be laid down
In the midst of its nightly creatures,
Not one of which openly comes

Into the golden shadow
Where the people are lying,
Emitted by their own house
So humanly that they become
More than human, and enter the place
Of small, blindly singing things,
Seeming to rejoice
Perpetually, without effort,
Without knowing why
Or how they do it.

JAMES DICKEY

Reading a poem can be experience. Sitting on a porch can be experience; indeed, all living is experience. But the value of experience depends not so much on what happens as on what you do with what happens. What Dickey did was to respond in an uncommon way. First, he was perceptive; he sensed for a moment the relationship between the temporal and the eternal. Second, he put his perceptions into words, and let the reader share the insights and intensity of the original experience.

Now, how do such things as a poem, or a story, or a mood

come about? Quite apart from the intimate accidental details that go into any creation, there is—to use computer language—"input," then "output." Although such an explanation may sound fatuous, it is nonetheless a truth at the center of artistic creation. In "New Light on Human Potential," Herbert A. Otto, psychologist and chairman of the National Center for the Exploration of Human Potential in La Jolla, California, says, "Japanese research with infants and small children also suggests the value of early 'maximum input' (music, color, verbal, tactile stimuli) in the personality development of infants. My own observations tend to confirm this. We have consistently underestimated the child's capacity to learn and his ability to realize his potential while *enjoying* both the play elements and the discipline involved in this process." Otto goes on to say, "Most people are unaware of their strengths and potentialities. If a person with some college background is handed a form and asked to write out his personality strengths, he will list, on an average, five or six strengths. Asked to do the same thing for his weaknesses, the list will be two or three times as long."

Dr. Otto's evidence suggests that personality development requires both greater richness of input and greater personal confidence in the worth of what we can do with what we have been given. We are too sensitive to our failings for our own creative good. By overresponding to temporary or permanent inadequacies, we tend to become less creative, less productive than our personal potential permits. Dr. Otto says of growth centers across the country: The experiences offered at these Growth Centers are based on several hypotheses: (1) that the average healthy person functions at a fraction of his capacity; (2) that man's most exciting lifelong adventure is actualizing his potential; (3) that the group environment is one of the best settings in which to achieve growth; and (4) that personality growth can be achieved by anyone willing to invest himself in this process."

Part of the process of "investing yourself" is to stop being afraid of your own perceptions, and part of the process is to stop being afraid of criticism. Too many students are not only afraid of criticism, they are afraid to create and through creation freely exchange feelings and ideas. This negative attitude results in essays, poems, and stories written for the bureau drawer. You can correct that fault by writing to be read and by welcoming the honest response of your readers.

Regular journal writing requires awareness and invites you to make creative use of common experience. The process of regular writing has a way of heightening your interest in ideas and of promoting the improved expression of them. You begin to look for material to see what you had not seen and to experiment with ways of saying what is to be said.

Fifty years ago William James estimated that a healthy person operates at less than 10 percent of his potential. Modern investigations have confirmed this guess with possible downward revisions. If you want to realize more of your personal potential and develop your own creative ability, one way you can do it without recourse to yoga and without waiting for further scientific discovery is to continue work with the journal. Keeping a journal may not prompt you to turn out a poem each time you see lights on a screen porch, but the experience of journal writing will help you to clarify your thinking and to be more perceptive.

Assignment 13

1. Read the chapter up to this point.
2. In your journal do *one* of the following:
   a. Write a piece of prose or poetry to be read in class. Aim at interesting your readers while presenting your own perceptions.
   b. Turn some of your journal notes into a full entry.
   c. Thoughtfully rewrite one of your earlier entries.

Assignment 14

One writes out of one thing only—one's own experience. Everything depends on how relentlessly one forces from this experience the last drop, sweet or bitter, it can possibly give. This is the only real concern of the artist, to re-create out of the disorder of life that order which is art.

JAMES BALDWIN
from *Notes of a Native Son*

Life presents both the usual and the unusual. The problem for the writer is to be happy with both, to adjust each to the other and all to his own vision. In practice this means welcoming experience but not assigning the same value to all perceptions, just as you would not read a newspaper with the same attention as you would give a history lesson. So you must sort out the value of your own impressions and give to each a different weight. Quoted by his wife, Florence Emily Hardy, Thomas Hardy puts this matter straight when he says:

A story must be exceptional enough to justify its telling. We storytellers are all Ancient Mariners, and none of us is justified in stopping Wedding Guests (in other words, the hurrying public) unless he has something more unusual to relate than the ordinary experience of every average man and woman.

The whole secret of fiction and the drama—in the constructional part—lies in the adjustment of things unusual to things eternal and universal. The writer who knows exactly how exceptional, and how nonexceptional, his events should be made, possesses the key to the art.

from *The Early Years of Thomas Hardy*

Howells and those of his school forget that a story *must* be striking enough to be worth telling. Therein lies the problem—to reconcile the average with that uncommonness which alone makes it natural that a tale or experience would dwell in the memory and induce repetition.

from *The Later Years of Thomas Hardy*

1. Read the excerpts for this assignment.
2. In your journal do *one* of the following:
   a. Copy out a passage in which you feel an author has succeeded in carrying out Hardy's advice. Then explain how the author has done this.
   b. Attempt "the adjustment of things unusual to things eternal and universal."
   c. Report an ordinary event that struck you in some way as extraordinary.

Assignment 15

When William James estimated that most healthy people operate at less than 10 percent of their potential, he dramatized the 90 percent waste that goes on in most lives. But if James was aware of wasted potential, he also knew some of the things that could be done about it. Here he explains one step that can be taken by any determined person. What he says has a direct bearing on writing and the writing habit.

The great thing in all education is to make our nervous system our ally instead of our enemy. It is to fund and capitalize our acquisitions and live at ease upon the interest of the fund. For this we must make automatic and habitual, as early as possible, as many useful actions as we can, and guard against the growing into ways that are likely to be disadvantageous to us, as we should guard against the plague. The more of the details of our daily life we can hand over to the effortless custody of automatism, the more our higher powers of mind will be set free for their own proper work. There is no more miserable human being than one in whom nothing is habitual but indecision, and for whom the lighting of every cigar, the drinking of every cup, the time of rising and going to bed every day, and the beginning of every bit of work are subjects of express volitional deliberation. Full half the time of such a man goes to the deciding, or regretting, of matters which ought to be so ingrained in him as practically not to exist for his consciousness at all. If there be such daily duties not yet ingrained in any one of my readers, let him begin this very hour to set the matter right.

WILLIAM JAMES
from "Habit in Psychology"

For the writer and for the concerned English student, one way to improve through experience is to get the journal habit. If you have kept your journal regularly, you are on your way toward improved perception and unified expression, but if you can't find the time to realize your own potential, "begin this very hour to set the matter right."

1. Read the discussion on "habit."
2. In your journal do *one* of the following:
   a. Review your own journal-keeping experience.
   b. Write an essay on disorganization.
   c. Present your own perceptions about any topic.

5 | Review

We all have to choose whatever subject matter allows us the most powerful and most secret release; and that is a personal affair.

T. S. ELIOT
from his Introduction to
Selected Poems of Marianne Moore

The following comments by Brewster Ghiselin are taken from his introduction to *The Creative Process*. He reminds us that invention and creation are in part a reflection of conscious, disciplined effort and in part a mystery beyond the control of human will.

A great deal of the work necessary to equip and activate the mind for the spontaneous part of invention must be done consciously and with an effort of will. Mastering accumulated knowledge, gathering new facts, observing, exploring, experimenting, developing technique and skill, sensibility, and discrimination, are all more or less conscious and voluntary activities. The sheer labor of preparing technically for creative work, consciously acquiring the requisite knowledge of a medium and skill in its use, is extensive and arduous enough to repel many from achievement.

Even the most energetic and original mind, in order to reorganize or extend human insight in any valuable way, must have attained more than ordinary mastery of the field in which it is to act, a strong sense of what needs to be done, and skill in the appropriate means of expression. It seems certain that no significant expansion of insight can be produced otherwise, whether the activity is thought of as work or not. Often an untutored beauty appears in the drawings of children, and we rightly prize the best of them because they have wholeness of motive, but they have scarcely the power to open the future for us. For that, the artist must labor to the limit of human development and then take a step beyond. The same is true for every sort of creative worker.

That step beyond is stimulated by labor upon the limits of attainment. The secret developments that we call unconscious because they complete themselves without our knowledge and the other spontaneous activities that go forward without foresight yet in full consciousness are induced and focused by intense conscious effort spent upon the material to be developed or in the area to be illuminated. . . . But though "inspiration" may be produced by such conscious labors, by what Katherine Mansfield called "terrific hard gardening," the procedure is not always successful; problems may remain unsolved, insights undeveloped, no matter how much effort is given to them.

BREWSTER GHISELIN
from *The Creative Process*

Review Assignment

1. Read the excerpt by Ghiselin.
2. In your journal do *one* of the following:
   a. Write an extended and unified entry on a topic of your own choice.
   b. At some length, present a character that reveals himself to your perceptions—a character you have *found* either through reading or through life.
   c. Write an original paper about the insights presented within a novel or story. In the course of your comments refer to at least five sources. Exercise special care in footnoting and in transcribing.

Index

of Authors and Titles

Very brief excerpts are indicated by an asterisk (*) preceding their page numbers.

A 1
B 2
C 3
D 4
E 5
F 6
G 7
H 8
I 9
J 0